DATE			

Actors on Acting

Performing in Theatre & Film Today

Joanmarie Kalter

Sterling Publishing Co., Inc.   New York

London & Sydney

Other Books of Interest
Exploring Mime
Getting Started in Film-Making
Make-up, Costumes & Masks for the Stage
The Shadow Puppet Book

DEDICATION
This book is for Lew.

CONTENTS

**"Actors—they'll tell you a lot,
but they'll never tell you all of it."—Rip Torn**

ACKNOWLEDGMENTS

My thanks to many people for many reasons:

—to the actors and actresses who so generously shared themselves, I am deeply grateful;

—to Ted Gottfried, Don Davidson, Irene Gershen, Ray Gill, Susan Milano, Vicki Kramer, Abby Gehman, and Dorothy Ross, for helping in myriad ways;

—to John Littell and Marvin Rosenbaum, for giving me work which paid while I worked on this, which didn't; Roz Zanengo and Judi Weinstein, for making calls when my telephone paranoia was most paralytic; Eileen Dent for *Backstage*; Mark for his patience; Rose, Bobby, and the Trix of the Trade for being the best there are;

—and most especially, to Gwen Lourie for her friendship; and to Gail North, my editor, for making this work a pleasure.

INTRODUCTION

The best way to learn about acting is from actors themselves. More useful than theory or technical analysis is wisdom gained through experience . . . and about 250 working years are reflected in these pages. Since acting is an art which cannot be separated from its artists, it was felt to be especially fitting that it retain its human dimension, and that these performers be allowed to speak directly to you.

An attempt was made, therefore, to talk to a broad cross-section of people; I looked for contrast, controversy, distinguishing features, and what I found was that I didn't have far to look. Each actor was so immediately and strikingly different in temperament, method, and outlook that it made only one concluding generality about actors possible: there are no generalities to be made. As Sam Waterston said, "acting is a person," and no straining toward grand theories or systems will ever do better than that.

Rip Torn's righteous anger is as understandable a reaction to his profession as Barnard Hughes' simple, humble delight. Lynn Redgrave is sparked by the differences between her characters and herself, while Laurence Luckinbill is fired by the similarities; Bruce Dern finds the keys to his roles in his own experiences, yet to Estelle Parsons, the inspiration comes purely from the text itself. And while some people have difficulty verbalizing the intricacies of their craft, listening to garrulous, gleeful Geraldine Page is like racing around under a shower of gold coins with nothing but a small hat to catch them; each time I read through her comments, I find another rare and valuable piece that flew by me the time before. So if all this makes for some unevenness in length, mood, and focus of the interviews—it also serves to reaffirm the richness of their art.

Rather than eliciting any juicy bits of Hollywood gossip, I tried to get at the essential elements of the acting experience: what impels a person to become an actor, how he creates his roles, how he polishes and sustains a performance, and how satisfied he is with his work. Along these lines, there were related questions: can acting be taught; what qualities are needed; how should an aspiring actor study; is the actor an original creator or is he the embodiment of the writer's and director's vision; is comedy more difficult than drama; is theatre more fulfilling than film; and what is the relationship between dramatic fiction and real life.

On the other hand, I tried not to neglect the more quotidian concerns of an actor's experience. After all, when I asked the acting students I knew what they would most like to hear from the people I was interviewing, the answer was fairly consistent: "How did they support themselves before they became established?" And so I have taken into account that once the decision to become an actor is made, it is not a life lived purely on inspiration and three pomegranate seeds a day. It is a constant struggle for economic survival and artistic significance in a world that is increasingly commercial and spiritually barren. There is a measure of anguish, fear, and disillusionment expressed in these pages; but to avoid the darker sides of an actor's life would be a dishonest endeavor. Besides, it's good to hear that even the top-ranked actors of the day had their rough times getting there; it's energizing to know that people can buck their hardships, and continue on in spite of them.

Yet there is always a question in doing such interviews as to whether the answers are really honest ones. Imagine that you've entered into the presence of a complete stranger, plunked down a tape recorder, and in the course of an hour or two, tried to elicit their most profound feelings about the work they do. The results are tricky at best, and particularly so when you're dealing with actors, who—after writers—are the absolute champions of self-concealment and self-creation. But I do believe that an actor's talent for illusion is overshadowed by his capacity for honesty, as the latter is one of the most important tools of his trade. How many people, when asked how they've grown after twenty years of work in their field, would respond by saying, as Bruce Dern did, "I'm more vulnerable." Concentration, discipline, imagination, observation, self-criticism—these are qualities needed in any creative endeavor—whether it be writing, painting, dancing, teaching, carpentry, or any other. But add to these, for an actor, the qualities of honesty and accessibility to emotion—these are needed most of all.

In the interests of honesty, I should mention that these interviews do not appear *exactly* as they were run off the recorder. What makes for acceptable conversation does not always translate into comprehensible reading and so, for greater clarity, I have cut, rephrased, and restructured. A good deal of my own comments have been deleted to make for less chat and more substance, and in editing those of my subjects, I have tried never to tamper with the meaning of their material.

It is my hope that these interviews provide insight and inspiration, whether to professional actors, aspiring actors, amateurs, or mere fans of the field. Since acting is drawn so directly from life, these conversations turned out to be as much about the creative process in general as about acting in particular, and certainly, they have given more to me than I could ever put back in. As Lynn Redgrave said, in speaking about classical roles and why they are so inspiring, "There is no end to them; you can never say, 'this is perfect.'" It amazed me that she appreciated difficulties rather than being frightened off by them, and in the times since, that one comment has lent so much strength. "They are a constant challenge that is never quite met," she said, and that's much the way I have felt about this book.

JOANMARIE KALTER
New York City

GERALDINE PAGE

Though Geraldine Page is known for the strict attention she pays to the inner detail of a role, in person, she's sweet, chatty, loose, and light-hearted. During this interview, which was held backstage at the Eugene O'Neill Theatre in New York, Ms. Page wore a long, wide, floppy dress, no make-up, and chomped down a tuna fish sandwich as we talked. She very much enjoyed discussing her craft, relating old stories about friends, teachers and colleagues—all the while gesturing animatedly in the spirit, as she says, of "a terrible ham." Her high-pitched, fragile-sounding voice dips easily to a deep, resonant one, and then into a child-like whisper; she mimics accents perfectly; shifts her shoulders and head to assume the poses of her subjects—and does it all lovingly and with great relish.

Ms. Page was born November 22, 1924 and grew up in Chicago, the daughter of an osteopath. She made her New York stage debut as the Sophomore in a 1945 Blackfriars Guild production of *Seven Mirrors*, but it wasn't until 1952 that she gained prominence as the small-town parson's daughter, Alma Winemiller, in Tennessee Williams' *Summer and Smoke*. The following year, for her performance as Lily in *Midsummer*, she received the Donaldson Award, the Theatre World Award and tied with Shirley Booth in the Variety New York Drama Critics Poll. Among the many award-winning roles which followed was that of the fiery, aging actress Alexandra del Lago, the Princess Kosmonopolis, in both the stage and film versions of Williams' *Sweet Bird of Youth*; Nina Leeds in the Actors Studio production of Eugene O'Neill's *Strange Interlude*; Sophie, Baroness Lemberg in *White Lies*, and Clea in *Black Comedy*, two one-act Peter Shaffer plays performed back-to-back; and Marion, the drunken banker's wife in Alan Ayckbourn's *Absurd Person Singular*. She has received two Emmy Awards as Best Actress for her work as "Sookie" in Truman Capote's childhood reminiscences, "A Christmas Memory" and "The Thanksgiving Visitor," and has received numerous Academy Award nominations for, among others, *Hondo*, *Summer and Smoke*, *Sweet Bird of Youth*, and *The Day of the Locust*. Ms. Page especially enjoys acting under the direction of her husband, Rip Torn, which she did most recently in two Strindberg plays, *The Stronger* and *Creditors*.

Before her marriage to Mr. Torn in about 1958 (neither claims to remember the exact date), she was married twice, once to violinist Alexander Schneider. She and Mr. Torn have three children—a daughter, Angelica, and twin sons, Jonathan and Anthony.

This interview took place on two occasions a few days apart, both backstage at the O'Neill. The movie *Interiors*, directed by Woody Allen, had just been released, but by an interesting and fortuitous accident, on the first afternoon we talked, Ms. Page had not yet seen it, and on the second afternoon, she had. A few months later, she received a nomination for an Academy Award—her seventh—as Best Actress of the year for that performance.

Part I

Could you tell me what originally motivated you to become an actress?

I remember that at first I wanted to play the piano, and then I wanted to draw. But when I got cast in a play at church, it was the first time that I felt I could express what I had in my head. So I concluded that my attraction to acting was pure laziness—it was just easier for me to act than to do either of the other two.

And how did your parents react to your wanting to be an actress?

My mother worried that I would starve to death. My grandfather made my parents send me to typing school to counteract the possible destitution in store for me. But my father, surprisingly enough, was very sympathetic. He was a doctor, but he wrote on the side, so he understood my ambitions. I was doing my third play at church, it was *Little Women*, and I was playing Jo. He thought I should have been playing Beth, because I was so shy; if anybody talked to me, I would go in the corner and blush. No one could hear me when I talked. So he said, "If you can convince me in the role of Jo, I'll let you go to the Goodman Theatre School." And I just put everything I had into that part. When my father saw it, he said: "Yeah, okay."

And so you went to theatre classes straight from high school? Your family didn't mind your not going to college?

No, my father didn't really believe in college. He fulminated against academe. He said that college was only for people who didn't know what they wanted to do. You could go to college and fish around for a while until it occurred to you, but if you knew what you wanted to do, you should specialize.

As a child, I had always daydreamed about going to the University of Chicago; it was such a gorgeous, fairy-tale place. But by the time I got to the age to go to college, I wanted desperately to go to Goodman. I was so happy to study all day long; every class had something directly to do with what I was interested in.

I did try, however, to get a degree. There was an agreement between Goodman and the University of Chicago downtown that you could get a BFA degree if you took extra classes. I wanted to study at least three hundred of them! Then they told me, "That's all very well, but you have to study English composition before you can study any of these others." So I tried. I went to a class conducted by a woman who was very bored with teaching and I stayed three weeks but I kept falling asleep. Finally, I said to myself, "I'll probably learn more about English composition if I read some good books." So I quit—and remain uneducated to this day!

Did you get a chance to play a variety of roles at Goodman?

Oh yes. In those days, the students played everything. When I was eighteen, I played Arkadina in *The Seagull* and Miriamne in *Winterset*. We played in children's theatre, too. The student directors could never persuade anybody to act in their productions, but I was always very happy to be in them. So I was in absolutely everything. The faculty must have gotten kind of sick of seeing me. In every scene that came up, I was in there playing something. But I'm a terrible ham. I'm still stage-struck to this day. I love it.

When I went back to visit many years later I was sad for the students. I found out the school was importing professional actors and all the students could do was bring on trays and say, "Tea is served, Madame." They were stuck being the spear-carriers.

After Goodman you came to New York?

Well, not directly. When we were graduated, I went to talk to the head of the school and I complained to him about being shoved out into the cold, cruel world. I said, "Where are we going to go? You teach us to have certain standards and now what are we going to do with all this?" He got very annoyed with me and said, "You people! You think all you have to do is sit around and someone will hand you a theatre on a silver platter. The kind of theatre that you want is one you're going to have to make yourself."

So thirteen of us put in thirty-five dollars apiece and we started a summer stock company. It lasted for quite a number of years. In the wintertime, I'd come to New York to try for a job here, but I'd go back every summer where I knew I could be employed and where my friends were.

Did you ever try teaching theatre as a means of supporting your-self?

Well, briefly. One of the teachers at Goodman was also with the De Paul University night school, and he asked me to come and teach in his drama department. So the following winter, I tried to teach at De Paul, but I was a total loss. I couldn't understand people who weren't as fanatic about it as I was. I had no way of communicating with them. I'd call rehearsal and they'd say, "Oh, I've got a date," or "I've gotta go to a Knights of Columbus meeting." I thought, who are these people? Martians? I couldn't understand them.

And how was it trying to break into the theatre in New York?

Terrible. Always has been and always will be. I had heard at Goodman there was a thing called the Blackfriars Guild which, because of their religious nature, was allowed to hire non-Equity actors. So everybody from Goodman, when they came to New York, would try to get into a Blackfriars show and then gradually work their way into the union. When I went to see about that, the person at the desk said, "We have all the people we need and there won't be any more casting this year." But on the way out of the office, I saw a pack of postcards on the end of the table. They were sending out cards to their file of people saying that they would be auditioning for their new show the following week at such and such a time. So I said, "Ah, hah!" And I showed up that day.

When I arrived, there was a long line of people and only two parts left. These were small bits to be played by the same person. I argued with the director to allow me an audition. He finally got so exasperated that he brought out a long list and said, "You see this list; there are forty names on it. Forty people are going to read for that one opening." I said, "I don't care how many names there are; all I want is a reading." "Oh, all right!" And he put my name down at the bottom.

I was lucky being at the bottom of the list because I could listen to everybody else read, and get an idea of what the part required. It was a scene with three college girls and their dates. They were at a dance. I could tell from listening to the dialogues that each couple was a kind of variation on a theme. I was up for the part of the sophomore, and everybody was reading it very dramatically, with much thigh-clutching, you know. But the senior, who was talking about the same thing, was being very serious about it; the ingenue had taken another kind of tack; and so I took a chance. When I read it, I gave it a comedic touch. The poor casting committee who had already listened to forty people, perked up when they heard me. And I got the part. So you see how there is an infinite reiteration of coincidence involved in getting any role. If I had come in the week before, the day before, they probably wouldn't have had the postcards ready, they wouldn't have been on the table, and I would've missed it entirely.

Did you spend a lot of time knocking around New York, going to auditions, making the rounds?

I tried to make the rounds but it depressed me so much I had to go to the movies to forget. I'd go to double features and hide in the dark to nurse my ego. I was bad at getting rejected. I'd come back every September and begin trying to get a job; by the time February came around, if I hadn't gotten anything, I'd really begin to get desperate.

How did you support yourself when you weren't acting?

Another thing that Goodman scuttlebutt taught me was that you should get a job checking hats. You can't get a regular job because people get outraged when they find out you're in the theatre; they won't hire you because they know that at the drop of any promise of anything, you will leave immediately with no qualms. They don't want to bother with people who aren't going to stay around. But what's wonderful about hat-checking for a concession is that you can call up and say, "I want to work tonight and on Thursday, and next week I want to work all week," and then you can change it at the last moment.

Did you ever get very, very discouraged and think that you were going to give up?

One time I almost did. I remember while I was going to Goodman and planning my campaign, I read everything I could about people in the theatre. The ones who stayed in the business for a long time and established themselves, strangely, took an average of about ten years to get a foothold. People who didn't stick it out that long just left early and went on to do other things. So I said, "Oh well, it'll take about ten years and the broader a base I can build, the firmer I'll be." But then the tenth year began to go by. . . . And I had always had this conviction that "I've got it and I'll get it. I'll get well-paid and I'll get recognition someday because I'm terrific." I'm still my best fan. So, the ten years were almost up, and I was talking to some of my acting friends and I heard this same firm tone of conviction from them. I thought, now wait a minute. Evidently this subjective feeling that you are *it*, that you are anointed and that you're going to live happily ever after is not a full guarantee. It's obvious that not all of us are going to have this good fortune. So I had to ask myself: what if nobody ever pays me adequately for this? What if I remain in crowd scenes and walk-ons Off-Broadway for the rest of my life? And I had to answer: well, I love it. I like being in crowd scenes. There's an enjoyable lack of responsibility and you can use your imagination in these small parts. The fewer lines that are written for you, the more you can make up your own character. So I really like it and I don't care if I never become rich and famous. I'll stick with it no matter what. And like magic, almost the next day or so, *Summer and Smoke* came my way.

It reminds me of a thing I always remembered from *The Great God Brown* by Eugene O'Neill. In it, Dion and Cybel are playing cards and she always wins. He says, "Your luck is uncanny. It never comes out for me." And she says, "You keep getting closer, but it knows you still want to win—a little bit—and it's wise all I care about is playing."

Did you have any inkling that **Summer and Smoke** *was going to be such a big hit?*

No, no. On opening night, I remember we were sitting around drinking red wine at the bottom of the theatre, and Ted Mann, the producer, went to get the newspapers. He came back and read this review by Brooks Atkinson. In those days, critics never went to Off-Broadway theatres; there was, comparatively speaking, nothing for them to look at. There was a mere trickle of activity, just showcases in the most literal sense, where actors got on stage and said, in effect, "Please buy me. See what I can do—look!

Don't you want me in one of your *real* productions?" Such desperation—no wonder audiences stayed away in droves. But the
Circle theatre group was different. They had decided that no one
would hire them anyway, and no one would come see their plays
except friends and relatives. So they did plays the way they
wanted to do them. They wanted to work. They did plays to
please themselves and because of that, people began to go and
look at them and talk among themselves about it. And that must
be the reason Brooks Atkinson ambled down there, saw the play,
and said something nice about it.

Now, Brooks Atkinson's wildest praise is pretty mild, so when
Ted read us this thing, he said, "You know what this means,
don't you?" We said no. He said, "It means we have a hit." And
we all howled: "Delusions of grandeur! What's the matter with
you, pretending you're a big producer. What is this?" But very
gradually a line started forming to see the show, and we began to
sell out. He was right. The play ran for two years. And it started
an entire Off-Broadway theatre revival. A whole world of drama
came back to life from that one production.

Do you ever miss that sense of freedom you had when you thought
you were acting in obscurity?

Well, yes. That's why when Rip did the Strindberg repertory I
had such a good time playing Kristin in *Miss Julie*. Nowadays, no
one would cast me in a role like that. They would feel compelled
to make me play Miss Julie or do another play, so I enjoyed that.
And I enjoyed a play like *Absurd Person Singular*, in which it was
very balanced. It wasn't a question of having one person hold up
the whole show. We all had to work hard.

You prefer that to having responsibility for the whole play?

Well, I like that, too. What is ideal, however, and what every
actor dreams of, is repertory, where you can play the lead in one
show and have a walk-on in the other. That way you can get a shot
at all of them. It's not fair that someone should always have to do
the workhorse role and other people are condemned forever to
bring out tea and then go home. It's not right. That's what we're
trying to do, Rip and I, to get a theatre together where everybody
can play everything and can direct, too.

*After **Summer and Smoke**, you were invited to Hollywood. I understand you had some problems there.*

Yes, one of the big studios asked me to sign a seven-year contract, and I said, "I don't want to. I'm a stage actress and I would like to be a stage actress who does movies once in a while. I don't want to be a movie actress who once in a while does plays." They got very angry with me. They probably thought, who am I, this little snippet who just came up from Off-Broadway in one little play to be telling them to take their seven-year contract and shove it?

Then a producer who was also an agent drew up a wonderful contract for me. The basic time limit was seven years but if I wanted to do a play for the whole year, he'd just add a year on to the end. "Your first three movies will be *Summer and Smoke*, *American Gothic* (from the novel), and *The Wayward Bus* by John Steinbeck with a treatment by William Saroyan." It sounded pretty good to me. So I signed.

Time went on and finally I said, "When are we going to start *Summer and Smoke*?" I was told, "Well, you know, they've just invented three-D and we can't do any of these intimate little stories now, because for three-D you need really big stories with wide open spaces. However, there's this Western with John Wayne. . . ." [She laughs.] I said, "I can't believe this. Not in my wildest dreams did I picture myself in a Western with John Wayne." It was incredible. He sent me the script for *Hondo*.

Then it was a number of years before you got back to do another movie.

Yes, I think it was seven years. It's as though they had a seven-year contract for me to stay away!

*When you accept a role, for instance, Eve in Woody Allen's **Interiors**, how do you proceed? Do you first study your own part or do you study the script as a whole?*

I read the script, and while I'm reading it, I envision it as if I were in the audience. And that's it. But I always hesitate to say that either to students or to anyone who will put it in print; people will assume that all you have to do is read something and then you can get up and act professionally. You can't. If you put down first that I am a graduate of a regular drama school, that I spent seven years in winter and summer stock, that I studied seven years with Uta Hagen and two years with Mira Rostova, and was at the Actors Studio for ten years, then if I say I read a script, put it away and don't think about it, it's not as misleading. The training that I have is in my brain and it works on material in not-so-conscious ways. I have all sorts of complicated, computerized knowledge stored away in the back of my mind. When I do then wing it, a lot of work has been done that I wouldn't have time to sit down and explain to everybody. That sounds pretentious, but the only alternative is to be very cavalier.

For instance, there was a time when the only thing that interested the media about acting was the "Method." The controversy was raging pro and con, and, for the longest time, journalists wouldn't talk to performers about anything else. We were working on *Toys in the Attic*, and the reporters would ask Wendy, "Miss Hiller, what is your method of acting?" She would say, "Well, I have a *bash* at it, and if it doesn't go, I have another *bash* at it." I thought that was marvelous, but it sounds almost haphazard. Yet I'm sure she was referring to all the years she spent in the theatre.

What was it about Uta Hagen's training that was particularly helpful to you?

I used to think, before I studied with Uta, that by the time we got to opening night everything had been done. My mind would get restless and I'd want to work on something else. It seems obvious, but when I started studying with Uta I found that there's so much more you can do when you're working with an audience. When you've got really rich material, you can explore it and work on it forever. And her war against cliché is absolutely thrilling. She would say, "People don't do that. That's what people on *stage* always do at a moment like that. The population of the world is so vast and we're all different, and there are so many ways of acting."

She'd say, "You've read the script, but in life we don't know from one moment to the next what we're going to say. We don't know what the person opposite us is going to do. We haven't got it planned out." Now, with *Summer and Smoke*, I took that lesson to such lengths that people began to caricature me. I didn't believe it, but Ted [Mann, the producer] and Jose [Quintero, the director] told me I added twenty minutes to the play one night. I was so enthusiastic about that new idea that I added time to every sentence. It was quite an innovation then, but now, you can't turn on a commercial on TV without hearing it. Everybody says, ". . . well, I, you, uh. . . ." And I say, "Oh God, what have I done?" But in those days, everybody used to get their lines down pat so they could volley them back and forth, hesitating not a moment. To change that was startling. Now, anybody who does pick up his cue and go right ahead gets this reaction: "Oh my, that's wonderful, it's something new."

That's one of the classic problems faced by an actor, isn't it? To give the illusion that these lines and these actions are actually happening, and not planned in advance.

There was another trick she taught us in that same vein. Because your character has not read the script, you go through your score (she was always comparing drama to music and noting how close they are), and whenever something's going to happen, you persuade your character to expect something different. That way, your character is continually surprised. If the person you're talking to is going to get up and go out of the room, your character should expect that they're going to stay—and vice versa. It helps give you the illusion of freshness. She taught us all these wonderful, magical, *practical* things.

You studied with Mira Rostova at the American Academy, too.

The things I learned from Mira Rostova were fantastic! It's easy for me to remember them because they were very concise events learned at a specific time, on a specific piece of material, with one sentence or two that's indelible.

Would you give me an example?

I'd love to! I was doing a scene from *The Girl on the Via Flaminia*, and when I got through with it, she said, "Geraldine . . ." (After every scene she used to look as if we'd killed her; she'd sit for a long time with her eyelashes on her cheeks and groan.) "Geraldine," she said, "you pause before you speak to think whether you should speak. You pause in the middle to think whether you should continue to speak; and you pause at the end to think whether you should have spoken." She was silent for another five minutes, and then she said, "People talk to each other. Please do this scene again and *talk* to the young man."

I thought, oh, this is ridiculous. Here in this scene, this girl is in fear of her life; half the time she's answering these questions, she's lying, and the other half, she's telling the truth. It's a matter of life or death. Any little miss or slip one way or the other, and she's going to her doom. You just can't go blah-de-blah-blah. I thought, I'll show her. So I started the scene the way she suggested and I found that all the pauses I had made so clearly before were now taking place in the middle of syllables. The character sounded so much more uncertain and anxious. It was so exciting—the class was amazed; the scene was terrific.

And it was a similar thing when we worked on *Notes from Underground* by Dostoyevsky. I played the prostitute and when her client asks about her life, she goes on and on about all the *tsuris* in her family. Everybody's blind and starving and dead and all these horrible things. Well, I played it out and after everybody was bored with the scene, Mira said, "Geraldine, you have done a great deal of work on the background, and this will not be lost. But my dear, you are a prostitute with a customer and if you do not cheer up this customer and make him happy, your madam will be very angry with you, and you will be even more miserable than you are now."

By this time, I knew enough not to question her. So we did the scene again and I was sort of bright and cheery, and I told about my little brother who had lost his legs, and how we didn't have anything to eat in the house, and how cold it was, and the roof leaked. And the more I tried to be cheerful about it, the more heart-rending the scene became. The prostitute was trying to cover up, or didn't realize that not everyone had had such a horrible life. It became much more poignant.

And what have been the advantages of Stanislavsky's Method for you, of trying to link your own personal experiences to those of your character?

Well, that everybody does, either consciously or unconsciously.

Stanislavsky was trying to get down what the best actors always do anyway; he didn't invent anything. So even actors who sneer at the Method, are militant against it, or, conversely, have never heard of it, when they get up and act, they use themselves. The Method is also a matter of who's teaching it, because Uta, Mira, Lee Strasberg and David Itkin from Goodman all taught the Method, yet in each case, it was filtered through their own brain.

But what happens when you study *that* aspect of acting (no matter who's teaching it) is that you find more analogies between yourself and the material than you thought you had. The Method allows you to discover less obvious connections between yourself and your character. You find some very deflected things that also relate. It opens up a whole field of connections you can *consciously* bring from yourself. You bring a lot unconsciously and automatically, but the Method widens your perception; you can then add more of your own colors to the tapestry of your character.

Trying consciously to establish connections between yourself and the character enriches the unconscious process that would happen anyway?

Well, it also depends on who's doing this work. For instance, you and I have seen actors who were so busy making conscious connections to their characters that they swamped the material; instead of enriching it, they smothered it. It can enrich if it's done right, otherwise it can hinder. People get so enamored with these techniques of exploring parts of themselves, that they forget what the object is. As an actor, you must do the fullest, best, most interesting interpretation of the *character,* and not the fullest, most wonderful exposition of your own discoveries of yourself. So, it doesn't necessarily help the end product all the time. But it's all fraught with interesting dangers.

It's sometimes said that this exploration of one's self can be dangerous. For instance, some of the biggest names out of the Actors Studio—James Dean, Marilyn Monroe, Kim Stanley—became rather tortured souls.

No, they were that way before they got there, and would have been that way if the Studio hadn't existed. They had complicated psyches. Jimmy and Marilyn and Kim . . . I know one of them and

knew the other two when they were alive . . . all great, complicated heads and wonderful people. I personally grieve that, with
such rich natures, they couldn't enjoy their lives and their talent
more. But that canker inside them had nothing to do with acting.
On the contrary, the fact that they did turn out to be actors probably relieved some of their innate grief, because acting *is* a release;
it is a way of taking anguish and making something beautiful out of
it. Yet, when you have so much, you can't meld it all into gold.

I thought that anybody who could act as well as Kim must love it,
just because I love it. We all project ourselves on everybody—
stupidly. I used to argue with her and say, "You must love to act,
underneath it all," and she'd say, "No." I never believed her and I
argued with her for twenty years. Then she came to visit us at the
house after having been out in New Mexico teaching. She started
talking about her work with those children and I saw her face,
listened to her, and I realized then that she was telling the truth.
Things that intruded on her head when she had to get up and act
were so painful that she really was more comfortable not acting
than acting. Whatever the problems with teaching are, they don't
impinge on her enjoyment; what she really *loves* to do, feels happy
and fulfilled and right doing is teaching. Just because I'm the opposite, I couldn't see it, but now I know that it's true. It's a loss for
those of us who want to see her act all the time, but it's something
marvelous for her.

*Do you notice any difference when you're acting in a play or movie
with people who have studied the Method as you have?*

Yeah. There's a greater freedom to explore the possibilities of
what you're doing. Most people who either have not studied it or
who actually fight against it are a little more set in their ways. If you
try a different tack on something, they're upset because they like
to get things set and keep it that way. It makes them unhappy to
change. And it restricts you if they won't respond to some new impulse that you have. When we're all trained the same way, if some
new color is rising at the moment, if your performance is changing
in a way that was not premeditated, the other person will respond
to that and a whole new drama can grow right on stage. Then afterwards, you can decide whether it was wandering further away
from the point or it was actually helping. You can keep it or
discard it or mutate it into something else.

So you're happy to see accidents happen on stage.

Well, they're fun. But I'm not the kind of person who thinks it's cute to make things go wrong. I hate that. But if some disaster does happen, it's a challenge and a pleasure to see if you can work it into something. You don't want anyone to notice that it's not part of what happens every night.

*You've played in some really long runs, like **Absurd Person Singular**, which you were in for about two years. Do you find yourself feeling bored with a long run?*

Well, I've been lucky. I've only experienced three long runs in my life, and two of them were in plays by Tennessee Williams. I really enjoyed *Absurd Person Singular*, too. Every audience was so different that it was a whole new ball game every time. It was funny, though, during the last week of performances, when I knew it was over and I had another job waiting, the scales fell from my eyes; I looked and said, "What am I doing? This thing has gotten so bad." I saw all the faults that had crept into it; how we exaggerated things because every time we added a little bit more, it felt the same as before, but actually it wasn't. I thought, this is terrible, it's a good thing we're closing. But up until then, all I had seen was the challenge of how to do things. I didn't have a really objective feeling for what was happening. Oh God, we were awful.

Do you still feel that you like stage work better than movies?

I do, though I'm more at home with movies now than I used to be. After *Hondo*, when I was still so shaken, in those seven years when I didn't do any movies, I thought, if I ever do a film again, I'm not going to worry about it. It's totally out of my hands. On the stage, if there's something wrong, you can do something about it. If you think it's going slow, you can pick it up, change the pace—you can edit yourself. But in a film, you have no control. When I started working again, I still fought for things, but then when I saw that I was not going to get anywhere, I dropped it and started struggling with the next problem and didn't brood over it. I've gotten used to movies now. If you're really used to stage technique and then you get into film, you think everybody's insane, they're doing everything backwards. You cannot understand how anything in the world is achieved in film; it's all a miracle. But now I've adjusted. I'm beginning to know how to do it. I enjoy film now. I enjoy it equally, in fact, but it took me a long time.

What is it that you like about movies that compensates for the lack of control?

The money, first of all. And second, it's very leisurely. It's much easier to do. Again, you have to get yourself in the frame of mind where you can enjoy the lack of responsibility—even though in film, that lack of responsibility means that your creative field is shrinking rather than expanding, as it would with a small part on stage. But there are advantages to film. On the stage when you're doing your own make-up, you cannot go out in the front and look to see if you've got the right color. The fact that in film you can see what you're doing means you can learn a great deal about yourself and your work. I was so appalled at what I learned about myself in *Hondo* that I wanted to go jump in a lake. But after you get used to it, you can objectively compare what you intended to do with the way it came out. Gradually, I'm getting so that what I want to do comes much closer to what I have done.

You haven't seen your performance yet in Woody Allen's **Interiors?**

I tried to. What I like to do, what is really good for me to do, is to go to the dailies. That way, I can see exactly what happened the day before so I can adjust my sights to see what I am doing now. Most of the directors I've worked with have allowed me to see the dailies. It's a general policy that actors are not allowed, because most people get shook and upset and then they start nagging about things that aren't essential. They get self-conscious and freeze up. So I can see why directors are against it. But I have proved to director after director that I am very good and I'm quiet and I don't then start telling them how to do things. I just learn for myself. And contrary to shaking my confidence, I always feel better. I say, "Oh. It wasn't as bad as I thought. Oh, I know what to do about that." And so I've had a marvelous time. But Woody, who is . . . well, he *is* paranoid. He would not allow it. I thought I'd finally persuaded him and he did say, "Okay, you can look at the rushes. They'll be

Saturday morning." I couldn't believe it. He's finally going to let me see some! Then on Friday he said, "Well, it's so close to Christmas and the projectionist doesn't want to come in. . . ." I never did see any of it.

Did you find that a particularly difficult role?

Well, in a way. I felt I understood the character; that part didn't bother me so much. But the execution of it was extremely difficult because of pleasing Woody. I would do a scene a particular way and he would say, "That's too . . . I just don't believe that." Me, the specialist in realism? Then we'd go back and do it again and he'd say, "Ah, it's just. . . ." He doesn't have any of the Method's verbiage or even the non-Method director's vocabulary at all. All he ever says is, "Well, I don't like it. . . ."

In other words, he didn't tell you in any specific way what he wanted?

Yeah, he'd say, "It's still like somebody you see playing an interior decorator in the movies. I just want the woman to come in and put down her handbag." It was exasperating and very difficult; I kept trying to simplify and simplify and take all the theatrical things out. But still he'd say, "No, that's like on the stage. Just come in and put the bag down." He didn't even go so far as to say, "Don't put the bag down like. . . ." He would just shake his head. I'd say, "What's wrong with that? How much simpler can I be?" I'd go back and do it again.

But what was wonderful was that I agreed with his taste. When he said he didn't like it, I believed it; I knew that if I saw it, I would agree with him. That's wonderful because you can't always trust those decisions, yet in this case, I knew. When people tell me it's some of my best work, I'm very inclined to believe they must be telling the truth. God knows, every director I've ever worked with has tried in various ways to get me to simplify, especially for movies.

You were playing someone who was coming apart at the seams. Was it difficult then to do take after take?

It was only difficult technically. I love to do someone coming apart at the seams over and over again. I love it. What was difficult was doing it ever simpler and ever simpler. Even if it was a happy scene, it would have been just as difficult to do it as "specifically" as he required. But that had nothing to do with the character at all. As a matter of fact, one of the scenes I loved the most was going in and getting knocked down by the waves—and I can't even swim. By the way, is that scene in? Do I walk in the ocean in the movie? I loved that. I can't understand these actors who talk about how they live a part, how they suffer. The poor things. Why don't they do something else that they like better? What a batch of complainers!

But to act such an emotional role—doesn't it drain you?

On the contrary, it makes me feel terrific. There's something about releasing all those tensions in acting that's very cathartic. It feels really good. If you take a dance class or a singing lesson, for instance, and spend that kind of energy, you feel great. I felt terrific after they dragged me out of the water.

What is a drag, what gets you down, gets you morose, is having to sit around and wait and do nothing—that is really killing. You get exhausted and irritable. But an emotional scene, even the most wrenching, is wonderful. It's a funny contradiction, but it's true. What drives everybody crazy is having to sit for a long time. And for that movie, we did have to sit. But we were a resourceful company, and we had Scrabble, we had backgammon, we had chess, a dart board, and Maureen [Stapleton] knew a wonderful word game that she had us all play. We had a wonderful time and it distracted us from the fact that we had to sit for so long. We thought Woody was a stickler for absolutely having things right, but Gordon Willis, the cinematographer, would look at the sky all day and say, "The clouds aren't right; they're just not right." So we'd go back to our games.

Part II

*What do you think about **Interiors** now that you've seen it?*

Oh, it's so compelling and I'm so pleased about my work in it. It's an unusual film. It's so spare.

Did you picture your performance as you saw it?

Well, I worried about a lot of things, and I see now that I didn't have to. I worried about the continuity of the character—for instance, exactly when she had her first breakdown, how much time passed between her relapses, etcetera. Woody told me not to worry about those things, so I didn't. And when I finally saw the film, Rip remarked what a lesson it was. We all have a tendency to think that kind of logical detail is so essential. But this movie proved that you can have an emotional understanding of the story without worrying about all that.

Are you generally satisfied with your performances when you see yourself in films or on TV?

I have a wide variety of reactions. Mostly though, I'm fairly pleased, although some things I like more than others. But I like the characterization in *Interiors*. I like the choices that I made. I really admired the degree to which I was able to convey that kind of covered and restrained behavior, where everything had to be almost unexpressed.

I thought it was very interesting the other day when you said that Woody Allen constantly told you to do less and less; the character was, in fact, evading so many things, and so that direction seemed to work very well for the role.

And that's why, when things did burst out of her, they were irrevocable. She never let off any of her steam.

How did you come by the facial expressions that you used?

Who knows? It's very hard to tell what knowledge and associations and skills went into it because there are so many. I think they always come from your subtext, your inner monologue; whatever it is that your character is thinking at any given moment. That's more or less what you see reflected in the facial expressions.

Do you carefully plan out what the character is thinking?

No. I used to, but over the years I have learned that if I preconceive what the character is thinking, it's not going to be as interesting or as varied as if I just go along and see what the character turns out to be thinking at the moment. Usually, if a line of inner thought seems to be working well, I keep it in. But if something happens to change, then I explore it. And it's wonderful with a role like Eve in *Interiors;* she's reminiscent of a character in a Chekhov play whose inner life is much more complicated than her outer life; it's just not expressed overtly. While she has very deep, complex inner thoughts, all she's doing is serving tea or something, yet her strong feelings come through even in that very simple behavior.

One of my favorite moments is at the birthday party when I'm sitting there but can't allow myself to show how straining it is to be surrounded by my family. When my son-in-law pours the champagne, I love the way it comes across how I disapprove, how I'm suffering through this: just the merest, tiniest fraction of a drop spills on my hand, but I wipe it off with such long suffering. I like that.

Did you draw on any particular emotional memories of your own for that scene?

Oh, I'm sure, but not in a conscious way. We've all been someplace where we had to behave nicely even though people were driving us batty. We couldn't protest, we couldn't get up and leave, we had to sit and put up with it. I'm sure that a variety of those experiences merged together in my mind, rose up to that part of the script, and responded to it.

Uta explained this one time in class when somebody was having a lot of trouble and saying, "I can't identify with this situation. It's too big; it's too tragic for my experience." She told us a story about getting on the bus to come over to the studio that day, and how she had been going back to her seat when the driver said, "Miss! Miss!" She realized he was talking to her, calling her back because she hadn't put her money in the slot. And she said the force of the emotions funneling through her at that moment, of shame, of embarrassment, of wanting to murder him, of feeling put upon against all justice, was enormous. There was enough emotion raging through her on that bus, she told us, to take care of this part, that part, and another part. It was a wonderful thing to be reminded of:

the kind of outsized emotions we can have over a small incident. All an actor has to do is remember that. So you don't have to be the kind of woman that Eve is to have lived intensely through the same kinds of feelings.

You don't have to have murdered to play a murderer.

To play Lady Macbeth, you don't have to go out and find a king and kill him.

I have the impression that, in fact, your identification with Eve must have been very remote.

Yes, I'm a very, very different personality. The fact that she's so completely neat, God knows, nothing could be further from me. I can't keep my mind on neatness; neat types find me terribly lax. It's very funny because I heard that Woody was amused—and maybe not so amused—that it took me so long to get ready. I spent so much time on my make-up, in making sure that every hair was in place. And he may have thought that was a character trait of mine. But if I were playing myself, we wouldn't have to do any of that. I'd be on the set saying, "Get away from me with that powder puff and comb. Stay away, I'm all ready." That's something I have done when they've tried to neaten up a character I thought should be frowsy. But with Eve, I thought that if there were one little thing out of place, she'd just snap. And so I deliberately would not get in front of the camera until I felt that things were exactly as Eve would want them to be.

Do you have any difficulty crying on cue? You really have leaky ducts in that movie.

I don't have too much trouble crying, yet that "on cue" business can be difficult. Sometimes I'll cry earlier or later, but not where the script says, "She cries." As for what it is I think about, there are so many things to make you cry in the world. It's endless. So many things to get upset about.

Do you remind yourself of some particular image that will make you cry?

You don't have to. If you go along with the story and you identify with the person you're playing and they're in a situation that is causing them grief and anguish, you just cry.

But if, on some day, your concentration is not completely there with the events of the script, would you rely on some image to make yourself cry? Has that ever happened?

Oh. Actually I use the more technical method. For instance, in a film, when they take and they take about nine thousand times because airplanes are flying over, finally your body and your nerves get so worn out, they can't function anymore. When that happens, I put my eyes in relationship to the lights so that they hit a certain angle, and it will make my eyes tear. If the moment can be conveyed without a physical tear, with a different expression in the eyes that conveys the same thought, then I do that. But real tears are necessary, it takes a minute. I have very hammy lachrymal glands. They just can't wait. I did *Something for Joey*, a TV show where I played the mother of a child with leukemia, so you can imagine. . . . And I made the crew laugh one time because we were redoing a scene from another angle where it had to match what we shot before. While we were still getting ready, the tears started rolling down. I said to my eyes, "Wait for your cue!" But we had to start over because the tears just came down too early.

It strikes me as being harder to be able to laugh on cue, particularly if you're supposedly responding to some joke you've heard a number of times already.

Laughter for me is harder. It really is a more complicated phenomenon. To make it sound spontaneous and really organic is tough. When people are first starting out in acting, it's a problem. Even to sit properly on stage is difficult. I remember back in the days when I was at Goodman, one of my teachers said, "I have such trouble with you. All the other students are so stiff with fright when they get on stage, they're all knotted up. I can't get them to relax. But you, when you get scared or self-conscious, you can hardly sit up, you're just overly relaxed. Now sit up and get yourself together!" I had to learn. And people starting out, they really have to learn how to walk. They can't think, "I've been walking all my life," because unknown, strange distortions take place when you're being watched that you're not aware of. When you think you're walking kind of normal, in fact, you're walking kind of strange. But for me, at this point, these are the least of my problems.

What are the kinds of problems you encounter now?

Well, most of my mental activity about acting goes into interpretation. It goes into working out an inner life for my character. That's what interests me most. If I have a certain line of thought going for my character, and then I have to deliver a line that doesn't seem to fit the mood or personality, a problem comes in. It's creating those links so the whole thing will make sense to me, that's the exciting and the difficult part. Now, with a character like the one in *Interiors*, I had almost no problem thinking up an inner life; it seemed very clear to me once I stopped worrying about the continuity. The only exception was at the end, where in the original script, there was a dialogue between me and Marybeth Hurt, who plays one of my daughters. I had a great deal of difficulty saying those lines because I felt that the content of them had already been said in the film; I couldn't find a justification for the need to reiterate them. So we talked about the scene and Woody listened to me, and then later he said, "I've changed the scene and now Marybeth will talk and you won't say anything." I really thought that was better, I felt Eve just couldn't have said another thing. And I think it plays very well. In that last scene, you don't know whether I am really there or whether Marybeth is imagining it. Then, of course, you find out that I am. So those are the problems that I have getting the emotional as well as the mental logic of it together.

Do you ever make notes of this inner logic?

A long time ago, I did a reading at the New School of *Hedda Gabler* and someone who wrote a magazine called *Off-Broadway* wanted me to describe the way I thought about the character. I started writing about what Hedda is thinking when the play opens; I'd written an enormous number of pages and Hedda hadn't even entered yet! So, it would take too much paper and too much time to write down this inner logic; there's so much variety and richness

involved. If I were to sit down and make notes, I'd only have time
or space to do one little thread, yet I've got in my head a whole
fabric.

For instance, one time I was working on *Macbeth* for the Actors
Studio and I tried to tell Lee [Strasberg] how I had conceived a certain part of it. "I'm working on the letters from Macbeth," I said,
"and I got certain ideas from talking to my husband Rip on the
phone while he was out in California. I always tell him about the
work he does and how wonderful it is, and he always says, 'Oh,
you're just saying that.' But then he called me up and said, 'Guess
what? I ran into so and so . . .' and I thought, some idiot-child of a
person, '. . . who thinks the thing I did on the tube last week was
great.' And Rip tells me all this with great enthusiasm. So it occurred to me that when Lady Macbeth gets this letter from
Macbeth saying, 'Guess what? I met these witches on the heath
and they say that I'm going to be king,' my reaction as Lady Macbeth would be, 'So what? I tell him that all the time; what's the big
deal about those damn witches?' Then, having made this connection between Lady Macbeth and myself, I began looking around
the room, thinking, well, if he's going to be king, I'm going to re-
decorate. When he's on the throne, we'll get some new hangings,
we'll get the place fixed up. . . . So part of my interpretation came
from lying in bed with the script just as Lady Macbeth was lying in
bed with the letters."

But Lee interrupted my explanations. "I don't know what you're
talking about," he told me. "Would you just do it?" So I did the
scene, and afterwards he said, "I want you directors to notice this.
Now you know perfectly well that when she was explaining what
she had in her head, she made no sense whatsoever, but you see
also that it worked for the scene. So it's a waste of time to tell your
actors what to think. If they're thinking something that's important
to them, it'll work. But give them thoughts that don't particularly
mean anything to them, even though they mean something to you,
and it won't." The point is to use something that'll work to feed
your imagination and not hinder it. That's all that matters.

What makes a good director for you?

A good director for me is usually a good director for all people. It's
a combination of things. Good directors, and Rip is an excellent
one, find out what each individual person has to work with and can

bring to the part. Then, with great open-mindedness and patience, a good director creates an atmosphere where people feel free to bring what they have to the roles.

Also important in a director is a great sensibility; an actor needs someone who understands what the material is about—on its deepest levels. It's very hard to be working on something and have the director tell you that the character you're playing is just sort of an irritating person. The director that told me that shall be nameless. But it's easier to act in a play, where you have more chances to go back and run at it. In movies, you have to make your decisions in a much faster way. Usually you rehearse and film it all in one day; you don't rehearse for three weeks as on stage. So directors who can keep away the distractions, the things that break your concentration, and get you to feel relaxed—those are the good ones.

Does it disturb you to act out of sequence in a film?

Yes, but I'm getting more used to it. Poor Marybeth [Hurt] went crazy. *Interiors* was her first film. She said, "Woody told us to play this scene one way, and then when we got finished, he said, 'Let's play it the opposite way.' Then we did it again and he told us, 'Now play it this way.' How do we know when we film the scene that follows this, which one of these was preceding it?" And I said, "In the movies you never know. The only way to keep sane in a movie is not to care. Let them decide." But it's terrible. In *Summer and Smoke*, Pamela Tiffin said (it was her first film), "But this is awful; it's like going to a banquet and they put a wonderful plate of food in front of you and just as you pick up the fork to take a bite, they whisk it away. You never get anything to eat."

Are you bothered by the presence of a camera?

It used to spook me. In one of the first live television shows I ever did I had a fairly small but crucial role. I had to come in and give the plot line that changed everything. When we rehearsed it, I was fine. But then it came time to really do it; the camera came up toward my face . . . and I went totally blank. I couldn't remember the line. I left it out.

What's especially awful is when you have to play a very intense, intimate scene with somebody who's supposed to be looking right in your eye, and you're looking right into the camera instead. The person's voice is coming from the other side of the room. But you have to pretend the camera is that person. The fact that I'm near-sighted helps a little bit.

Do you know how much of your body the cameraperson is seeing—whether it's all of you or just from the neck up?

It's so hard. I remember when I did something on TV, somebody said something to me and I responded by turning my foot. On stage, that would have been a very telling gesture. But the camera was only filming from my chest up. It looked like I had no reaction at all. So I finally learned; when they're setting up, I ask, "What's your frame? How much of me are you going to see? Do you see my feet?" Sometimes the crew gets annoyed and they don't want to bother telling you. You have to make a nuisance of yourself.

You must have worked very hard on the development of your voice for the stage. You have a very frail voice. Is that an adjustment that's second-nature to you at this point?

It's not second-nature. I have a really rotten voice for acting. It's so feathery, there's nothing to it. I have to make a conscious effort to put any tone in it so that anybody can hear me—even on camera. It takes a great deal of work and I always ought to do more than I do. I had a wonderful voice coach who was terrific when I did *Sweet Bird of Youth*. I remember a line I had that would make me so out of breath. I'd say, "He ffflew and he ffflew as fffar and as. . . ." That would be all I could get out. And the coach said, "Well, that's simple. You're just fluffing all the air out on the f's. Concentrate on the vowels." So I did. "He flew and he flew as far and as fast as he could." I could go on for forty-five minutes and still have plenty of breath. It's those little technical things, they're just like magic. Then I had another sentence later in the play and again, I was out of breath. The sentence ended with a "me." He said, "In this case, you have to stay with the consonants." So instead of saying "meeee," I said, "mmmme," which saved the breath. Then I thought, do I have to go in and ask him about everything? Well, I did—or just about.

Do you have breathing exercises to do?

Yes. I have a terrible tendency to leave off the ends of sentences. If the sentence is, "I've got to go home now," you get, "I've got to go ho. . . ." The critics are always after me. But, you know, I listen to Colleen Dewhurst, Julie Harris, Jess Tandy, and I say, "How can they possibly talk about *my* voice mannerisms?" I mean, you can instantly recognize the strange voices of those other women.

I'm always able to do better, vocally, when I've made the choices about what I want to do with a line. If I can say, "This is right, this is how it should be," then you can hear the whole line, but if I'm exploring around and I haven't quite decided yet, it's more likely to be lost.

There's so much energy needed on the stage. Is there anything you do to keep yourself physically in shape?

That's a matter of rest and food. I have to have a steak when I'm performing. And there has to be the right amount of time between when I eat and when I perform. If I eat too early, then it all wears off, and if I eat too late, I'm too full and can't get going. So if I have my steak at five for an eight-thirty performance, I'm fine.

What makes you decide against taking a certain role?

I'll turn down any part if it's like the one I just finished. No matter how great it is. I look for contrast.

I turn things down, too, when I think that the content is contrary to what I believe in. If I think it's selling rotten ideas to people, I'll turn it down, even though it's a good part. Of course, economic necessity sometimes causes me to have to do something that I don't idealistically approve of, but I say, "Well, at least this project is less obnoxious than some other ones," and I have to take the lesser of the evils. If I were only to play in things that I believed in—every syllable of them—I wouldn't work much. For instance, I enjoyed being in *The Happiest Millionaire* even though that movie was all about adorable Detroit and the wonderful automobile industry and I don't go along with that. But it was just a wonderful part. I had a good time. And it helped us buy the house. So I don't want to try to pass myself off as this great virtuous, pure thing because I haven't been able to achieve that. But I've tried. God knows, I've tried.

Do you find comedy harder to play than serious drama?

No. I find good things easier to play than bad things whether they're comedy or not. Things that are well-written, that are soundly based in real human behavior, are easier to play.

There is an extra added challenge to comedy because the relationship to the audience is different. In a drama, you can feel the attention of the audience and you can feel that they're getting bored, but in a comedy the relationship is so intimate and it's like that [she claps time] all the way through. The science of getting the people to respond the way you want them to in comedy is terribly intricate and tricky. And mysterious. A line you've done the same way will get a barrel of laughs nine times out of ten, but then the tenth time is different. You become so involved that nothing seems to get the kind of response you want it to, and you play around with it, varying it constantly. In that sense then, it's easier to play a drama. But that's hard too, because you need to create a longer attention span for people. If people don't laugh at something in a comedy, within two seconds, you will have another joke, whereas in a drama you have to slowly build a certain atmosphere; when you lose it, it takes longer to get it back together. They're both devilishly difficult things to do. I guess if acting were easy, then we wouldn't do it. We'd find something else to drive ourselves crazy with.

It's fascinating that you see acting as problem-solving.

Oh! I love the problem-solving. I do love it. I even love it when the scenery falls down, and you have to think of wonderful, witty, apt things to say to cover for it. I love all that.

What happens when you're working in a drama and you feel the audience's attention slipping? How is that problem solved?

There are so many things you have to think about all at the same time. You have to change the rhythm of it. Like if it's very *largo*, you must for a minute quicken it, so as to bring people's attention back. That's a very technical thing to do, but at the same time, you have to conclude that your own concentration must be slackening. Ordinarily, if your concentration in a performance is really intense, people will be drawn into it. Even though they disapprove of the content of the play, or they don't like the actor they're looking at, if it's really intense, it's like hypnotism, and it will bring people into focus.

I saw a strange thing done when I went to the Jewish Community Theatre in Brooklyn; I saw Jacob Ben-Ami playing *Detective Story* in Yiddish. I don't understand the language but I understood what people were doing through their body movements. It was an audience as in the Oriental theatre were everybody brought their lunch; they'd all greet each other with, "Hello. How are you? How are the children?" They'd sit down, open their lunch and if there was a fight on stage, they'd stop and look for a while, but they would pick parts that they liked and listen only to those. I thought to myself, "What kind of a community is this?" But Ben-Ami went on and played the part of this jealous man, paying no attention to the mayhem. It seemed that he neither knew nor cared whether anyone was listening. Yet he played so quintessentially the core of the character that I said, "I'm watching Othello. This is not a detective in a modern story, this man is the pure thing." And it was breathtaking. It seemed to me it didn't have anything to do with the play and he had no connection to his audience; it was the strangest experience. I said, "What a lesson. You see, you shouldn't get all flustered and give up and worry if everybody is not hanging on your every word. You just do your work."

You were nominated a number of times for Oscars.

I was nominated six times.

Do you put much store in those kinds of awards?

Well, they express something, you know, but I don't think that anybody who misses getting an Academy Award should go drown himself or give up the business. I think it's nice, the popularity contest, but it's not too important beyond that.

And I think it's terrific as long as I don't have to get up there and make one of those embarrassing speeches. I love being nominated because that means that a certain number of people have approved of my work. But my ambition is to get so many nominations, more than anybody else has ever gotten, and yet never get the award. There's just no way that you can get away without making a fool of yourself if you win. If you don't go, then you make a pretentious idiot of yourself. If you do go, and you start thanking people, you're not going to be able to thank all the people unless you take up a whole hour; you're going to leave out somebody and you can't do that. There's no way you can win by winning. You just have to get nominated forever. It's much better.

You won two Emmys when you played a very lovable character. But how do you feel about playing the unlikable ones?

I love it. It's fun. It's such a release to be able to be naughty and not have to go to jail for it, not have to die for it, not have everybody hate you for it, but on the contrary, to admire you for it! You can act like the most rapacious, selfish person, and, instead of saying, "Get rid of her quick," everyone will say, "Oh, it's wonderful." But there's a similar kind of release with the good guys. Just think, to be able to play Saint Joan, to be a saint without really having to burn at the stake. Terrific!

One thing that you learn working in the theatre is that there's a lot of good guy in every bad guy, and there's a lot of the bad guy in all the good guys. Your ambition is to represent a well-rounded, real human being. If you have a good guy, you don't want to make him all sweetsy-peetsy because no one would believe it. You've got to have dark colors in your good characters and light in your bad.

You've mentioned a number of times now a sense of color in your characters. Do you feel that an appreciation of other arts feeds your acting?

Oh God. It's so nourishing. I think an appetite for one gives you an appetite for all of them. And I'm a culture-vulture. I walk around with my cassettes playing classical music. The other day, I was walking down the street listening to *Manon Lescaut* and I was carrying this big book I got on sale about Toulouse-Lautrec. I have the feeling, a real strong conviction, that almost everything an actor does contributes to his skill. I used to go to museums and tell my mother I had been working. She'd say, "What do you mean you were working? What did you learn?" But I couldn't explain what it was. Sometimes, I just walked down the street and watched people. You know, I'd sit on the bus and notice how people behaved. I always feel as if I'm learning a lot, but still, I can't explain what it is that I learn in very specific terms.

Do you ever feel that you'd like to take time off just to recharge yourself?

I always have time off because one doesn't get employed that often. There was one time, however, that I really felt the need for a rest. I was in Chicago and I played three plays in a row for three weeks each. And I thought, I've had enough. I wanted to just sit down for a minute. They were three very difficult plays all of which I'd always wanted to do. That's when it's most frustrating; the chances of being able to do it the way you want are so remote. If it's something that doesn't mean that much to you in the first place, then you can enjoy each piece of it. But when it's a great play that you've always wanted to do, your vision is so big, so immense, that you can never fill it, and you're always feeling inadequate.

Can you tell me why you love acting, what it satisfies in you?

Well, it's a way of communication. Quite often I've tried to explain things to people who I thought were quite sympathetic, and I'd talk and talk and then realize that they hadn't comprehended a single word I'd said. It can be devastating. When you get a lot of thoughts and feelings that you can't communicate, it's very constipating— you should pardon the expression. And so it's wonderful when you can do something that gets it all off your chest.

The wonderful part about acting is that you can convey these very, very complex things quite graphically. If you're a musician, you can evoke wonderfully complicated things, but music is open to many more interpretations. You can't be too specific about what you're saying. I suppose writing is the most specific, except that it's more linear; you can convey more accurately, but only so much at a time. It's like when I was trying to write down what I wanted to say about Hedda. It would have taken such reams of paper. But if I walk on the stage with a certain attitude, people will understand immediately what it would have taken all that time to explain in words.

RIP TORN

Interviewing Rip Torn is more or less a matter of turning on the tape recorder, warming him up, and getting out of the way. He is generally acknowledged as one of the most uncommonly talented actors in the country, but his uncommon mixture of outspokenness, political involvement, and refusal to be commercially packaged makes his career one of the most turbulent and his ideas some of the most unique.

Elmore Torn, Jr. was born on February 6, 1931 in Temple, Texas. His father, who nicknamed him Rip, was involved with the agrarian reform movement and was at one time associated with the black botanist, George Washington Carver. This influenced Torn's decision to study agriculture, but he later switched to architecture and finally decided on acting. In 1952 he became an apprentice at the Dallas Institute of Performing Arts under Baruch Lumet (father of the film director, Sidney Lumet), and after enlisting and serving in the Army during the Korean War, he came to New York in search of work.

Torn was given his first break on Broadway by Elia Kazan, who hired him as understudy (and eventual replacement) in the role of Brick in Tennessee Williams' *Cat On a Hot Tin Roof*. Although he was under tremendous pressure to change his name, and risked the loss of a number of roles in refusing, in the years that followed he appeared regularly on the live television shows that made up the medium's most Golden Age: "Omnibus," "Playhouse 90," "Kraft Theatre," "Hallmark Hall of Fame," "Alcoa Hour," and more. He won the Theatre World Award in 1959 for his work in *Chaparral*, and created the role of Tom Finley, Jr. in the original stage production (and later film) of Tennessee Williams' *Sweet Bird of Youth*. He took over the co-starring role of Chance Wayne in the touring company and appeared with Emlyn Williams in *Daughter of Silence* by Morris West.

But from roughly the time of Kennedy's assassination to the fall of Nixon, Rip Torn was *persona non grata* among the powers-that-be in the film and theatrical worlds. For the most part, the jobs he did manage to get were as the typecast villains of such TV series as "Bonanza," "The Man from U.N.C.L.E.," "Route 66," "Mannix," and "Ben Casey." He began to involve himself in the more off-beat assignments that an image-conscious actor would shun. In 1969, he directed and starred in a multi-media production of Shakespeare's *Richard III*, playing the title role in Nixon costume. He won an Obie award for his portrayal of the sleazy, bisexual pimp in Norman Mailer's *The Deer Park*, portrayed a redneck storekeeper in James Baldwin's explosive *Blues For Mr. Charlie*, and was an exuberant Henry Miller in the film, *Tropic of Cancer*.

Although Mr. Torn's performances have almost always received kudos from the critics, the productions as a whole have often met with their disapproval, and this has been true of his directing forays as well. Despite disdain from critics, he won a second Obie for his direction of Michael McClure's *The Beard*, and he won a third for his staging of a double bill by Israel Horovitz, *The Honest-to-God Schnozzola* and *Leader*, although the latter plays ran for only eight performances.

Recent years have found his opportunities once more expanding: he was a guest artist with the Yale Repertory Theatre in the title role of Strindberg's *The Father*, played Walt Whitman in the critically acclaimed CBS Special, "Song of Myself," and had an important supporting role in Nicholas Roeg's film, *The Man Who Fell to Earth*. Still, because of his desire for greater artistic independence, he has been working to establish his own company. The Sanctuary Theatre Workshop's first production in 1977 of two one-act Strindberg plays, *The Stronger* and *Creditors*, was directed by Torn and included among the cast both himself and his wife Geraldine Page. In interpreting these pieces with more grim humor than some theatre critics believed them to have, Mr. Torn was as unconventional as ever—and still criticized for being so.

He has one daughter from a previous marriage to the actress Anne Wedgeworth and three children with his present wife, Geraldine Page. They own a house in the Chelsea section of Manhattan.

Ms. Page has been—and continues to be—fiercely loyal to her husband, and upon meeting him, it is easy to see why. His intensity and intelligence are not to be subdued; he doesn't hesitate to say exactly what he feels and doesn't shy away from his own strength. Mr. Torn is obviously upset about his former reputation for being "difficult," but has not been defeated by it. With a rich, resonant voice and a faint Texas drawl lurking at the edges of it, he suggests a proud figure from the American frontier. There is a sense of drama about him, as if he were a character in his own autobiography. And it would be difficult to walk away from meeting him without seeing one's vision of the world in more vivid colors.

You began acting as a child, I understand; you were a great ham.

Oh yes, I was doing shows and benefits even when I was a little kid. I can remember, as a teenager, putting on neighborhood shows, and not only acting in them, but organizing and writing the scripts. I think all of that is a very natural thing; a lot of kids do that. But most kids grow out of it; they become serious. I never did. I like to have a good time. That's something that I share with Gerry [Geraldine Page]; we're actors because we have such a good time doing it. I don't see any other reason for practicing an art. So many of the side effects or the environmental effects of being an artist are unpleasant and painful, so you'd better enjoy the work, or do something else. That's the way I feel. And I always have a good time. When people come up to me after a performance they've seen, they often say, "Gee, you looked like you were gettin' off." And I say, "Yeah, I was."

You went originally, however, to agricultural college.

I did. I had a major in drama and a minor in agriculture, which is probably one of the more weird degree plans that anyone has ever been graduated with. I was studying advanced farming procedures and it finally dawned on me that I didn't even have a farm. So I said, "Well, I'll go into the movies and make a lot of money and I'll get my ranch." Somehow, I tripped myself up. I got more interested in the actual art of acting than in making money from it.

Was acting considered a respectable profession when you were growing up in Texas?

Oh, no. In those days in Texas, saying you wanted to be an actor was like saying you wanted to go straight to hell! My family, the neighbors and friends, none of them liked it. But after I had served in the military, I decided I'd paid all my dues. I'd done what my folks wanted me to do, what my country wanted me to do, and I was going to do what I wanted to do.

Do you think their respect for acting has grown in the years since?

Yeah, I think so. For movie acting particularly. My cousin, Sissy Spacek, is a big star. She's terrific. But I think that I made it easier for a lot of people that came after me.

You have studied acting and dance and speech and voice with some of the greatest names in the fields. But do you think that acting is a skill that can be taught, or is it basically an innate talent?

I think it can be taught. It's just like painting, though. You can be taught all the rules, the perspective, how to use the colors, how to buy the paints, and you can become quite competent. But to really affect other people—that's where the innate artistry comes in. It's why some paintings have a tremendous impact on people while others don't. And it's the same way with actors. You have to have a scenic talent. You have to have something that makes people look at you when you are on stage. There are some people who are very fine movie actors, but who only have an acting power for the camera at a distance of five feet, close up. They don't have that force on the stage. They don't have that kind of energy. People who really have it carry their own spotlight; others will look at them no matter what they're doing.

There *are* great teachers, though—like Jim Moll and Sanford Meisner. Lee Strasberg is one of them, too. He can teach you how to relax on the stage. Tension, he says, is the actor's occupational disease. And in the area of sense memory, he's a true pioneer.

Do you find the same satisfaction acting in films as on stage?

I love to do it all. To make a distinction would be like a fisherman saying he would rather fish for bass than trout. I like it all; I like to fish.

Does it bother you that plays are so ephemeral? All that work . . . and then after a certain number of performances, it's gone?

Yes, I think that is the worst aspect of plays. At least film is an artifact. But you know, we have the technical ability to record everything with videotape; it's just that the union situation is so bizarre that you cannot even make a record. It's not so much the actor's unions; it's mainly the stage hands who want the extra pay. But there is obviously a difference between what is commercial broadcast tape and what is just record. I feel that we actors are cheated. If the tape becomes a commodity, if someone wants to buy it, then the union could demand that the people who participated in it get some compensation for it. But to *a priori* just cut it out and say, "No, we don't allow any kind of taping," is just ridiculous. I see marriage counselors using videotape, the cops use videotape, firemen use it, golf pros, training programs for J. Walter Thompson use tape, and yet the very people who can use it most—the actors, the stage people—are not allowed!

When you're acting for film, does the jumbled shooting sequence disturb your sense of the development of a character?

Well, I have a very visual imagination and before I started doing shows, I studied to be an architect. I actually see my own performance as a film in my mind. That doesn't mean that I always do what I envision, but at least I always have a plan. I know in an instinctive way what should go in a certain scene.

Certain scenes, you know, are "key scenes," and they are usually shot the first day. I used to think that was some kind of weird practice, but now I know why directors do it: in case you can't play the key scene, they can fire you in time to get somebody else!

Do you feel that you don't have much control over your own performances in a film?

Well, you don't have much control, it's true. This may be apocryphal but there's a story about Rock Hudson who was supposed to get on a horse and ride it. The horse shied, reared up, and ran out of the scene. Hudson could barely stay on. But it was printed in reverse, and therefore looked like a wild horse that he gentled. So, certainly with film they can do a lot of tricks. I once did a film where a guy was reaching out and getting fresh with a woman; he put his hand on her and she pushed it off. But if you ran it backwards, it looked as if she reached out and put the guy's hand on her. Film is still the same now as it was at its inception: a magic show.

You did a lot of television work in its early days, when it was live.
What was that like?

It was very much like the theatre. You'd rehearse for a couple of
weeks and then you'd do the show live—literally in front of mil-
lions of people. To me that was a wonderful experience. I felt I
was visiting with friends of mine all over the country. I really
could feel a kind of kinetic energy; I could feel people coming
through the camera. It sounds silly, I guess, but when the red
light was on, I knew that my relatives were watching me down in
Texas or friends of mine in San Francisco were visiting with me. I
loved live television. But the producers and sponsors didn't have
enough control over it. They cut it out.

Most people think that the quality of television has declined since
those days. Does that affect the opportunities available to actors
today?

I do think that when you had live television, it was a great training
ground for a lot of people. Sidney Lumet came out of that, John
Frankenheimer, writers like Paddy Chayefsky, Rod Serling, and
many others. And the live TV in New York subsidized the
theatre. Actors could support themselves on television work, and
be free to appear in plays that paid little. Certainly, in every
theatre capital except the United States, cultural activities are
centrally located. You don't have, for example, the theatre in
Paris and the movies in Marseilles. You don't have theatre in
London and films in Birmingham. You have one cultural capital.
But in this country, it is divided between New York City and
Hollywood.

Do you think there's a pressure to choose between forms—to be
either a movie actor or a theatre actor?

Oh, there's a tremendous pressure. You have female theatre
stars in New York, but what male stars do you have? You've got
one or two. There's Jason Robards. Pacino comes back and does
a date, but he probably won't do anything for a year or two.
Actors today are fearful of the theatre. They don't know anything
about it, and in California, they don't want to know anything

about it. They say to me, "I've never heard of anything that you did," and I say, "Well, that's because you live in a very provincial town."

Do you think, in fact, that the techniques of acting are different from one medium to the other?

Yeah, I think so. Again, you take an example like Jason Robards who used to be great on stage but not in films. Well, it's not that he was rotten, it's just that he wasn't that good. But he's also somebody who has really discovered how to just *be* on the screen. You don't catch him acting. I saw him in *Julia* and he was just sensational. He's finally reached a point in his life where he accepts himself in front of the camera, and he's just content to be there and that's terrific. He has the kind of technique now that doesn't show. So there is a difference between stage acting and film.

But always, the best training for actors, even if they're going to do film-work, has been the stage. That's true of all Bergman's people, for example, and that was true of the actors who appeared in the films of the thirties, forties, and fifties. When people talk about the Golden Age of filmmaking, one of the reasons it was so good was that all of your supporting players were star stage actors. The character actors were well experienced on the stage and they were tremendously valuable in every scene. They made all the difference. You look back on some of those movies that Peter Lorre made . . . imagine putting somebody else in those roles— there would be nothing there! He was a guy you could put in a Simonize commercial and make it a classic. You just can't get that anymore. An actor can have talent, but if he hasn't done the work, he's not going to be able to do what a guy like Peter Lorre did.

What is the difference really between stage acting and film acting? Would you make your emotions and expressions larger on the stage than you would if a camera was close on top of you?

It's not just making it large. A lot of times it's the intensity. Stage energy is a more intense energy than we need for talking here. This conversation can be captured on a tape or video recorder, or on film, because the camera can move up and see the expression

in your eyes and actually get down inside you. On the stage it's
more your *body*, the way your body is moving. In film, it's your
face. There are film actors who couldn't walk from one chair to
another on stage without stumbling. They're just very clumsy
people. They haven't had that kind of training. But their faces are
eloquent. Perhaps you could say that stage acting requires more
of a totality.

I was in Francis Ford Coppola's first film, *You're a Big Boy
Now*. He was a student director, it was a student project, actually.
He had a scene with Julie Harris, and everybody knows Julie
Harris is a fine actress. I brought him to the Actors Studio that
day. He was very interested in a lot of techniques and I'd given
him books on film rehearsal. Pudovkin, a Russian theorist, had
set up a scheme for having film rehearsals, and Francis wanted to
try them. He wanted to rehearse the hell out of Karen Black and
some other people but I said, "We don't need it, not for film. You
may need it for the younger people, but film is improvisation."
Then we got into a scene with Julie and he'd rehearsed it so much
that she didn't know what he wanted. Professional actors, when
they see that a director is puzzled or seemingly unhappy, don't
give him less, they have a tendency to give him more, more,
more. So Francis said, "What she's doing now goes way, way
overboard. It's too big for the screen." I said, "Why don't you just
give us our marks and let us do it? And," I added, "tell everybody
to underact." He said, "I can barely talk to her anymore. I don't
know how to say anything to her." So he came in the next day and
he had a T-shirt that said UNDERACT on it. She laughed and, of
course, she did a terrific job.

*Do you have to go through some sort of routine before you go on
stage to get yourself in the mood to perform, to prepare yourself for
putting out all that energy?*

Gerry likes to get there very early and take her time, and she likes
to be the last one to leave. Unless I'm doing a character that
requires a great deal of costuming, I like to just drop in and do it.
When I was a younger actor, I would prepare for hours, summoning up the concentration. But people told me that when I got
older, I'd be able to get to myself and get into these things much
quicker, and I find it's true.

One thing I like to do is to go to the gym every day—particularly when I'm working. I went yesterday. I was completely exhausted, but I felt that if I went to the gym and worked out for at least half an hour, then it would really refresh me, no matter how bad I felt. The best actors, and I've talked to many about this, feel a similar need. Olivier, for example, used to work out at a gym; he felt that that was the single most important quality for an actor—physical strength. Keep in very, very good health, good shape. And Michael Redgrave, writing in his book, said that he found it obligatory to work out, whether it be running, or swimming, or weights, or fencing. He needed a physical workout, then a nap.

Do you find that there's a conflict in your life between being an artist and being a father? Has that caused you any problems?

Having children is a wonderful thing. A lot of actors say, "Gee, it's going to ruin my art." But to think that you have to choose between your art and real life is bull. The artist has been sold a bill of goods about that. Mainly, I guess, the worry is an economic one. You think, how can I do my art when I have to worry about supporting a family? But I've gotten at least fifteen, twenty characters by just watching my kids. I get so many ideas. They put on shows. We don't push them to do anything, of course, but we don't discourage them. When people say, "Do you want your kids to be actors? " I say all kids *are* actors. It's one of the basic human impulses. I think the more you are tied into life, the better an actor you will be, not the reverse. The idea that the artist must live in an ivory tower and hold himself away from all kinds of responsibilities is just talk. I know I'm a much better actor for having had children.

One of the concerns for many people, I suppose, is that an artist needs solitude in which to concentrate and create.

No, my powers of concentration are much more highly developed as a result of the children. I mean, I can actually learn my lines and rehearse in that bedlam! So, you see, it's helped.

Could you tell me how you go about preparing for your roles—for instance, with Walt Whitman? What was your procedure for creating that character?

With Whitman I read about fifteen or twenty books, maybe seven biographies, all of his poetry, all of his prose poems, particularly *Specimen Days*, which has a lot of fragments of different essays. When I'm doing an historical character, I really feel that that person's presence comes around. I think they're interested in how they're going to be presented, especially a guy like Whitman.

Do you consciously sit down and try to establish what you have in common with the character?

I used to do it very much that way, but as I get older, I do those things instinctively. In the case of Whitman, for example, I knew that when he was only twenty-eight, he was the editor of *The Brooklyn Eagle*, and he built two houses in the same year because he was a carpenter, too. And he learned to be a printer when he was eight years old. He may have called himself lazy—but that was just a pose. He liked to sit out on the grass on his lunch hour and say, "Oh, I'm *so* lazy." But in fact, he thrived on work.

I felt I understood that about him because ever since I was a kid, I was always working, too. I was in great demand to take care of yards and flower beds and stuff like that. I also worked at a grocery store after school, I had a paper route, then I had a little wagon with a concession, and I'd sell sorghum syrup. I was always busy, making my own way. I never had money from home. So with Whitman, I would make these identifications. I even understood a lot about him from the description of the way he would say one word. I knew he was a poet who didn't say, "I want you to hear my 'po-em.' " He would say, "I want you to hear my 'pome.' " He was that kind of guy. So I learned from the descriptions of his contemporaries the way he looked, the way he acted. And from all those qualities, I chose the ones which would best represent him.

I think I have a great deal in common with painters, and many of them are interested in my work. I once asked Larry Rivers why that was so, and he said, "Well, we look upon you as an action painter." I like that. I feel that's what I do. I do paint characters. I select my elements by the way I choose to walk, the way I move, the way my voice operates, the actual pitch of it, the sound of it. I select those in the same way a painter takes colors from his palette to create an impression. So while my identification is instinctive, my selectivity is conscious; that's where the artistry comes in. And I never believe that I *am* the character. I might believe it for a moment in the scene because I'm concentrating as the character would be, but that's about it. When I was doing Whitman, they'd call me at the desk in Baltimore and say, "Time for you to wake up, Mr. Whitman," and I'd say, "He ain't here."

You differed over your conception of Whitman with the people at CBS. Why was that?

The people at CBS said, "We're going to bring Walt out of the closet." But to me, Walt Whitman was never *in* the closet. They thought I was making him too noble, and I thought they were making him a dilettante.

I started out as a writer, and I guess that's part of it. I worked on the high school paper and in college I worked on the college paper. I studied journalism along with a number of other different subjects. (I was accused of going to college not to get a degree but to get an education.) A play is like any other kind of construction; the script is only your blueprint. And sometimes, when you work with a blueprint, you have to say, "Look, this isn't right; we're going to have to readjust." There are times when you are readjusting everything to the very last minute.

I am an actor whose friends are basically writers. I've been lucky to have known the major poets and playwrights and novelists of our time. I count them as acquaintances and friends. They haven't been people whom I've pursued, because that's not my style. But I know Norman Mailer and Terry Southern and Jimmy Baldwin because they wanted me to work with them. They wanted someone to do their work and they know I'm very respectful of the role of the playwright, of the author. I think that I have gotten in much more trouble in California attempting to hold onto the original script, yet my reputation is one of somebody who comes in and tries to change it. I don't do that. When I make changes in the script, they are only slight, and I do it to sharpen the work. I don't do it as some kind of strange subjective thing. It's just that I've worked long enough to know what will wash and what won't. I just know it from experience.

When I accepted the role of Whitman, I told them what I
thought about that particular script. I said, "The skeleton of the
script is very good, but Whitman himself was not a verbose person. He was very laconic, very terse. He was a listener more than
anything else." And what I fought to do was to keep him from
being the *idea* of the poet. Most good writers are always picking
things up; they're walking recorders—they're listeners. They're
not people who are always displaying themselves. And Whitman
wasn't that way either. So I did differ with them in that area. But
it wasn't changing the script, it was mainly cutting down on the
verbosity. And that feeling of mine came from all the research
that I did.

*In the case of a fictional character, where you do not have access
to research material, to first-hand descriptions, how do you go
about building the details of the character? Is it more difficult?*

Sometimes you have a complete picture of the character right
away. I've done characters where, from the first reading, I had a
sense of the entire personality. I don't know where it came from.
It could be that the character reminded me of somebody I might
have known in school or when I was in the army or when I was
doing different kinds of jobs. I just did a film with James Brolin,
for example, where I play a guy that dips snuff, an old country
man. To me, that character was Sweeney, a guy from Ashdown,
Arkansas that I knew when I was working in the oil fields almost
thirty years ago. I'm sure that Pop is no longer alive, but he
reminded me of the character I was called upon to play—a kind of
folksy philosopher and a very good guy. In that sense, I act in the
same way that everybody acts.

I know that one of my uncles, for instance, is a great storyteller
and my mother is good at imitating people. I think we all know
people who, especially when they start gossiping, will do imita-
tions of different people. Like if they have a fight with a neighbor,
they'll say, ". . . and then she came . . ." and they'll proceed to
mimic that character. So everybody does that. We're all experts
at the preparation of characters. What do you do when you gird
yourself up to go ask the boss for a raise? You've already played
the scene out in your head, right? Sometimes you've got the
wrong preparation. You get down there and get into an argument

right away. But that's basically my method: I give my impression of the way that I think somebody else is. And I don't try to separate my work from the body of my associations in life. All those things—my friends and my family—they feed into my work, they're a part of it.

Have you ever felt the need to visit a locale?

Yeah, I do that. I use a tape recorder a lot, and when I did *Desire Under the Elms* I went grouse hunting in New Hampshire. I found this guide, gave him twenty bucks, and told him I wanted to record his voice. They have a very funny accent up there; it sounds a little Southern, but it's just what I wanted. I got a bottle of whiskey, we sat down, and I got him to record the entire script. When I have people do that, I don't get them to give me their interpretation, I just want their speech patterns. I said, "Do it kind of flat, just read it." I did the same thing in order to play Hartogs, the Dutch psychiatrist; I worked with a man who was a publisher. (If a character you're playing has a different kind of accent, you want to, first of all, get someone who is of the same class. Obviously, if I was playing a Dutch psychiatrist, I couldn't go and get a Dutch machinist. I might, of course, if the machinist were very educated, but I guess it was more propitious to get a man who was a publisher.) He said to me, "Well, I have never acted," and I said, "I don't want you to act, I just want you to read the lines," which he did. Before each scene I would listen to the tape and then be able to have the correct kind of accent. My editor and producer told everybody in town, "It's uncanny the way Rip never made a mistake, he kept the continuity of the accent all the way through." Well, I could hear where I slipped, where I made mistakes, but they couldn't.

Do you ever get insights into a character from listening to a piece of music or seeing a painting?

Of course, theatre is a synthesis of *all* the arts, so the more you know about them the better off you are. With a fictional character, in particular, you're a kind of detective, and you look for hints all around you. Say you're playing a character from a certain century; you have to dress and behave and talk in a completely different way. One way to study what poses and stances people took at the time is to go to a museum. That's why I like to be a character actor: it's a continuing study, and a continuing discovery. In that way, it's very thrilling to me; you keep very fresh. You don't have to do the same character over and over again.

There was a period of about ten years though, when you were limited to the same kind of character.

Not on stage and not in my early days of television. I had a very wide range then. One week I'd be playing an old Irishman, the next I'd be playing a wetback. But when television moved physically to the West Coast, all the good guys, the heroes, were the people under contract. They played the sergeant or the detective or the lawyer. The people who were the guest stars were always the troublemakers. They were the bad guys, the impossible cases the lawyer had, the weirdos. Those roles were a lot of fun, but they were basically the villain roles. And that's when I began to get type-cast as a villain, but so did *everybody* that did not sign a contract and become the contract player. There was a lock on all the good-guy parts. And I got a reputation that way.

Is there, in fact, a kind of role that you do best?

Yes, actually, I think the thing I do best is comedy. I'm a clown. Yet when you're considered a dramatic actor, producers are always surprised that you can *do* something like that. They don't think of you doing comedy. But all good dramatic actors are also comics.

You're saying that the two talents are not as distinct as they may appear?

All the best actors have always said, as Charlie Laughton said, "You play a tragedy like a comedy and you play a comedy like a tragedy." With a funny role, if you don't play it for real, you're not going to get your laugh. If you keep saying, "Ha, ha, ha, isn't this funny?," you can be sure that it won't be. And in the same way, if you present a drama with an "isn't-this-sad" attitude, it won't attract anyone's sympathy. The art of a good performance is in combining them both. It's like the combination of extremes in a Rembrandt painting—the very dark and the very light combine to make a dramatic portrait. Say you're playing a character, a kind of down-in-the-mouth, sad person. To make an effective portrayal, you're going to have to find the places where he's not like that, you're going to have to dig for those moments when the character feels joy. Even the great clowns, like Emmett Kelly, realized that principle. A lot of them had a tear painted on their cheeks. The things that were tragic to the clowns were the things which were funny to the rest of us.

The great writers have always known that. If you play a Shakespearean character, particularly in the tragedies, you want to get the humor. After the murder of Duncan by Macbeth, there is the scene with the porter who's talking about getting drunk and pissing and carrying on. And with Strindberg, everyone thinks of his plays as being grim, but they are just as funny as the proverbial rubber crutch. He wrote them that way. In his journals he said, "I want comic actors." That doesn't mean that to look for the comic aspect of a character is to make the character shallow. Laughter is the glint off the surface of the waters, but the waters run deep. And a laugh is just as meaningful as a tear. You can't go on the stage to be funny. You can only go to do certain actions and say certain lines, and you *hope* it's going to be funny. It's as Bernard Shaw said, "I tell the truth and people laugh."

You say that a comic actor has to play his part "for real," but isn't there a detachment implied in the very fact that he's on a stage in a theatre, and the audience knows it's "for laughs"?

There's a fancy phrase from Coleridge: the willing suspension of disbelief. I don't think you can come out on stage and say, "I'm really in this room." You've got to say, "I'm on this stage and those are people out there watching me. But they're watching me to see how I would behave *if* I were really the person in this room." Once you take that all in, then you are ready to play-act.

*And that strengthens the relationship between the actor and the audience who have to participate **together** in overcoming the illusion of the theatre.*

Yes, the audience loves those breaks back and forth between the actors and themselves. That's why live television was so good. The producers used to worry about the fact that sometimes the camera got into the shot or the actor had a coughing fit. When Maurice Evans did *Hamlet* and when he said, "Now I am alone," the carpenter walked on and looked around right in the middle of the scene; it got a big laugh. Yet my friends said, "I like to hear actors cough; I like to hear somebody drop the nails or the hammer or see a camera come into the shot." Basically, the play is *real* because it's happening right there. It's the immediacy of it which makes it so exciting. If all the sports shows were to be broadcast a week or six months after the games were played, they wouldn't attract nearly the kind of interest they do. People like to see things happening right in front of them. And that's why events on the stage are much more powerful many times than on film. People will say to me after a theatre performance, "I really saw you do it. You were really there!"

Having first been an actor, then a director, you must have a good sense of what qualities in a director bring out good performances.

Well, I, of course, have great respect for actors, and the kind of director who is good for me is the kind of director that I try to be. I try to cast a play well and although I have very specific plans for the play, very specific ideas for each actor, and how they should do their role, I keep those things quiet. It's like the beginning of a poker hand: I keep my cards to myself and I let the actors play out *their* cards. I want them to come and bring their own creativity to it. If I come in and show everybody how to act, how to talk, how to stand, and what to do, they only become the puppets of my imagination. While that might be very good with a very imaginative director, the director would be robbing himself of the people that he has. Theatre is a collective process; it is, as I've said, a synthesis of all the arts. And if you have seven or eight very talented people, why rob yourself of their creativity?

Work itself is a very good editor. I try to remember very, very precisely what the actors do and then I can maybe, very diplomatically, come up the next day and say, "Gee, that's terrific, but the other night you did a certain thing . . ." and I will describe it to them. You must be careful not to ever act out an actor's bit better than he does it—if, in fact, you can. (I myself never felt that I could.) A lot of directors make the mistake of saying "no" to an actor's idea, and then coming up the next day to present the idea as if they thought of it. You have to be very careful not to do that. That's one thing that'll turn an actor against you. And a lot of young directors do that. They want to act the role of the director instead of just *being* the director. Some of the finest directors say very little. But they are there, and they watch.

I just finished acting in a film where the director demonstrated to me how to make love in the love scene! I thought it was kind of bizarre. It made me furious at first and then I thought that maybe he just wants to get off on it; he seems to be so crazy about the leading lady that I guess I shouldn't worry about it. But as a director, I do not like to intrude upon the actor's fantasy. I like to protect it. And the finest compliment I got as a director was from Michael McClure, who said that I build a protective bubble around my actors, working with them. No matter what, if an actor says something is disturbing him, I honor that. A lot of directors say, "Oh, these temperamental actors!" But who the hell has more right to be temperamental than an actor?

Do you think that the power of the critics has grown too great?

The theatre in this country is no longer an industry of actors—it's an industry of critics. It's gotten to the point in American theatre where the tail is wagging the dog. Critics have emerged as stars themselves. I think they really hate the actors because they know that they fatten and feed off their work. When Corelli was singing in the opera and he saw the critic who wrote about him, he said, "He's the guy who did it!" and right in the middle of the aria, he jumped off the stage and punched the guy out. I thought that was terrific. People will say, "Oh, well, that's part of your upbringing, Rip, your idea of frontier justice." But I'll admit there are some good critics—the best are people who are also engaged in the work that they are talking about. You take a man like Truffaut, for example. Or take Bernard Shaw, who was a music critic for many years and a theatre critic but was also working in the theatre. Let's see some of those others write a script. You find that some of these people are flawed artists. They can't get their play on, they can't act, they can't direct. It's like the old saying,

"Those who can, do; those who can't, teach." In art, it's "Those who can't, criticize."

Criticism may be valuable as an historical record, but I think it's gotten way out of hand. When I did Strindberg, some of them complained I was too emotional, too fiery. They said, if anything, Strindberg was icy. Strindberg!—a guy who had all those tempestuous relationships with the leading feminists of his day, who jumped off a boat, who tried to commit suicide when he was about eighteen, who was always in a wrangle, in a fight—he was a tremendously volcanic personality. To say that he was glacial shows the most amazing ignorance! Icy is how Olivier played him and that was Olivier's style. But it means nothing beyond that. And this is the kind of thing that's wrecked the theatre to a great extent.

Critics should at least give a play two weeks before they review it. Let it have its day in court. I've seen so many plays that the audience loved and then the reviews came out and told them they shouldn't have liked what they saw. I've even had people write me letters that say, "I saw your production and I thought it was wonderful and then I read that it was terrible. What am I to think?" This shows you how brainwashed we have gotten. Everyone complains about the Russians and how they only follow the party line, but isn't this following a line? The critics decide about a play's worth and it has nothing to do with what people are really seeing. That's why we don't have a theatre today, or why it isn't as good as it was.

So you feel that the quality of plays being written and produced today is declining as a consequence?

I most certainly do. It used to be that when you went to the theatre, you got an education; you went there to come out as a better or wiser person than when you went in. The whole purpose of art and of the theatre was to reflect the times. That's why all of the best playwrights were always in a jam, whether it was Aristophanes, or Molière fighting the Church, or Shakespeare. Shakespeare didn't stop writing because he had male menopause; he was involved, peripherally, in the great conspiracy of his time. Southampton and Essex were trying to mount a coup to get rid of Elizabeth. The night before they were to make their attempt, to gird themselves up, they commissioned that Shakespeare play *Richard II*, which was about the deposing of a king. Southampton and Essex were caught, of course, and Shakespeare, as a consequence, went home to Stratford. Essex got his head chopped off, Southampton (who was Shakespeare's patron) went to jail. So Shakespeare got into a jam, but he was doing *real* things. It wasn't just because some critic all of a sudden said, "Well, he's not writing very well anymore."

I once talked to Tennessee Williams, and he was worrying about what the critics would say. He told me, "I thought they'd like this one. I wrote it for them." What an abomination that such a great spirit as Tennessee Williams was worrying about what these people would say!

Do critics have that power because the pressures of the commercial theatre are so great? If it takes so much money to stage a play, then the bankers must want only sure-fire hits.

The critics control the dispensing of the grant money in the so-called non-commercial theatre, too. And everyone—the critics, the bankers, the foundations—are afraid of stirring people up. They're afraid these plays might have a few socialistic or humanist ideas. So what have you got? The theatre these days is about swapping your wife. Isn't that what it really gets down to? Think about it: *I Love My Wife; Same Time, Next Year*. They're little pieces of sexual titillation. I think that we ought to have plays and characters that deal with the serious issues of our own time.

When you think that during the Vietnam war, there were no plays about the subject at all. . . . Toward the end of the war, there were a few, like *Sticks and Bones*, but during the war there were none. There have been maybe one or two plays about what happened in Mississippi during voter registration and civil rights—*Blues for Mr. Charlie* was one of them—yet at every other age there have been plays that reflect the society. And now there just aren't. The reason is that the arts are controlled by the critics; they determine who gets the money and the grants. That's why a man like Norman Mailer, who wrote a couple of plays, *The Deer Park*, for example, doesn't continue with it. James Baldwin doesn't continue with it. Lillian Hellman doesn't write anymore;

Arthur Miller hardly writes anymore; Tennessee Williams doesn't write anymore. I think it's wonderful that a guy like Arthur Kopit has continued, but he had a long time between plays. I think something's terribly wrong in that whole scheme of things; that's why we have to remove ourselves from our present way of doing things. We have to do things in a workshop where we, the artists, have total control.

Twenty-five years ago, all those people you mention were creating plays. In your opinion, does the dearth today have anything to do with the anti-Communist purges back then?

I think so. I think everyone was so afraid, and that attitude has remained—it sours and affects *all* our arts. Certainly today, no one would give a grant to a Diego Rivera for a painting. Yet what was the content that the McCarthyites considered subversive? All those purges accomplished was to turn the content of film from being anti-Fascist to anti-Communist. And what are we left with today?—the harmless. *Real* art is anything that puts a crack in all that garbage and cuts through to reality. I guess there are people who are afraid to do that, but I think it's very healthy. In fact, it's what the theatre is all about. The ancient Greeks knew it: they knew that what is put on stage is what we are afraid to talk about. Good drama engages us and our emotions, and seeing those fearful emotions acted out purges us of our own. We come out of those experiences as better human beings. Good plays are therapeutic. But they don't want that anymore.

You have been trying for many years to set up a repertory theatre apart from the commercial system, but non-commercial theatres, you are saying, are under the same kinds of pressures. Is there, in fact, much of a difference?

Well, the problem is that when so much money is at stake, people act very bizarrely, and in the commercial theatre, there are always a lot of firings. I don't believe that you should ever hire somebody if you're going to fire them. What's the point? You rarely get a replacement that's much better. There seems to be this psychic need, however, to make a few sacrifices, hurt a few people; it's going to propitiate the gods and then you'll sail by.

You've got to fire somebody. And I despise that. Being replaced in a play is a great death, it's like being killed.

The kind of theatre you envision is one which will allow actors to feel secure about their jobs and themselves?

That's what is really needed. I did *The Father* at Yale and the critics and many of the people who work up there said it was one of the finest productions they ever did. On opening night I got a tremendous ovation. I was sitting with Bob Brustein and he said, "This must be one of the happiest moments of your life; you're like a god." But I said, "No, all I can think about is that in a couple of months I'll be looking for another job." Actors have no continuity. We are really like gypsies. In the old days actors organized themselves into families. They traveled around and they took care of their own. Even today, all beginning actors usually pool their money, get together, get a house. They share their food and share the work. I remember during the sixties kids would say, "What you need is to live in a commune," and I'd say, "Actors have always lived in communes, they've always worked together collectively."

At this point, I want my own home. I want a workshop, a place where I cannot be fired, where I will be treated as an artist. If someone were to commission a work by a painter like Larry Rivers, can you imagine them coming in when he was halfway finished and saying, "Ah, wait a minute Larry. Let me have the brush. Here's the way I want it." But producers do that to actors all the time. So the commercial way is not the way to do it; it's too nervous. And I don't want to work with non-commercial groups either. I work for very little money, and then they get big grants. I just want my own place. Joe Papp often invites me to work with him. I'd be happy to do things at Papp's Palace, but I'm still a guest there. A person who has no home does not solve his problems by visiting someone else—and actors have no homes.

Actors do not receive the same respect in this country that other artists do.

Actors are a very underprivileged minority; they've got about an eighty-percent unemployment rate. There's a fraction of the work here in New York that there was twenty years ago. It doesn't make sense logically because populations have grown. Why should there be less theatre; why shouldn't there be more? Acting is the Appalachia of the arts.

I came to the theatre after having been an officer in the army, having worked in journalism, having done a lot of different kinds of work and I couldn't believe the way actors were treated. They were treated like children! I was doing a television show the other day and the director kept saying, "All right, children, all right." Here I am, a man with a twenty-two-year-old daughter and three other children, and this guy was saying, "All right, children." It's ridiculous, but that's what many, many people think. I'll tell you right now, it's not so: actors are people who are always in action, who like to work. But they have learned that being children is what's expected of them. No one wants them to act like grown-ups. The idea that's promulgated is that the actor is a drunk, the actor is a child, the actor is basically doing something frivolous.

Is that attitude some sort of holdover from a Puritan age?

Yes, I think it is. Adults are supposed to be controlled; they're supposed to repress their emotions; that's our Puritanical background. But an actor must go through the emotions in a night that some people only go through two or three times in their life—at weddings, funerals, and by the side of death beds.

You yourself once had a particularly bad reputation; in the past you were considered "difficult."

I had a reputation for being temperamental and difficult precisely because I always fought this kind of treatment. Rumors were spread about me that were untrue. For instance, people said, "you always quit." Well, as a matter of cold fact, I've never missed a performance, I've never missed an entrance, I have never quit anything. An actor doesn't quit for one basic reason: if you quit, you don't get paid. Then people say, "Oh, you want to be treated better than anybody else." No, I want to be treated as well as a carpenter or a plumber—no better, no worse. I want to be treated in a way that's commensurate with what I'm doing.

Do you find that actors in other countries are treated with more respect?

Yes, actors in England are treated as respected members of the community. They're professional people, just like dentists. Everybody in England is interested in the art of the actor. It's something they grow up with. They know that an actor paints a picture, that he creates a character. They don't think that Olivier is Coriolanus, or that he's Archie Rice in *The Entertainer*. They know that he's an actor, and that acting is a human art. It's only in America that you hear the phrase, "Oh, actors are like that." In other countries it's understood that they're all individual artists, and that they are worthwhile citizens of their society.

You bring up an interesting point. Why is there such a cult of personality in this country? As you say, in England, no one thinks that Olivier is the character he plays. But here, someone like Steve McQueen has entirely become "the Steve McQueen character."

Well, I like Steve McQueen and he's not as tough as that guy he plays. But the Steve McQueen character has become a commodity. It's very valuable at the banks to say, "I've got McQueen for this picture." You know what he's going to do. That's why he, in a way, is a more stable commodity than a guy like Brando. You don't know what Brando is going to do when he gets in there. Brando doesn't know what he's going to do when he gets in there. It makes it exciting, but to some people, it also makes it very frightful. So it shows you that art has nothing to do with it.

In the schools, character acting is not even taught anymore. You are taught, instead, how to present your own personality. People figure that that's the way they'll get the commercials, that's the way they'll become a star—just by playing themselves. There have been other movie actors who have played me; Paul Newman, when he did *Hud*, said, "I was doing Rip." Jack Nicholson has said the same thing. But I don't do Rip.

I have created characters and people have said to me, "You could make a million dollars off that character." They have said, "We just want you to be 'Old Sarge,' " or "We want you to be this doctor," or "Oh, you really play this lawyer great, you look so

good in the suit," or "This is a wonderful character, we can do
this for five years." But that's not what I'm interested in.

*It's fascinating to hear about the commitment a person has to his
work, and the struggle to remain true to it.*

Friends of mine say, "If you hire Rip, you're going to have to let
him do the role his way. If you just want him to personify an idea
that you have in your mind, forget it. It's not that he's difficult,
it's just that that's the way he does his art."

*Just before this book went to press, Mr. Torn found a home for his
Sanctuary Theatre Workshop at Greenwich House, a community
settlement in New York.*

LYNN REDGRAVE

Sometimes called "the reluctant Redgrave" or "the white sheep," Lynn Redgrave always wanted to distinguish herself from the others in her family. Because her parents, Sir Michael and Lady Redgrave (better known as Rachel Kempson), have long been giants of the British theatre, and her sister Vanessa and brother Corin were early enthusiasts, Lynn's childhood interests were emphatically elsewhere. After delivering one line during a school nativity play ("There's a star!"), she resolutely turned her attention to cooking and horses, and even preferred cartoons on the "telly" to watching her father play Hamlet. Then, as a teenager, she saw a production of *Twelfth Night* at Stratford-on-Avon (coincidentally the same play she herself was appearing in when this interview was conducted) and decided suddenly to become an actress. Since that time—and though she still dislikes thinking of herself as part of "a royal family"—she has, in fact, assumed her place in the fourth generation of a theatrical dynasty.

Ms. Redgrave was born on March 8, 1943, the youngest of the three children, and trained at London's Central School of Speech and Drama. She made her first stage appearance at the Royal Court Theatre at the age of eighteen, playing Helena in *A Midsummer Night's Dream*. Her first film role was a small one in *Tom Jones* (directed by Tony Richardson, the man who was later to meet, marry, and divorce her sister Vanessa), and on the basis of that performance, Laurence Olivier hired her for his National Theatre Company. There she began with small walk-ons, but gradually worked up to the larger roles, and made a particular impact as Jackie Coryton in Noel Coward's *Hay Fever* and as the mute daughter, Kattrin, in Brecht's *Mother Courage*.

She made her Broadway debut in Peter Shaffer's *Black Comedy* and in the same year, when only twenty-three years old, received an Acad-

emy Award nomination as Best Actress for her work in the title role of *Georgy Girl*. For that part, which she gained fourteen pounds in order to play, she was co-winner (with Elizabeth Taylor) of the New York Film Critics Award, and though she was quite happy to be praised for her work as "an inspired young elephant," she was concerned lest she be typecast forever after as the floppy loser she so brilliantly portrayed. In fact, Ms. Redgrave has consistently taken care to avoid being boxed into any kind of category. She has hosted the syndicated TV talk show, "Not For Women Only," has received a Tony nomination for her work as Vivie in George Bernard Shaw's *Mrs. Warren's Profession,* and has acted the role of the infamous Xaviera Hollander in *The Happy Hooker*. She would like no one ever to be able to say, "Lynn Redgrave could not act in *that* kind of role. . . ."

She and her husband John Clark initiated the production of Shaw's *Saint Joan* in which she starred and he directed. Mr. Clark was a child star in England, is a photographer, an occasional actor (he understudied for the Broadway play, *Comedians*), and is now his wife's agent. They have a young son and daughter, Benjamin and Kelly.

It would be difficult to find two more down-to-earth, friendly people than these. As we pulled into the driveway of the Connecticut home they were renting for the run of her play at Stratford, Ms. Redgrave came to meet us at the door. She is tall (5' 10") and slender, a supple line in contrast to her sister's angularity.

Ms. Redgrave gave careful thought to many of these questions; she obviously takes her work very seriously, is steady and determined, and while she is wildly in love with acting, she is also very much attuned to the traditions and responsibilities of the theatre. As for her sister Vanessa's political activism, it is an interest Lynn does not share; she has claimed that politics "bewilder" her and that while she loves her family, they "are not in one another's pockets." The adult no less than the child, it seems, insists on being distinguished.

Coming from such a theatrical background, it's interesting that you didn't always assume you would be an actress, and that there was, in fact, a moment of decision.

Oddly enough, I decided I wanted to be an actress in a very unrealistic sort of way. I say "oddly" because I do come from such a theatrical family; I should have known the practical side of acting and yet I didn't. But when I was fifteen, I saw a production of *Twelfth Night* (which is the play I'm doing now), and I just fell totally in love with it. I thought, if that's being an actor, being in something like that, then that's what I want to do. But at that point, I really hadn't acted; I'd done only one school play, and didn't know either that I *could* act or that I would even like it. I just really fell in love with the image of it, and I think, too, that I fell in love with actors themselves. I was with my parents at Stratford-on-Avon when they were acting there, and I'd been there during other seasons with them as well; it just looked like a wonderful life.

It's strange that I went into acting more on the basis of that one strong feeling than on what I knew from my own family's larger experience. When you see a play really well done, it looks effortless, it looks wonderfully, gloriously happy-making, and there *are* those moments, those high points in the life of an actor. But the low points or the medium points are far more testing of one's real love of it. I said to my parents, "I want to be an actress." And my mother said, "Do you want to be an actress so much that if we said we won't help you at all, we won't put you through drama school, we forbid you to do it, we turn you out of the house—if we were to put all these obstacles in your way, would you go mad and still do it?" I said, "Well, I don't know about that . . ." and she said, "Unless you feel that strongly about it, don't even *think* of being an actress."

So every day I would wake up and I would ask myself: "Do I really care?" After about a year, I decided that, yes, I *did* really care, and I started going to a lot more plays and thinking a lot more seriously about it. I tried to think about what it really meant to be an actor—still without having tried it. But I did come to the conclusion that that's what I really wanted.

Once you got into it, were there moments of doubt and indecision?

There were a few along the way, during my training and for a while afterwards. I was in a play on tour which was quite miserable—the company and the places we traveled to were all miserable—and I thought, so this is being an actress, eh? Do I really like it? But I always counted on the fact that it would get better, and indeed it did. I hadn't been wrong about my addiction for it and, of course, the more I did, the more addicted I became. I'm a total addict now. I don't think I could live without it; in fact, I *know* I couldn't.

What is it about acting that gives you such pleasure?

It's being other people. That's the best, the biggest satisfaction for me. Performers always talk about the egotistical side of it— enjoying the applause, the laughter, the tears of the audience, enjoying those hushed silences that fall (if they do!)—and I agree that there's nothing that makes you higher than a wonderful audience who has loved everything you've done. That's very, very exciting. But to me, the chance to be another person is the most interesting aspect of all.

You say that as a teenager you fell in love with other actors. Has that attraction remained?

Yes, I liked the way actors were with people and that feeling has remained, even though there are times when I say, "Oh God, actors. . . ." You know, we are such boring people sometimes. And even though very few of our friends, our real friends, are actors, I still like actors' company very much. There is nothing better than that first day of rehearsals—meeting old friends, making new ones.

There's sort of a family feeling to it?

There is something about combining with a group of people in a common cause that is very lovely. There's a sort of intimacy that you feel, even though you don't know each other very well. It's unusual, and actors are so lucky that way. I think it must be hard being a writer because it's somewhat solitary; the hardest thing about writing for me would be sticking to it without any company. That must be very difficult. I love the gregariousness of acting.

Do you find it painful, when the play's run is over or the movie has been completed, to leave those friendships behind?

Oh, yes. If it's been a happy experience, which it often is—although that does not necessarily have to do with how successful the show has been—then splitting up is very sad. Sometimes there are a lot of drunken tears shed on the last party. Sometimes you never see these people again, and sometimes you don't see them for ten or fifteen years; sometimes you work with them on the very next job. What's nice is that those you get along with, those you have a good working relationship with, you can meet twenty years later and pick up as if you have never left them. I don't know if there are too many other jobs where that happens, and so I think actors are very lucky.

Was drama school a waste of time for you?

No, I didn't think it was a waste, but I was a little too young for it. You see, having gotten the bug to act, I kind of insisted and pushed my parents to let me go right away. I was sixteen and really, it was a little too early. I think I would have gained far more from it had I been a little older, but I really can't tell. If my own children wanted to act, I'd try and dissuade them from going that young unless they were much more sophisticated than I was at sixteen—which is extremely likely because they're much more sophisticated at eight and ten than I was. But at sixteen, I was very emotionally unstable, and learning to become an actress is a very emotionally unsettling thing in itself. It's only when your own emotional stability is better that it becomes possible to be an actress, and before that it can be very hard to handle. It's difficult to act other people if you don't know who *you* are. It's confusing and disorienting. So drama school was not a waste for me; I was just not ready for it. But in terms of what I did learn, I couldn't have done without it, that's for sure.

The generally accepted myth is that actors tend to be flighty, unstable, temperamental people, and yet to be a good actor, as you say, you need to be a rather stable personality.

Yes, I think that myth has come from the people who have fallen apart in a celebrated way. And of course, you're more likely to

hear about the actors who have trouble than about your top exec-
utive who has fallen apart from strain. You don't hear about the
others because it's only the actors who are well followed by the
press. But it is a very unstable profession because the employment patterns are so peculiar; you never know when you're going
to be constantly employed. And there are some things that you
can make money at, while other things don't pay at all. Many actors have a very hard time just making a living. So from that point
of view, it's very up and down. Unless you happen to be in a hit
show and get a year's contract, you don't know where you're going to be three months from now. That part of it you just have to
learn to handle. And I rather like that aspect. I hate knowing
what I'm going to be doing too far in advance; I'm afraid I'll have
changed my mind by the time I get there.

*You say that the best part of acting for you is being other people.
But that must have its difficult side effects.*

Yes, it *is* hard; it's hard to cut off. And the more successful you
are at submerging yourself in someone else, the more schizophrenic it can make you feel. Depending on the nature of the
character you're portraying, it can have a very strong and strange
effect on you. After you play a very neurotic person, if you've
played the role for a long time and played it very successfully, you
can have withdrawal symptoms. I found that when I did Saint
Joan; I played her for six months, and it was probably the hardest
role I've ever done. When it ended, I was terribly sad because it
had been a very special experience, and because it had been
something I'd wanted to do for so long, but my depression was out
of all proportion.

I'm much helped by having children; they bring me back down
to earth. You come home and the child's sick and that becomes
your focus. So, apart from the fact that it's lovely to have children,
it's also very leveling, and it stops you from getting too involved in
these pretend-roles.

*I was wondering how you arrived at your particular conception of
Saint Joan. You played her as being very arrogant and yet other
versions, Carl Dreyer's for instance, have made her so vulnerable
and pained.*

Well, while we were playing Saint Joan, the company had a screening of the Dreyer film at the Museum of Modern Art, and I must say I thought it was fantastic. Marvelous! But the Joan that Maria Falconetti played—and she played her *impeccably*—could never have been Shaw's Saint Joan, and I doubt she could have been the real Saint Joan either: she could never have led an army. This is not because I think I was necessarily more right about the character than any other actress, but just that Dreyer did not deal with the problems of who Joan really was. I mean that girl in his movie would have fallen off her horse at the first bugle blow. I don't think she could ever have persuaded any king or duke or landowner to give up his castle. But Falconetti wasn't given that situation to portray; she was only given the trial and what she did with it was remarkable. Incidentally, that film apparently did terrible things to her; she died. . . .

Yes, I think she went off to the desert in Mexico. . . .

She went completely off her rocker; it was very, very scary. But different people's Joans have been different things. Anouilh's Joan, the one Julie Harris did, reads totally differently; again, I think he created a character that was not historically true at all. He made her his own wonderful little person: she never stopped saying how small, frail, and young she was. Not only does Shaw's Joan not do that, but history's Joan does not either. Her life is documented better than almost any other person's of the medieval times; it's amazing how much is known about her, far more than is known about many of the kings of the time. She wrote these incredible letters, all of which exist and can be read in translation. For my characterization, I read a lot of histories of her and parts of the trial. I learned a lot of unexpected details. Far from being shy about what she would wear, for example, she insisted on wearing the very latest fashions in men's clothes. She believed in a hierarchy of people and since she was a "chosen person," everyone must know *immediately* what she was by the look of her. She wore the best jewels, the finest gold cloth, and the finest furs.

So in researching an historical character, you must be sure that the playwright has also written with the true historical character in mind, or your conception will be in conflict.

Yes, I had to keep checking to make sure that this would be playable in terms of Shaw's drama. Sometimes you can do wonderful research and it's just not playable with what you have. That's often the problem when you do historical persons. But in fact, this was about the only time that Shaw allowed himself to be ruled by real history.

Shaw described her as—and in fact she was—insufferable and boring; she talked too much, she harangued other people. But you see, she had to have been extremely arrogant—in a good way—or she couldn't have accomplished what she did. She must have had enormous physical strength. The chain mail alone which she carried weighed over fifty pounds, and that's without the outer armor. So she would carry, all together, over a hundred pounds of metal into battle. She had superhuman strength; she was big, she wasn't frail, and while she admitted to being a physical coward, it was in the sense of "I can't bear being hurt, but I carry on anyway."

Can the memory of your own experiences possibly come into play when doing such a character, one so removed from the rest of us as Saint Joan?

It comes in quite a lot, though it's often hard to know in a conscious way what you're using. When I played Saint Joan, I wanted at times to regress to being a baby again. I felt that that would be a way to play her. She was full of all these amazing strengths, but when she changed, during the trial scenes, for instance, it was almost a schizophrenic split; she would regress totally to that basic self that we all have in us, the self we put layers over when we grow up. And so, before I went on stage for the trial, I used to go into a sort of mental trance, a meditation where I would try to remember, as clearly as I could, tiny flashes of incidents from my childhood. I would use those ten minutes of intermission to regress into that long-ago world. I had never thought of doing anything like that before; usually I try only to think about things that are directly related to the character. But I found with this play, I just couldn't come to the trial scene in the right frame of mind unless I had reduced myself to something much smaller than I was. I had never tried it before, but the more I did it, the better I got, and the more that I thought I had forgotten resurfaced in my mind. It was a very peculiar experience.

It worked incredibly well, because there was such a change in your appearance when you came on for the trial. The look on your face was wrenching; it was so full of emotion.

I really had to think to get myself in that state. The company was wonderful about it; I never had to say, "Please don't talk to me." Everyone was very sensitive. I would go into my dressing room and literally not talk to *anyone*. When I came out, I'd stand off on the side and the "soldier" and "executioner" would put my chains on in a kind of silent ritual; I never said a word, but they understood and never intruded on my concentration.

Is this why you consider Saint Joan your most difficult role?

It was difficult for me, an agnostic, to play someone of great faith. I came nearest to understanding religion, though, than I ever had before. I *had* to believe, and I suddenly thought, "How wonderful, to believe in something that strongly." I'm much more open to what religion can do to people now. I haven't rushed out and become a church-goer or taken up any faith in particular, but it changed my whole view because I realized how much imagination plays in one's faith and how good that can be. I'd always looked on religion as a rather repressive thing, as something that only uneducated people could really use, but I began to see it in a different light. It's hard to come to such strong convictions in life. Imagine what it would be that could make you say: "I will die for this." It doesn't come in most people's experience; it certainly didn't come in mine.

Acting must be a very personally expanding activity; it stretches you to see life as someone else would see it.

It is, but it's awfully difficult and that role took a long time arriving at. I could have gone on for much longer with Joan; I didn't ever feel that I'd finished with her. I played the part quite a while in Chicago and then in New York, but it wasn't until the last month in New York that I felt proud of it; I hadn't been proud of what I was doing before—I'm often not—but by the last month I finally was.

So you do find that your performances evolve beyond opening night?

Oh yes, they always do, but how much they evolve depends upon the part. With some roles, you have to beware of going too far. You try and complicate it and make it too difficult; you end up pushing something that is better left as a simple statement. That's why these massive, classical parts are so good to do. There is no end to them; you can never say, "This is perfect." That's why they are very satisfying and so good for an actor to play. They are a constant challenge that is never quite met.

Faced with a new role, how do you begin? Do you first learn your lines?

First, I read the play a lot. That is, I read it if I have the time, if I'm not offered the role the week before I have to begin. Ideally, though, I study it and I begin thinking about some physical aspect of the character—how I think she looks—and I often learn a lot from that. Of course, there are times when the playwright's description of a character can be off-putting, particularly if you've been cast against type; it can be discouraging to read about the small, blonde person you're supposed to play when there you are, tall and dark. But sometimes the other characters will loosely describe her, or she will give a description of herself, and that will often stimulate my imagination. Sometimes I get a very clear image of the character; that will often change later on, but there have been roles for which my initial picture was the one I stayed with.

And then I do try to learn the lines. The bigger the part, the more I like to know them. It's the biggest bugaboo of my life that most actors, through sheer laziness, do not do the same. I know it sounds arrogant, but it's true. Many actors justify their laziness with excuses like, "Oh, I can't possibly learn my lines, I have to know my character and my moves along with it." But that is absolute rubbish and it's the biggest time-waster in rehearsals. It *is* boring to learn your lines; it's dull and repetitive to sit with pages and pages, and just memorize them. Dreary. But thousands of wonderful actors have done it for years, and it pays off one-hundredfold the minute you start rehearsals.

You see, you cannot really act with a book in your hand and so it's a great thing to hide behind. As long as you can say, "I don't really know my lines," you can get by without really giving a performance, without really attempting one. Then, come the last week of rehearsals, the books are finally down, and only *then* is there that tiny length of time in which to get the role together. But by that time, everything's panicky; you're going to get the costumes and you're going to have an audience soon and the producers are coming in and all the rest of it. So by then, you don't *dare* attempt anything. And, of course, the first few performances are not the time to be daring, either. This is a point I feel so strongly about, yet I can rarely find actors to agree with me.

Perhaps there are a lot of actors who have a genuine problem learning lines. That much memorizing could be incredibly difficult.

It's only those who know they have a problem that bother to learn them in advance. Of course, there are some who have a genuine problem and still don't do it, so, come the last dress rehearsal, they still don't know them. To me, lines are there to be used any way you want to use them; but unless you know them as well as you know your name, address, and phone number, unless they're fed into you like a computer, you become their servant. Not knowing the lines makes you want to reach for the most obvious ways of saying them, because that's all you've got time for. Yet the lines should be serving you; there are any number of ways to bend them to your character.

Then there *are* a lot of people who have been poorly trained; they learn their lines the way they're going to say them. It becomes a habit they cannot break. So, come the day the director says, "You know, I have a feeling that that line could be a lot more interesting if you gave it a different stress here," they find they are strait-jacketed into their own reading. They become paranoid about changing the way they're going to stress a single word. Poor training is difficult to overcome.

Having studied the play and learned the lines, the character is fermenting inside you. Are you trying to develop a train of thought below the surface of the lines, too?

Yes, that's the subtext, and it's as important to the part as the lines themselves. Sometimes what I'm thinking is the total opposite of what I'm saying; you know, we often don't say what we

mean. That's another problem of not learning your lines early—
you seldom get a chance to explore what you're *not* saying.
Maybe you're lying, maybe what you're saying is all a facade.

*How do you develop that subtext? Does it just come automatically
from your identification with the character and the situations
she's in?*

It becomes apparent as one goes through the rehearsal process.
The bits you haven't filled in, the lines you haven't understood
the motivation of—they stand out like cracks in plaster. I can
know the lines and know the moves, but when I come to a spot
where I don't know what I'm thinking, it's like a great gap. I feel,
"something's missing here." The better the play, the easier it is
to fill in. In bad plays or in badly written TV scripts—there
are a lot of those—you often have to invent stupid bridges for
yourself. Perhaps the script was hastily written, or the writer was
not too terrific, or somebody just made a cut without realizing
that certain lines and actions did not link up with the sense of the
character. Once you're reasonably experienced, you can manage
those gaps without making them too apparent to an audience.
You don't just stop and look an idiot. But *you* know they're there
and you don't feel comfortable. I'm sure it shows in some way;
the audience may not notice the particular line but they will see
that the character lacks a certain reality.

The hardest thing about developing a subtext is not to get too
wedded to one way of thinking. Sometimes you see a situation
very strongly in a particular way and you set up a whole load of
conditions surrounding it. In order to fulfill those conditions, you
desperately want the other actors to react in a certain way, but
they may be off doing their own interpretations, and those may
not coincide with your own. That's my biggest problem: I have to
try not to superimpose something that doesn't fit with what the
other people are doing. People *are* unpredictable.

Isn't that where the work of the director comes in?

Yes, a lot. Quite often it's just a matter of being reminded that if
the other actor does this, then you must do that; or maybe he
doesn't want to do this, so you must not do that. You have to fit

your parts together somehow. But of that exploration, wonderful new insights can come.

Do external elements help build your sense of the character—working from the outside in? For instance, is costuming an important part in the development of a role?

Yes, the internal and the external work together, really. I always try and approximate in rehearsal the sort of costume I'm going to be wearing. I find that it's less panicky when I finally get the real thing, and bits of business—problems or difficulties—come out of it. In other words, if you're going to be in a long dress and you rehearse in jeans, you will just automatically sit differently, no matter how much you try to be aware of the difference and take it into account. Everything about the two costumes is different—the way you walk, the way you stand. The same is true if you're going to be in a high heel and you're rehearsing in a low heel. Not only does it throw you when you finally get into the right costume, but you miss out on all the possibilities you could have worked with. Maybe the character doesn't walk very well in high heels, but you're never going to find that out if you leave it until the moment when everything else is hitting you. If it's a modern play and no one is sure what they're going to be wearing, I try to persuade the designer to hold off deciding until I have time to experiment. If it's a classical play and the designer has decided all these things, then either I try to get the real costume—which is almost always impossible—or I duplicate it out of junk I have at home.

*Your husband directed you in **Saint Joan;** how is it to be directed by someone that close to you?*

It was very good. I think he's a very, very good director; he's imaginative, but he allows the right amount of input from the actors; he's helpful but not restraining, and yet he doesn't just let it all go. He does that indefinable something that good directors do—he creates an atmosphere in which the actors feel free, adventurous, and bold. He's got an unbiased eye, too. Yes, he's got an excellent combination of all the things that directors need to have.

And you felt he could be objective about your performance?

If anything, he's probably more critical of me than he would be of another actor because he knows me better. He knows a lot of what I can do, and so he always wants me to go further. Sometimes I find that difficult because I can't believe there's further to go—but he's usually right.

In the case of a disagreement with a director, do you defer to the director's way of thinking?

Well, what I'm no good at is doing something just because somebody tells me to. Some people can say, "Oh, okay, fine, I'll do it that way," and it comes out very well. I'm just not very adept at that. So I try and rethink it or talk it out so that I can understand why it is they want this of me.

It's very different in film; there you really *do* have to just go by what the director says—sometimes to your doom, and sometimes to your great elated success. Sometimes it all depends on the editor; he can make a dreadful moment appear to be much better than it is. I've been on the receiving end of both good and bad from movies. I've had a wonderful time making a film—the director seemed marvelous, everybody seemed terrific—and then the final result was awful. It's happened exactly the other way around as well.

Do you feel torn between doing film work on the West Coast and being a part of the theatre world in the East?

I think there's more of a choice that has to be made between the theatre in New York and television on the West Coast. Films get made all over the place, even though people in California always say, "You should be out here because this is where the decisions are made." You know, the big brass of all the top movie studios tend to be out West. But television, that really is all done in California and because of the huge span of the country, a lot of people have to make a conscious decision to pursue television at the expense of their theatre possibilities. A lot of stalwart New York theatre actors finally say, "I can't make a living. I've got to go where there's more money and more jobs." So off they go. It *is* difficult to work in a combination of fields.

That's the only aspect of acting in England which is easier: the country's so small that you can combine a career in all three mediums. Of course, there's precious little filming done over there, but what there is is done down the road. You can't go very far; there's nowhere to go.

How did you happen to settle in the States?

John settled here in 1960; we met and married in New York and then I persuaded him to come back to England with me. It had never really occurred to me that I could live anywhere else. I hadn't been in America much at the time and I feared that I wouldn't work enough here. I still felt tied to my family; my roots were with them in England. But as I grew up and things began to change, we became more and more dissatisfied with English living. We moved to Ireland for a while and tried a sort of idyllic life on a cliff, which was indeed idyllic but was also totally impractical. I mean, unless you and your family are where the work is, you end up with the family having a wonderfully idyllic life while you're on a plane—which wasn't what we had in mind at all! I either had to turn things down or be prepared to be away. And then a play came up over here which we decided we'd do, and towards the end of the run, we said, "Well, are we going back or not?" And we felt that, honestly, we didn't want to.

How do the opportunities for an actress in the United States compare to those in England?

I've *felt* that they've been less restrictive here, though I really can't prove that. In England, people had a certain image of me and of my place in my family. It affected their thinking. I was "the baby of the family." The press is very familiar with the whole lot of us. And I felt, perhaps wrongly, that most people and most prospective employers saw me in a certain mold which I didn't want to be in, Over here, no one saw me in the context of anybody else; they just saw me as me because they weren't so familiar with "the Redgraves." And so I've felt that I've been able to do many more things here than I could have done in England.

You've taken some roles purposely, I think, to do the unexpected, to break out of molds—like the part of Xaviera Hollander in **The Happy Hooker.**

Partly just to see if I could do them, you know, and because I am
fascinated by roles which are so outrageously outside myself. Occasionally, sense will get to me, and I'll say, "No, I don't think I
can do that." But on the whole, I've always had this dream of being able to act anything; I don't think one really can, but ideally
one would like to. People are just not as likely to be convinced
that you are an eighty-year-old as they would be by an eighty-
year-old actress. There's something that stops them from totally
believing. There are times, though, when people offer me things
that are very unusual, difficult, and outside of myself, yet I feel
that I can bring them off, that I know a way to do them. And to a
certain extent, I want to stop any remnants of people thinking of
me as Georgy Girl, which some people still do. I hear: "Ahhh, I
loved *Georgy Girl*," and it's very nice but it's surprising, you
know what I mean? People say: "I've seen everything you ever
did . . . I've seen *Georgy Girl* and 'Hollywood Squares.' " And I
think, "What happened to all the rest of it?"

*Why do you do game shows on TV? I mean, "The $20,000 Pyra-
mid" is my favorite show, but I'm always surprised to see an actress of your stature as one of the "celebrity hosts."*

Well, I do game shows for two reasons. One, because I do genuinely enjoy them—not all of them, of course, but I do have a
wonderful time on the "Pyramid." So that side of it is pure indul-
gence. The more important side of it, however, is the practical
aspect: it makes people come to the theatre. When I go outside of
New York to areas that are not normally heavy theatre-going
areas, if people have seen me on the "Pyramid," they'll tend to
come to the theatre even if they've never been before. I hear a lot
of people say, "I never saw a play before but I saw you on the
so-and-so and thought I'd come see you now." It extends my
audience.

*Do you enjoy touring, going to those out-of-the-way places where
people don't generally go to the theatre?*

I love touring, yes. Even though I hate to pack. It's an unfortunate thing to hate when you like to tour.

*Touring is a very traditional part of being an actress; it's one of
those traditions that's dying out.*

Yes, it's part of all that stupid old show-biz stuff about another opening. It's so exciting, though. Even if you're only walking into some dingy little theatre in the middle of nowhere, there's something about getting into your dressing room and having your first performance. There's something quite thrilling about it, even if it all turns out to be ghastly. I've played a lot of dreary places as well as a lot of nice places, and I've always liked it. I like the idea of arriving in a place and having people come to see a show— people who perhaps have not seen much before. It's sort of adventurous, and has that end-of-the-rainbow feel about it, even though what you find usually isn't the pot of gold.

Does the transition from being a stage actress to doing films pose any particular problems for you?

It's such a whole different process, really. My biggest problems with films happen when a director rehearses me too much. With a play, when you rehearse, you go through what might be called a gestation period: you begin with a fresh view of a character you don't know, you work through all the possibilities and then you come around to a way of doing it that appears to be acted for the first time. But there are moments during the rehearsal period where it not only looks like you're acting this for the hundredth time, but it also looks like the hundredth *bad* time. You're just not able to make it spontaneous or fresh; you haven't decided how you're going to play it. But there was also that wonderful moment when you *first* did it, when you did it just the way it hit you.

Now that's what filming is, I think, from an actor's point of view. You have to have figured out your blocking, of course, you have to know where you're going to sit, where you're going to stand, where the director wants you, where the lighting man needs you to be, your mark, and all those technical things. And you need to have had some discussion or thought about how you're going to play the scene if it's of any complexity. The best film acting seems to happen when the camera prints that first revelatory moment. That's why I'm much better in early takes than in late takes, although my theatre background has prepared me to be able to do takes forever. If the director says, "let's take 54," I don't fall apart, I keep on trying. I know that the best things I've done on film have been my first or second tries—that's when it's been fresh and truly spontaneous.

But you say that the rehearsal period does you good when doing a play . . . what's the difference?

The difference is that you can rehearse a play for about four weeks; you can go through a whole exploratory process and come out with a solution at the end of it. But in a film, you're only going to have one week—and that's why I'd rather have nothing at all. You only get halfway through the exploration of the character in a week's time, and they'll *never* pay you for anything more than a week. You're caught between having rehearsed it too much, and not enough.

How do you react to watching yourself on film?

I don't enjoy it, no. I can do it now and be objective, but at the beginning, I couldn't watch myself at all. I was just hopelessly self-conscious. It never looked to me like what I thought I had been doing. I've always hated going to the dailies, and still don't much like to, but I'm getting better about it. I can now stand to see myself be bad and to say, "That's what was bad about it." I used to be so upset that I would have just collapsed.

It's important to be objective because that way, I can help myself; I can correct my own mistakes. It's really pride and ego that stops me from wanting to see myself look bad. Sometimes, it's just sheer vanity. I've got a pimple or something; it's kind of distressing to see it all blown up, and as I watch, that's all I see; it becomes a scene about a pimple. Of course, everyone sees themselves in that magnified way. The lighting man is watching that great shadow that came across the screen just at the right moment, and he doesn't care what I did. There was a time when I couldn't stand to even hear my own voice. If I was in a TV studio and we were taping a show, sometimes they'd have to roll back and pick up the end of the previous scene and I'd hear my lines broadcast over the speakers. I used to block my ears because I couldn't listen; I couldn't stand it. I just thought it sounded so terrible that there was no point in going on.

I've heard that you felt your voice was too high and childish. How did you work on changing it?

I've been working in New York with a teacher for about four years, and I had various teachers in England, too. It used to go up from nerves a lot; it was fairly thin and didn't have much body to it so I tried to extend it in both directions until it got better. What I hadn't realized was how badly I had used it for a long time; I started to lose it even when I wasn't pushing it very hard. It was horrifying to find that my voice wasn't reliable. It can be as bad for an actor as·for a singer, but people think only singers have to worry about their voices. If you're using it wrong, it can be thrown out so easily; a bit of nerves, you tighten and that's it.

How do you learn accents? For instance, in the Garson Kanin play, **Born Yesterday,** *you had to have an American accent, and yet you weren't living here at the time.*

Oh, that I got off a cartoon show. There was a certain character who had the exact type of voice I wanted, so I taped some of it and just listened and listened. I find, in general, that accents are fairly easy to do. It's just luck that I can pick them up without much trouble. My father envies that because he finds accents very difficult; he'll work on an accent for months and months before he gets it, though when he does get it, he does it wonderfully. He always used to say how lucky I was that I could hear something, pick up the essence of what made it different, and transform that into sound. I have a knack for it.

Your father is known for having an almost religious devotion to the theatre. Do you think you've inherited a similar devotion yourself?

I have almost the same feeling, yes. I really love it, I get excited by it, and I feel that seeing a really great performance on the stage is one of the most wonderful experiences you can have. I can't think of anything more uplifting or more amazing. And while there's lots of good work about, those nights when you're present at something extraordinary are very rare; one can remember them on one hand. But it's something marvelous to aspire to. It's a very elusive thing to achieve; when you think that so many good people can't do it all the time, you realize just how elusive it is.

Your father once played Macbeth with a freshly broken ankle; to go on stage in such pain shows a very rare devotion indeed.

It's mind over matter; it's like those yogis who lie on a bed of nails or walk on hot coals; it's like natural childbirth. When you're concentrating very hard on something else, you are unable to feel pain. I've seen people, and I've done it myself, hobble to the theatre, sprint their way through a performance, and have to get on crutches as soon as they're off. I haven't ever broken anything, but I've had cuts, sprains, hurts, whatever. And I literally didn't feel pain at the time.

Is this devotion to one's craft getting more rare?

Well, it's become curiously voguish nowadays on Broadway for an actor to take time off, and I just don't understand it. Why would anyone want to take time off? I mean, if people have paid to see you, then you ought to be there, and if you have a contract to do a job, then you should do it. That's an old-fashioned attitude, but I believe it's good and right. Then too, I'd feel very jealous of the person who took over for me; there have been occasions when people have, to their detriment, allowed someone to take their place, and then found themselves out of a job. But I hate to be off; I find it unbearable. I feel like I'm missing something, and I can't imagine not going on unless I had been in a car accident or was giving birth. There *are* no other reasons. People think that's stupid, though, and maybe it is. They laugh now about that show-must-go-on business, but I find there's an element of the reassuring in something that *has* to happen.

What is the relationship of an actor to an audience? Are you very aware of them when you're on stage?

Oh yes. They're the missing ingredient that you're working towards, and only when you finally have an audience do you have a play. They're part of it. The live theatre is special in that it's the only medium that depends to that extent on an audience. Ballet and opera are ruled by the music and will tend to go on regardless of what the audience does or does not do. But the participation of the audience in theatre is essential, and what they bring to it or don't bring to it alters the nature of the performance. It doesn't matter what people do in front of a television set or movie screen because their participation is nothing. That's why it's lovely and very relaxing to go to a movie or watch TV; you don't have to join in. And that's why a lot of modern audiences are difficult to play to; they don't know, for example, that if they talk, the actors can hear them, or their fellow audience can hear. People are so used to talking through a TV performance.

It's best when you're playing in a theatre where the audience all has a good seat. It makes their involvement so much greater. Nobody is saying, "Who is that dot down there?" You can sense every change of mood, every bit of how much you're holding their attention, and how much you're not. In a big house, that becomes difficult; you can't judge it as quickly.

Do the reactions of the audience generally surprise you or is the situation more controlled than that?

Oh, it's very unpredictable. For instance, the things that audiences find funny are always a big surprise, and the "yuks" you got in the rehearsal room are nothing. There's an old saying on movie sets that if the crew laughs, that for sure will be the dead spot of the film. And it's the same on stage. When your fellow actors laugh themselves stupid, that's invariably not what will get the laughs in the theatre.

Do those reactions vary from night to night?

It's altogether different every night. There are times when something's happened, like the air conditioner has broken or they've all had a lot of drinks, and you could be Olivier playing King Kong, but you're not going to keep them. Other audiences, as soon as the curtain goes up, you know you have them. They're there; you just have that sense. The weird thing is that you can tell a cold audience before you've even begun. There's something about the level of talk—it's quite scary sometimes, you can absolutely feel it. You can feel their disinterest. It's crazy what vibes human beings can make. But you can never rely on anything either; if the first scene goes well, you can't assume that the second will. You let up for a moment and it all goes away.

Do you find comedy more difficult than serious drama?

It's much more difficult; it takes more energy and a stronger concentration. You have to put an edge to every line; given a different reading or a different set of circumstances, that line would not be funny; you have to find the particular slant that makes it funny. It's not just the words, because there are some actors who are not very good at comedy—their strong point is something very emotional, very deep—you could give them the same lines and it wouldn't raise a laugh. So it's not just the juxtaposition of words or the situation or where the characters are. (Of course, some roles are going to be funny no matter *who* plays them; those are known as "actor-proof.")

Comedy is like walking a tightrope and running an obstacle race all at the same time. The pace of it, the speed of your reflexes, the method of controlling a laugh—it's all so tricky. You have to have your wits about you so sharply. For instance, sometimes you don't want to get a laugh at a certain point, you want to stop the laughing, and if you take a breath too long, they're gonna laugh and you'll have killed your next moment. Or, what are you going to do if they cough on the one word that makes sense of the sentence? When you get tuned up to it and you've played it for a while, you can hear a cough start and bring the word out stronger; that's why it's nice to play in an intimate house. It's a bit of a contest in a way, and that makes it very exciting when it works. Yet it's awful when you don't hang on top of it. There's nothing worse than playing a comedy that the audience doesn't find funny. Terribly depressing.

It must be even more difficult to do comedy on film, where you don't have your own timing; the director and editor control that.

It's the hardest of all. In the end, the question is: does the man in the cutting room have a sense of humor, or does he have the *same* sense of humor?

Do you think that acting is an instinctive ability? Or is it something that can be taught in a classroom or learned from experience?

You learn everything from experience, really. I don't think you can learn to act without doing it. No amount of class acting can compare. If you can't get a job, then it's better to be doing something; I'd advise going to class and learning. On the other hand, you could work in class for twenty years and not learn what you'll learn in a week of professional work with an audience. Doing it in any form, though, is better than not doing it at all, because your acting ability is something that atrophies, it doesn't just stay with you. Your instincts may stay with you, but your abilities are lost if you don't exercise them. Singers know that they can't stop; dancers know that if they stop for three months, it will take them three months to get back to their peak. Yet people think that acting is something you can pick up and drop—you can't. It may be possible with television work, but it's not so on stage. You have to be able to make something you're blowing up appear real to fifteen hundred people. There's nothing natural about it, yet you have to make it look natural, and it should feel natural to you.

What do you consider truth in acting, then, if the theatre is entirely such an illusion?

Hmmm. That's a really difficult question. It's not just being truthful, because truth isn't always interesting. Reality isn't always interesting. But you *do* have to stay truthful. While it might be truthful to pause for ten minutes on stage because your character has a sudden thought, the demands of the playwright and the interest of the audience require that you do not. So you have to look for another truth, because that one is not interesting theatrically. It might be truthful to cry all the way through a scene because you're feeling very sad, but if you can't be heard then it's no good. That would be entirely self-indulgent. And it's probably very truthful to stand with your back to the audience, but if they don't see you all the way through the play, then that's no good either. Yet you can't be theatrical at the expense of being truthful, or I think audiences will know it. It can't just be your own truth, however; you have to find a combined truth—one that's true for you, that says something to the audience and that best puts forward the play.

Even film acting, which is so hung up on being natural, is not natural at all. If the camera's on you very close and you're going to sit down, you have to sit down like this [she lowers herself onto the chair very slowly]. That's not natural and it's not truthful. It *appears* on the screen as if I had a perfectly natural sit-down at a perfectly normal speed. But it isn't at all. And if I think it's truthful for my character to cross the room in a great fury, I'll have to check that at a certain point because the camera won't be able to follow me.

You have to draw your actions from observed reality, but first be loyal to the intentions of the film or play.

Yes, and each actor's version of that will vary. Really good plays can be reinterpreted so many ways. Different people's truths may each be equally truthful.

What are the qualities one needs to be able to do all this, to be a good actress?

Strength and stamina—good health. I put those before talent, because I think practically everybody has some talent they could use as an actor. Yet they don't have the other things—the concentration and, literally, the physical strength. Acting is tiring; it requires a lot of work, a lot of muscle, an enormous amount of voice. As I've said, you have to blow something up while making it look normal, and do that for eight shows a week. There are an awful lot of talented people—practically every high school or college group will have a few of them. They stand out, they shine, they're attractive, interesting-looking. So why aren't they all big stars? Luck is some of it, but they've got to have that strength, because acting is just hard, hard work.

LAURENCE LUCKINBILL

Laurence Luckinbill is, as he says, "always stirring things up." In 1961, as a drama specialist for the State Department, he was sent to Khartoum to produce and direct plays at the National Theatre of Sudan. For his first production, he chose George Bernard Shaw's pacifist play, *Arms and the Man*—a choice the authorities in that military dictatorship greeted with less than enthusiasm. Mr. Luckinbill was quickly transferred to Rome.

In 1970, he did it again with an article he wrote for *The New York Times* entitled, "The Irrelevance of Being an Actor." He had, at that time, spent more years training for his work than many doctors do, had been in seven Off-Broadway plays, including the·very successful *Boys in the Band*, two Broadway plays, had spent a year touring with *A Man for All Seasons*, had appeared at Lincoln Center in *Tartuffe*—and had made in ten years as a working actor an average of $3,700 a year. The article spoke also of his disenchantment with the small size of the theatre audience in this country, and the fact that, to the great majority of the American population, "the theatre never speaks and [they] couldn't care less if it did." Acting, he concluded, is neither economically feasible nor relevant to society. His comments remain, to this day, a subject of heated discussion among actors.

When the piece was written, Mr. Luckinbill was starring Off-Broadway in *What the Butler Saw*, a comedy by the late Joe Orton. He has since collaborated with Herbert Berghof on the translation from the German of Czech playwright Pavel Kohout's *Poor Murderer*, and has acted the lead on Broadway. Though the play's short run was a major disappointment, his subsequent role, in Michael Cristofer's Pulitzer Prize-winning *The Shadow Box*, was a triumph. As Brian, a man who reacts to his terminal illness with a manic redoubling of creative energy,

Mr. Luckinbill performed with what one reviewer called "a passionate intensity." He later founded the New York Actor's Theatre and played the title role in their production of Brecht's *Galileo;* several months after this interview, he and his wife Robin Strasser took over the leads in Neil Simon's Broadway hit, *Chapter Two.*

In addition to his stage work, Mr. Luckinbill has appeared in the film version of *Boys in the Band* as Hank, the married Ivy League homosexual whom he portrayed in the original Off-Broadway play. He has co-starred with Dyan Cannon in Otto Preminger's *Such Good Friends,* and has appeared with Kathleen Quinlan in *The Promise.* His TV work includes a stint as Frank Carver on the daytime soap, "Secret Storm," and a starring role in the nighttime series, "The Delphi Bureau."

Mr. Luckinbill, who was born on November 21, 1934 in Fort Smith, Arkansas, now lives in a townhouse on Manhattan's Upper East Side with his wife and two children. On the day of this interview, a hot summer afternoon, Mr. Luckinbill was relaxing comfortably at home in a polo shirt and gym shorts. His living room appeared furnished with an eye to being child-proof: scattered toys, a big dog, and a lazing cat were the only easy movables.

Mr. Luckinbill is warm, casual and, like Brian in *The Shadow Box,* he takes great pleasure in the flow of ideas. He is, however, without his character's desperation, and instead is straightforward and honest, able to speak with equal ease about his limitations as about his ambitions. Of the latter there are many—"so much to do in one's life," he says—and they lead him to voice some surprising (therefore Luckinbillian) feelings about acting.

It's interesting that someone who planned a career in science ended up in the arts. You had wanted to study medicine, then you switched to dentistry. How did you ever get into acting?

I flunked my premedical school application and though I could have gotten into dental school, I decided that I didn't want to do that. I was two years into college and my mother thought I should find out what I wanted to do with my life; it was critically important for up-from-under poor people like us that I find out. Now, this was the 1950s, the age of aptitude tests, when people thought that the key to human existence could be found through rat psychology. So my mother insisted that I take a series of these tests. We went to the University of California and took an eight-hour (or was it an eight-day?) battery of exams and when we came back a few weeks later, the evaluator said, "Well, I have to be frank with you. These tests indicate that you have no taste at all in the normal sense of the word, or else you have the worst taste that I've ever encountered." What he meant was that I didn't conform to any of the possible categories; my choices had been entirely an enigma to him. And he said, "I really recommend that you get into the performing arts."

Where all the weirdos go.

That's right—the loony bin, the chute to oblivion. My mother took all that information in and was stunned; she could hardly believe it. Yet for me, it clicked; I said, "Yeah, okay."

Had you done any performing at that point?

I had not been a performer at all. I had absolutely no dream of myself as an actor, knew nothing about the stage or how you went about it. And in the period of time that I'd been at the university, I don't think I'd seen even one play.

Nevertheless, I went back to college and switched my major on the strength of that aptitude test. I took all of the drama courses that were offered—about forty of them—in a year and a half. I had found where I ought to be. It was amazing. I was in every play after that; I took any and every part that came along. If people said they wanted to do a reading in class, I was the one

who did it. In the space of two years, I became very well known at
college.

That was another incentive, you see, because before all this, I
had been an absolute nonentity. Worse than that—I had been a
failing nonentity. I was the one who had to ask my friends for help
working the slide rule. Everybody knew I was hopeless; they
were all sorry for me and very kind. But do you know how it feels
when you're the one who has to ask for help, when you've got to
grab the sleeves of people going by in the Student Union and say,
"Please explain this assignment because I have no idea of how to
do it all"? Now, of course, from the vantage point of many years
later, I can look back and say, "What the hell difference did it
make if I didn't know physics?" I *would* have been a good doctor,
I have all the attributes: I'm cautious, very conservative, meticu-
lous, I care very much about people, and diagnoses of any kind
interest me—whether they concern cooking, character studies,
or diseases. But at the time, I agreed with them. I thought, okay,
it must just be the white coat that I'm after; I like the drama of
being a doctor.

It's such a marvelous accident that people become what they
become. I'm at the point in my life where I feel I could be anything tomorrow; I could drop all this acting and go on to something else. (And an actor never feels that more than when he's
doing television!)

*What was it about that early acting training you had as an under-
graduate that clicked? Was it just the recognition you got from
your fellow students, the thrill of doing something well that trans-
formed you, or was it something beyond that?*

I grew up in a very small Southern town, sort of a Faulkneresque,
redneck town, and there was no scope for imagination, at least
not for the kind of imagination that I had, being a dreamy sort of
person. The only way out of that environment was if you were
lucky enough to find something like the theatre which put you in
contact with great ideas—and by "great," I mean the fundamental, wheel-turning ideas of our culture. The contact that I got with
dramatic literature, with Shakespeare and the Greeks, left it up
to me whether or not I advanced culturally. I got the chance to
become a civilized person, somebody capable of relating to my

own children, and I became concerned with how they should be as human beings. All of that is very important to me. And so in a way I've always considered the theatre a kind of sideline; it's a detour on the road to becoming a civilized person.

I take it then that you're not altogether happy with being an actor, that you think there's something greater you could be doing.

I frequently have the same reaction that a lot of people do—that acting is not a fittin' occupation for a grown man. Not the theatre so much, but particularly television and film. The theatre is so demanding that it does seem a proper occupation, although I do think that it would be better if we could limit it to a festival once a year, something that had a kind of religious connotation.

That's the way theatre was in ancient Greece, wasn't it? And why we still use the expression, "the theatre season."

Yes, and it meant something more than it does now. We would be able to train for that festival all year and then doing it would be like a great climax. When it was over, we could go back and start training again or just go live our lives for a while. To me that's the correct idea. I mean, it's not so correct to get yourself into a holy state of mind for the benefit of the Shuberts, but that's the nature of being an actor today in the commercial theatre.

I'm still a bit puzzled about why you say acting is a detour for you.

It's a detour away from my ultimate goal, which is to create, to really do something that is mine. I'm not the sort of actor who is totally happy reading other people's lines. And it's the nature of the business that a play has to run a certain amount of time to make its money back; and so if you're really going to be a Broadway actor, you have to resign yourself to committing several months a year to a given play (if it's a success). You have to commit yourself to six or eight months at the least. Most people like to get a play and stay a year or two, but I find that to be totally uncongenial. I can do it fairly successfully, but there's something about it that's so mechanical after a while.

I'm unhappy with the fact that the best you can be as an actor is a combination between a very personal and very objective interpreter. If you go too far out of the general understanding of what the part should be or what the words mean, you're wrong. You may entertain a lot of people, as Zero Mostel did in *Fiddler on the Roof*. When I saw him do that, I was absolutely astonished and delighted; but I saw Zero, I didn't see Tevye. I was familiar with the Tevye stories and they were very different from what I saw Zero do. Yet Zero's light was incandescent; he was like a thousand-watt bulb on stage, and I no longer cared who Tevye was, I just loved who Zero was. But I'm not a performer like that. I'm the sort of performer who likes to do what the role is; I like to be very specific and analyze very closely what the play really says and then do that.

There's a limited amount that comes back to you after you've done a play for a while. There may be an infinite variety of audiences, but there's a certain pattern that develops between you and them; you know that tonight is going to be such and such a type of audience, and so your performance moves in that direction; it becomes a pattern, an imprint, and that's when I start to go crazy. I always devise ways and means to get sick; I am hypochondriacal, I leave shows, I quit—and I know this about myself. So I think that maybe the way out is to become closer to myself as a writer.

Writers, though, operate under all sorts of commercial pressures, too.

I know. All of my writer friends laugh at this idea of mine because they have exactly the same commercial pressures and problems. When you are in the publishing world, it's: "When will you do this? Will you sign this book cover? Will you do this review? We need a book on a certain subject, can you do it in this amount of time?" And you say to yourself, "Well, I'm really working on the big novel, but I'll take three months or six or eight and I'll produce something to order." So writing becomes the same game as acting.

It's a rare life that is lived in complete self-expression. People laugh now and say Picasso was a factory, but he had that rare combination: he believed that what the world needed, what the gallery dealers needed, was what he in fact produced, what he wanted to produce. And the most successful theatre artists are those people who really have an absolute need to do what the public absolutely wants. I mean people like George Kelly and Stephen Sondheim—they're totally on a track with the audience. There's no falling off into lack of art because they are expressing exactly what they are; and it's brilliant.

To be a first-rate actor, does one have to be born with the talent? Is it something that can be taught or learned through experience?

To be a first-rate actor takes a combination of training and talent. You must be born with a certain perception of life but also born into an environment which forces you, drives you, to be the best there is.

*Much of this being first-rate is a matter of the role. I think Barnard Hughes feels that, though he's been an actor for forty-five years, he's only now first rate, and it's because he's finally got a role in **Da** with which he can connect, as you say, in that balance of personal and objective interpretation.*

Yes, it does depend about half on the role and the other half on the fact that a guy like Barney Hughes has been first rate to the rest of us all along, just maybe not to himself. It's true, though, you can't do it without the words and the play and the successful production. It's got to be a hit, you see; no absolutely glorious critical successes will do if it's a commercial failure. I've had lots of those; people say, "This will be long remembered," but it is long remembered by about four people.

It's part of the nature of the theatre, and it's what drives everybody mad, but it *is* a mass art, a mass craft. We come together in a group to develop something that must look unified in the end; there may be thirty of us or there may be two of us in the cast, but we're still a group. It's not just one guy musing with his pad and pencil, or his paints, sitting on a hillside in Arles.

That brings us back to theatre as a religious festival—as in a mass—where an entire group of people act together; they take the communion as one body.

Yes, there must be that shared perception; that's what it's all about. I suppose I'm not quite serious when I say it's a detour, because it's one that's been going on now for thirty years. It would be a great relief to me to finally be able to say, as Olivier said in an interview recently, that at the age of seventy he finally considers himself an actor because there's nothing else he can do—it's too late, he's passed too many options by. There would be a great happiness in my saying I'm an actor, in coming to that unity with myself, but I'm not quite there yet. I feel there are too many other things I want to do: I want to produce, I want to write, I want to develop television news shows. . . .

What is the impulse behind all those yearnings? What is the common denominator to your various ambitions?

Everything I want to do involves reaching out to other people, finding out what they think and telling them what I think. Some of the best theatre in my life has been a conversation with one person in a room, and yet it's curious because I've always been a loner, and I'm still a very alone person. It's a paradox, as everything in life is a paradox. I'm not needful of other people, but I can't get along without them. The best in me does not come out to me, it only comes out to other people. If you can give an answer to someone who asks the right question, that person doubles and you double, you amplify yourselves. And that, in a sense, is what a great performance should do: it should leave open ends.

Is that something you can consciously strive to do, to leave unanswered questions in the minds of the audience? How does an actor manage to leave those ends open?

You can only do it by not going into a performance having calculated everything. The best performing I've ever done was when I just put on the clothes and went on stage. In effect, I did not rehearse. When people asked me what I did, how I got this effect or that effect, I wanted to say, "Shut up, get away, I don't want to talk about it." I am aware that if I try to hang on to the role too strongly, I will strangle it.

For instance, I had a running difference with the playwright when I acted Brian in *The Shadow Box*. He saw the character differently than I did, and in that division of opinion was the electricity that made the character work. But he kept saying to me that Brian was a bad writer and I kept saying, no. You see, if I had said, yes, Brian is a bad writer, that would have been a comment upon Brian from me, the actor. Yet for me to insist that Brian was a good writer meant that I *was* Brian, and was incapable of standing apart from him in judgment.

An actor then who does not make comments on his character is more likely to create questions in the audience because he leaves those judgments up to them.

Yes. And the biggest questions in life, the ones that relate most to successful theatre are the unanswerable ones, the ones that come from the family. Those are the questions we all ask: Why did Daddy do that? Why is Mama like that? You can never answer those questions, and they are more serious for the older people· who largely make up theatre audiences because Mom and Daddy are dead, or they're too old to tell you. A play like *Oedipus* is a perfect example. It's a story that interests people less today because they perceive it as being a play about incest—which indeed it is. I think we're out of touch with our own incestuous needs and desires. Yet it's impossible not to identify with a man like Oedipus who doesn't know what a horrible mistake he's made— particularly when the man is powerful, arrogant, but also very vulnerable and hopeful and handsome and in love with his wife. All those things are woven so powerfully into the fabric of that play; it's the clearest play in the world, and yet every statement it makes raises at least ten questions.

*How do you feel about the kind of theatre then that someone like Robert Wilson does—*Einstein on the Beach, *etcetera?*

I happen to like Robert Wilson, but on the other hand, I don't think what he does has anything to do with theatre. It just doesn't reach me; it "pings" like those television games; you can feel rhythms, you can hit a point and make a score, but the audience does not ever once come together and say as a whole, "*Wow*, I understand," or even, "I don't understand." That has to happen in the theatre; the audience has to come together, they have to feel something in unison.

You worked for a while with the Open Theatre. Don't they work along a different philosophy of what theatre is all about?

Yes, but that was in the '60s, when everybody was distrusting what the traditional theatre could do, and that, of course, is a very healthy thing. We just were not interested in traditional stories anymore. And the Open Theatre was a very creative thing to work with because the actors were providing so much of the improvisational juice for it. We were making up the pieces, using our own bodies, voices, minds. The interaction of the actors was the most important part of the evening. But that's why the Open Theatre work seemed to me a bit closed. It was much more for the actors than for the audience.

At one point, I was teaching at Queens Community College and I got the Theatre a gig to go out there. The audience was made up of people who hardly ever got to the theatre. They didn't understand what was going on. They watched the movements, heard the sounds—the "arghs"—and afterwards they asked a lot of stupid but legitimate questions. "Why do you make those ugly sounds? What the hell do you think you're trying to accomplish?" They weren't hostile about it, yet everybody in the workshop *was* hostile; they responded with, "Leave us alone; what right do you have to ask these questions?; what you see is what you get; it doesn't have to mean anything. . . ." Those were all the answers of conceptual artists, which indeed the Open Theatre actors were. But that's a dead end. It's a dead end for actors to work only for other actors and to develop techniques that don't include the audience. I came away feeling that I had had enough.

Is there a difference in audiences, say between a New York and London audience?

I think quite honestly that the New York audience is simply the best theatre audience in the world. The London audience is awfully good, but the New York audience is less parochial. We don't have our Sirs and our Dames who can appear in anything and still get an appreciative crowd. There's no actor in America who can appear in *anything* and still get an audience. It's very democratic that way. If George C. Scott's in a turkey, people will say, "George C. Scott's in a turkey—goodbye." But in London,

Gielgud can run in a turkey for six or seven months; people will say, "The play's awful, but how many times are we going to be able to see Sir John before he dies?" That's lovely too, of course, but I prefer the slightly more *a priori* attitude of New Yorkers.

You do, though, get bored with a play even though the audiences are responsive?

Well, for about three months you can continue to be surprised by the audiences themselves. You can sense the differences in each audience every night. You're like a lion tamer who senses a different mood in the beast, and so each night it's a different beast to you. In a comedy sketch, the beast will not laugh at certain lines that the one last night laughed at, that every night for the previous two and a half months got a laugh, so you say, "My God, exactly what kind of beast is this?" You start to categorize them and though that's not correct, unfortunately, that's what we are as human beings; the combinations are infinite, but our capacity to absorb them, to relate to them and deal with them isn't.

You've described yourself as being relatively loose when you play a character; you try not to calculate everything or rehearse the part too much. Does that mean you have little work to do in preparing for most of your roles, or is this only for a scattered few?

It's an interesting thing, but you get to a certain level of competence and you can open a play (and naturally, you start to look for those plays) where you can read ten pages and say, "Okay, I know who this is, let's just do it, let's get rid of all this stuff like rehearsals, let's just get to opening night. I know what I want to do." You forget how long it took you to arrive at that point, but you know technically what you can do. You don't even have to think about your voice, your body; you just know how this character looks and you can automatically go ahead and do it. Now, that's a high level of competence; you don't have to worry about what to do with your hands or what you're going to sound like or whether you're going to sit down, stand up, cross the room—none of that is important. Yet there are other parts that you don't feel such a connection with, where *all* of that is terribly important, and where the mechanics of the part have to be worked out precisely because you're fighting to create an illusion.

The parts I've done most successfully have been those that were not an illusion; they have been the parts where I felt immediately that I *was* that person. For the two hours of *The Shadow Box*, for instance, if you were to talk to me as Larry, I wouldn't know who you were talking to—I was Brian. That's an exaggeration to a degree, but in a way it's not. You *do* take on aspects of the character and carry them into your life.

This is a trade truism, of course, but you would hesitate to play Macbeth for too long if you were in the mode of Macbeth, in other words, if Macbeth came easily to you. Not that it would make you go out and murder someone, but it would bring out the characteristics of an emotionally plunging person, which Macbeth was, and that's a dangerous state of mind to be in. So all you can hope for when you do play a character with whom you identify closely is that the person's a good person and relatively easy to be around. Otherwise, it can be uncomfortable.

Did the fact that Brian was a terminal-cancer patient take an emotional toll on you, even though your identification with him was so easy and complete?

Yes, it did. It was just very depressing to play over a long period of time. The play was uplifting for the audience, and the ending resolved matters for them, but for the actors, it did not. We went away with that tension, those indigestible feelings of fear that the characters have. Nevertheless, I liked Brian the best of all the characters, and if I could choose a way to die, it would be Brian's way. He was the silliest; he just went on and on, making a joke of everything. His sense of self was the same as mine: I thought he was an absolutely marvelous, entertaining, unimportant human being.

You acted the role of Galileo in Brecht's play, and there, the playwright ***wants*** *you to feel distanced from the character, doesn't he? That way, the actors and the audience can have a critical, political reaction to the drama.*

Yes, Galileo is somebody who fascinates me and as Brecht writes him, I feel very connected with him, but at the same time, very objective about him. He makes certain errors that I tend to think of myself as not making, and yet there's an enormous childlike fun in showing this guy make his mistakes; you feel yourself saying, "See what he did!" In Brecht, you must retain that objectivity about the character because it helps you be clear to the audience about exactly where the guy goes wrong; and in every Brecht play there's that situation.

What about the characters with whom you feel little in common? Do you try to stay away from those parts, or are the differences between you ever an attraction?

Well, speaking as a professional actor, you can and very often you do perform roles with which you have no connection at all. You do it for the money and because it's your life; you need work. If it's work that you're serious about, you have to have some sort of hook and if you *don't* have something to identify with, then you'd better stay away from it, because you're not going to be happy acting it and you're not going to do a very good job.

*You played an insane actor in **Poor Murderer**. What kind of a connection did you feel there?*

Actually, that was a curious play because the real basis of that play was not the plot or characters, but the fact that it was a metaphor for the political state of Czechoslovakia in 1968. It was too dangerous a statement for the playwright to do as anything but a very covered metaphor, so while it was a very clever play, it was not as immediate or direct as it should have been to be effective. I couldn't ever feel that I was getting out of myself what was there inside.

You were making an intellectual identification with the role rather than an emotional one?

Yes, that's all I could do. And certainly the same was true of the audience. Although we were reaching a group of highly intelligent people, people concerned with the suppression of freedoms in Eastern Europe, the story was not as moving as it could have been. They felt removed from it, and so did I; but there wasn't much I could do but play the play.

The people who went to see it were those already concerned about the situation in Czechoslovakia. That's similar to what you said in your **New York Times** *article a few years back, that the people who go to the theatre are those who already care about the theatre, and that acting in the theatre is therefore like a group of people trapped in a closet, shouting at each other. Do you feel the same way now?*

Well, I think that theatre audiences have expanded enormously in the last few years. All of a sudden tickets are available cheaply the day of the performance, so people who used to be entirely outside of the theatre have had an opportunity to start caring. In the years since that article, television has become rather déclassé and very few movies make it these days, so that adds to the glamour of Broadway.

Ever since *Hair* and *Boys in the Band*, a whole new group of people have been brought into the theatre—the kids. Kids went to see *Hair* who normally wouldn't go to the theatre, and because a lot of people came out of the closet to see *Boys*, there has been a splintering of the market. Today, even a play about two West Indian lesbians will have a market; it can run awhile somewhere, someplace. But five or ten years ago, that sort of play would have been done for a couple of nights at the most—in somebody's loft. Now there's an audience, and people will be standing out in the street to see it if you get the word out.

In other words, because of those plays in the late '60s, people see the theatre as being more relevant?

Yes, yes. Somebody told me, "You must come and see a play about Modigliani," and we went down to some gallery on Grove Street or somewhere, and it was jammed, just jammed! Here were all sorts of people interested in a play about Modigliani destroying himself. I mean, that's a subject that a lot of people couldn't care less about, and yet it ran very successfully; it was an okay play, not that great, but I was astonished. So really, I no longer have that feeling I once expressed that it's only four percent of the upper middle class who goes to the theatre. I believe the audience has expanded.

And yet even with the greater interest in theatre these days, acting remains a very insecure profession for you.

It's insecure because you're selling yourself all the time, and who the hell are you? Just what is it you're selling? You open your sample case some days and there's nothing in there. And most of the time, you open it and they ain't buying what you really are. So you fix up your case to have all the shiny wares on top, and underneath you put the bugs—your good, true stuff. If they buy the shiny layer, you feel slightly violated. If they don't buy the shiny layer and you can't show them the other stuff, then you don't know what to do. You feel totally rejected. That makes you insecure.

Even if someone hires you for a play that utilizes your true talents you may not be able to support yourself from it—is that still the case?

The economic situation still, today, is that you can be a Broadway star and not earn enough to support yourself; the only way to survive is to do commercials, television, and films. I myself would prefer to be able to devote my time to the theatre because I'm best at it, and because it's deserving of my best—it's a place that is still an open forum, one in which you can say anything you want to say—but I can't. Most of my time is spent hustling around, trying to earn the money to be able to be in the theatre. Now, I'm lucky because I have a certain commercial viability in other areas, so I can make it. But there are many people who are not commercially viable and who still cling to the theatre—those people are the bravest souls around. I was just talking to a friend who works in a garage parking cars; he was in *Galileo,* and he's a very good actor but he is not a commercial type, so he has absolutely no money. Now that's an absurd situation. It's waste; it's the sort of casual waste that is typical of America. We say, "Well, there'll be ten more of those tomorrow, so throw that one away." But it's a false premise and gradually, we're going to learn, to our cost and our discredit, that there aren't enough talented, valuable people around that we can afford to throw any of them away.

These are the problems of being an artist in a capitalist economy. Yet given the fact that we don't want a state-run theatre system, what are the solutions?

I think the people who control the theatre have been very profligate in the very fact that they don't do market research, they don't continually strive to set up means of expanding the audience and lowering the price of tickets—those should always be their goals. They're really responsible and there *shouldn't* be these problems; the theatre *should* be possible in a capitalist mode. I think, for example, there could be a value tax added to ticket prices that would go into a general fund for the development of the theatre.

Wouldn't that added cost of the tickets discourage audiences?

No, because it would only be ten percent, or five percent. There's nothing wrong to me with the idea of hit shows supporting other kinds of theatre. It's just smart capitalism. The theatre is an industry like timber; if you take an option on ten thousand acres, cut it all down and don't reforest, you're in trouble. People like the Shuberts should be smart enough to know that they've got to reforest now, they've got to open up avenues for new people; they've got to build new audiences.

You see actors as a sort of conservative force, don't you? You've said they're "in the preserving business, they're holding back and building hedges." Would you explain that?

Well, actors are conservationists because most of us, in this generation of actors, studied the classics. We got our training from digging into the best of the past, trying to reinterpret it for now, and as you do that, you begin to carry the baggage of the past with you wherever you go. And you tend, like people who understand history, to want not to repeat it, not to make the same mistakes. That makes you a conservative, a cultural right-winger.

There are certainly a lot of actors who consider themselves left-wingers out there trying to make their impression on the cultural world, trying to change it as the Open Theatre tried to change it in the '60s. How do you react to them?

I think it's very healthy when there are left-wingers out there who want to break things up, who say, "Now wait a minute, it's all very well to do a season of Shakespeare, but let's also re-examine the relationship between the audience and the actors and the playwright and director. What can we be doing? Can we be learning new things?" That's the process; that's how the theatre becomes richer. We are richer for having had an Open Theatre, for having had a Living Theatre, and now we understand how to do those things. We can now go in and create an Open Theatre situation in rehearsal, and teach those techniques to new actors who are always eager to learn what has been developed before them.

The more things change in the theatre, the more they stay the same; the ultimate goals remain constant.

Yes, because the ultimate goal is always, and has always been, to expose an emotional vein of human relationships; to show one person to the other, us to them, them to us—that is unchanging. But that goal is the opposite of anarchy, you see. You can't have anarchy in the theatre. You can't have fourteen people working in fourteen different styles and arrangements. When the playwright gives you the work and you sit down around a table to read it, there's got to be a unity of purpose.

But a particular role can be interpreted by the actor and perceived by the audience in any number of ways. One line can be almost like a Rorschach test in the variety of its meaning to different people.

I disagree. I believe there's an absolute meaning to things, that in a given scene of a play there's an irreducible meaning. Being an actor is a matter of finding that irreducible meaning and then presenting it clearly. And if the play is great, if the writing is great and the acting is clear enough, that meaning will reverberate and resonate and move everybody to get on their feet. It's like a line of music: it's irreducible that that note is a C-flat, that it goes on for six measures. You've just got to play it and play it right. Now, there are a whole lot of ways to get into the playing of the note; there's the playing itself, and there are any number of ways to finish it off. All those variations can leave the audience saying, "It's never been done that way before," even though it's been done a thousand times, a million times. And somewhere within that process of getting in, doing it, and getting out lies the art to me. In two lines of dialogue in a scene by Molière, there is a relationship built between two characters; you can't say, "It means this or this or that." It's *not* infinite. You have to say, "He wrote what he meant, now let's find out what it is."

How do you find that true meaning then? How do you approach the task of deciding how you'll play a part? Do you rely on research about the type of character you're playing, about the author of the play and what his or her intentions were?

When I find myself doing research, I know I'm in trouble. No, I don't. Research is objectivizing. Oh, it's nice to know that somebody wore cork-soled shoes, and okay, if you go get me some cork-soled shoes, I'll find out how to walk in them. That may take me a day or two or maybe a month—but it's all technical stuff, you see. You have to find what you need from inside; you have to find what the role means to you. You have to connect with what you think each line really says, and then simply develop a technique for getting it back every night. That's the research I do— it's finding the character in myself.

But how do you go about making your soul accessible in that way? How do you develop that capacity?

I have inside myself an unchanging, undying need to be somebody else—that's being born to be an actor and maybe that's being born to be an artist in general. That, however, is paradoxically coupled with the unchanging desire to express *myself*. So while I want to be somebody else, I also want to give voice to who I am; while I am *only* myself, I am also other people, and somewhere in the dim relation between those statements is my understanding of others and my capacity to act them. An actor qualifies everything he sees with that understanding. He says, "Well, yes, I could have been Hitler." It's the there-but-for-the-grace-of-God-go-I syndrome. You start asking yourself all those questions that you can legitimately ask any human being. "Well, could I have been Hitler? Could I kill people? Maybe Hitler didn't think he was killing people; maybe he thought they weren't really people." You might ask yourself, "What would it be like to be a paraplegic?

Maybe I'd get off on the idea that people would always be kind to me. . . ." Suddenly you find you have whole new modes to deal in, whole new keys to play.

This is different from the Actors Studio approach, it seems, because you're not developing your own personal emotional responses as much as you're developing your imagination.

Again, it's connected with that need to be other people that goes through your life all the time, daily. You are asking yourself: "Would I do what that bus driver just did when he kicked that old lady down the steps? Yeah, I might. But would I really?" I go through life asking myself those questions all the time.

Einstein once claimed that he thought of the theory of relativity because he was so slow to grow up—he didn't even speak until he was three. He said that other people gave up thinking about why things moved; they matured and started to deal pragmatically with objects as tools; they accepted the fact that, yes, that moves, that's X. Yet he kept thinking, why X? Why does it do that? Like a child, he never gave up asking those questions and following up the answers with still more.

So you think artists are children in that way, too?

Definitely, yes. By that I mean in the Christian sense: you must become as a little child again. You must become very wise, very direct, very Zen. It's the difference between being childish and childlike, I think; it's what people mean when they refer to the greater thing that a child is. It's never having given up asking the basic questions. Why am I a man? What would it be like if I dressed completely differently and ran a vegetable store or tried walking backwards or talking another language that didn't mean anything to me? I do things like that and other people who are actors do, too. It's not peripheral to us; it's fundamental. It's what life is; what it's all about. It's that kind of experimentation, and it's not with self so much as it is with others. It's always trying to reach other people.

Some call it the need to be loved.

One psychiatrist said it's the need to cover your fear all the time: being an actor is like being a tightrope walker, the audience is so terrifying.

The actor has a fear of the audience, but the audience has a fear of the actor, too. You people on stage have a great power over us; you can show us parts of ourselves we'd rather not see.

Yes, and people will cover their fear with a kind of contempt. People treat actors very well, but often it's just a way of dealing with that contempt. It's a little pat on the head. It's like saying, "I'm not really interested in what you do; it's not really relevant to my company of eight million shares of Katangese Copper. . . ." And yet it's wonderful to walk out of *Boys in the Band* as I did one night, and find a guy clinging to the railing of the steps while his wife was trying to drag him to a taxi. He was wearing a four-hundred-dollar suit and she was wearing a three-thousand-dollar mink coat, and he was saying, "I can't move, I'm terrified, terrified. . . ." I stopped because I thought maybe he was having a heart attack and needed help, but then I realized that *we* in the play had terrified him. We had scared him out of his wits with questions about life; we had opened something up for him. Yes, there are a lot of people who don't take kindly to having their eyes opened that way and they don't want actors taking credit for doing that.

In what sense is what an actor does "play"? When is it "work"?

Oh, it *is* play. If it's successful, then it's play; if not, then it's work.

What was the value of doing soap operas to you? Did you get much out of it beyond the financial rewards?

It had a terrific value. First of all, I got to see myself in instant replay. I could compare what I thought I was accomplishing with what I *really* was accomplishing. I could see my body and my face and my voice and my general attitude toward life as it was projected on screen. I could measure that against the character which, in my heart and my head, I had *thought* I was presenting. I could see how my personality had shaped that character. And I started to see that, well, I'm not too good at this kind of a scene, but I'm really good at that kind. It's great for actors to see who they are, who their public selves are.

The action of soaps is so furious that very often you don't have the time to learn your part properly; the bigger the role, the more you are at a disadvantage. But ironically, that gives you a better chance to learn: you fail more often to accomplish what *they* want you to accomplish, and you see what you really do with your face and body.

I would imagine that just being employed as an actor would have its psychological benefits . . . it gives you a certain credibility, makes you feel that you are a "real" actor.

That is a great plus. It makes you into a successful actor right away. From nothing to success is very heady and very nice; you go from no money to a steady salary, from no job or the prospect of only a series of weird jobs, to one with a routine. And it *is* acting—it's the real stuff. Generally speaking, the scripts are not too horrifyingly bad. The worst part of it is the repetition—you have to repeat scenes so many times in various ways in order to keep people up on it.

Would you say that acting in soaps is difficult work?

Very. Technically it's very hard to learn and memorize continuously like that. And it becomes destructive in a way because you start to treat all material like that—as easily memorizable but easily forgettable. Your mind becomes a bit of a sponge, a sieve; you develop colander-brain. But if somebody wrote me a great part, I'd certainly do a soap again.

How did you feel about the filming of **Boys in the Band** *after you'd originated the part on stage?*

I felt good because I made a lot of money. It was wonderful—but it was also very strange. We all thought it was going to make us major motion picture stars and it didn't happen that way, so it was a head-wrecker for a lot of people. But it was great to be able to do as your first movie a play that you knew inside and out; you knew what every character thought and felt at any moment. The camera could come to me at any time and I would know exactly what I should be doing; I would never have to search for it.

With most movies, you get the script and you may have some time to read it, but it's by yourself. Movie acting is you and the camera. It's not even a question of missing an audience because there isn't even any reciprocity between you and the other actors. You can't develop the drama as a whole—work your roles in with each other—because you don't have time. You arrive on the set; you have had the script for two months or more likely you've had it for ten days; and as soon as you get there, the director says, "Okay, get on top of her now and make love to her." Or, "Kill her," or "Drive the van over the bridge." You have to stretch for the emotions; you have to push to get the part. There are great movie actors who can absolutely analyze a script and figure out what the audience needs to see on their face in any given scene, and then absolutely do it. That's a technique I haven't learned yet, but I admire it enormously. Pacino's like that; he's learned it. Then too, a lot of people handle movies by doing nothing, by just letting what they are be photographed. But that's the safe way out. I like performers who dare to take chances with themselves—like Dyan Cannon. She's taking enormous risks now, she's terrific; it's nice to see someone go just a little overboard like that.

How do you react to seeing yourself on the Big Screen?

Oh, I don't like the way I look very much, but it's curious, you begin to isolate your characteristics. I like my left profile. I don't like myself in tight close-ups, fullface, because I have a full face and I tend to look a little bit like the moon. But the camera lies all the time, you know, especially about really seeing deeply. What it can see, though, is a spirit in your eyes, and you've just got to keep yourself fluid enough to let that spirit shine clear.

An Indian friend of mine just did *The Chess Players* and when he told me, "All I did was try to keep it fluid," I knew exactly what he meant. There may be two weeks between shot A and shot B, but in the final film they're absolutely continuous. You can't plan for that. You shouldn't try to repeat what you thought you felt, you shouldn't try to rebuild it. It's completely different from the theatre where you must rebuild the same thing constantly.

Is the theatre, in your opinion, more true to life than films?

Well, films are both very true and very false. They tend to enhance the idea that life is a series of unconnected moments; and what we see on the screen draws us in very powerfully because we ourselves have that same sense. We think of life as relatively unconnected fragments because we don't understand how to connect them. But the theatre is really more like life. This scene of our talking right here has an art to it; it has an exterior and an interior; the arcs of our lives are intersecting, and that has significance. Movies can only enhance the glamour of the moment. You know, the gigantic head goes down to meet the other gigantic head and the two of them have a gigantic moment of gigantic kissing which is all made so gigantic that you feel the moment must have meaning. Whether or not it *has* meaning, or whether or not it has the kind of gigantic meaning that it inevitably has on a movie screen is another matter.

So you agree with Susan Sontag's thesis on photography.

Yes. Photographs are fragments of reality and therefore no reality. Life has a continuity, a flow, and that flow *is* the reality; the pattern is the reality, not the individual moments.

You said that you are best on screen when you are able to project your humor. I take it then that you prefer doing comedy to more serious things?

I like to do a role that's serious because it's funny—a comedy-drama, and there are very few of them around. When a character is making very serious points in a comedy, the points are being communicated without his having to make them. *Macbeth* is a very serious play so it's not really in the same category, but I recently saw Albert Finney play the part at the National Theatre, and there was a moment that relates to this. His Macbeth was not a success; it was the first preview, a dreadful night, he just wasn't cutting it; but he knew it. When he came to "Tomorrow and tomorrow and tomorrow . . ." he laughed all the way through it, and I got a glimmer of brilliance! It suddenly dawned on him that Macbeth is a man who makes a choice for total evil; he *knows* it's

wrong and yet he goes ahead. So what other reaction could he
have, seeing his own low estimate of himself justified at the end,
and speaking falsely when he says, you see what we are, we're
worse than nothing, we stink. There's such a deep bitterness
about it that it becomes terribly funny in a very cynical way. It
was wonderful! But the reaction in the audience was uneasy because Finney didn't go all the way with it, and his laughter was
coming from a different source. Had he been consistent with it, it
would have really been funny.

*Do you like a strong director to guide you when you work, or do
you prefer to figure things out on your own?*

I like to work things out on my own, and I do not like directors—
period. But the worst kind of directors are those who come in with
something all laid out for me; I can't work with them anymore.
I'm getting to the point where I fight with them so continuously
that it isn't even fun to do.

There are also lots of very good directors around. Bob Moore,
who directed *Boys in the Band*, is a fabulous director. He did
have a very concise plan, but it wasn't about what people felt or
thought; it was only about what people were picking up and putting down. That's a different matter. Most really good directors
trust the actors enormously; there's a certain humility in that,
though it's a false humility, because a director knows that the actors will solve his problems.

I haven't had that many good movie parts, though I just had a
good one in a film called *The Promise*. I felt that the director was
really looking to me to find out what the character could be. His
attitude was, Who is this person? Let's find out. A few times I
thought I went wrong. I told him and he agreed; he said he
wouldn't use those parts. There's a danger, you see, in trying to
stay fluid, too. You make mistakes, you do something that the
character really shouldn't be seen doing because you weren't
totally concentrated that day.

*You spent three years in Hollywood. What would you say are the
differences in opportunities between New York and Hollywood?*

Well, the difference is that in New York due is given for work

done. You can do a play in a loft downtown and if you're successful at it, you will get better offers. You can progress. Therefore, your motives for doing any kind of showcase are rather impure: you expect it will advance you. And yet out of that impure
motive comes the best work. In California, you can do theatre
with the purest motives because there's no other way to do it: it
means nothing, it gets you nowhere. As someone once said, "You
can play *Hedda Gabler* across the street from Universal and get
fabulous reviews, but it won't get you into a television sitcom."
There's no connection between the two. And in California, you
can be a much more successful actor by working less, by reserv-
ing yourself.

*You make yourself a commodity for which there's little supply and
hopefully, much demand?*

You make yourself hard-to-get, whereas in New York, the more
work you do, the better off you are. The more you plunge in and
take chances and be seen and be hungry, be amenable, be juicy,
the better off you are, the more happens to you. In California, it's
the opposite. The less happens to you, the more valuable you become. It's a perverse place. They like you to be "laid back"; to be
"laid back" is to be a good human being. I think that's a normal
and probably a rather good reaction to the hunger of ambition—
but everybody there has that hunger deeply and desperately.
They're all ambitious, they're killers, and so in order to deal with
that personally, they lie back; they lie back further and further
and further. In effect, it's a good human impulse to say, "I'm not
as hungry and ambitious as I really am." But obviously, it can be
terribly dishonest. It's like saying, "Please don't think I'm so awful as to be here only because you're here; I need you to see me
and sleep with me and do whatever in order to get a part, but it's
okay because I really like you." Now that's perverse.

Here in New York, it's okay to be hot, to be like that character
in the *I Can't Hear You When the Water's Running* routine: You
want me to be short? Tall? I'll take off my hat. I'll take off my
clothes. I can be fat, thin, I can be this, that. . . . Here, people
acknowledge the fact that opportunities are slim and that the best
actors are the kind of all-out, "Here I come! Take notice!" type of
people.

Yet the theatre jobs in New York are not as well paid as the television work in California. The price of living here is high, and actors often end up living in very difficult conditions.

Yes. Theatre people are generally subletting illegally and driving a broken-down old car that they park in somebody's lot in Jersey; they're scrambling, scuffling. Yet I know that I could not leave this city; it feeds me.

What do you find most difficult about being an actor?

The most difficult thing for me is feeling that I'm not in control, in charge, not being the primary artist.

Being an interpretive rather than a creative artist?

Yeah. I have very strong impulses to be the prime mover and an actor, no matter how successful, is almost never in that position.

*With **Galileo,** you founded your own company and produced it yourself. Do you think that's becoming a trend for actors?*

Yes, it is. It's become that way for a number of reasons. Actors are better educated than they used to be, they generally understand money better. And the field is wide open; producers are not producing, they've dropped out. But being a producer is largely recognizing a property and getting hold of it, and actors are beginning to think that they could do that as well as other people. It's a good idea, the actor-manager.

Did you feel that acting the role of Galileo was more fulfilling because you did have that control?

No, I felt that I did the role less well, that I wasn't as fully in it as I should have been.

Because your concentration was scattered?

Right. If I ever acted again with the company, I would cut myself out of the production process much earlier. I mean, for the first two weeks of rehearsals in *Galileo*, I was writing an article for *The New York Times* about the company; that was much more important to me because it was primary, you know, I was *writing*, and so I couldn't give total time to the part. But you do what you can, that's all.

Yet you must feel that founding a company has brought you closer to your goals now?

Closer, yes. My friend who was in *Galileo* told me that when he was at the Equity office the other day, people would grab him; they were thinking that our company was going to be the next A.P.A. [Association of Producing Artists], and there's a kind of delicious responsibility in having stirred up so much. Yet I stirred it up like I do everything else, just blindly, because I've got to be busy—and because I do so enjoy the stirring!

IMOGENE COCA

Imogene Coca, with the sadly wistful quality of a female Chaplin, is one of this country's most well-known and well-loved comic actresses. She was born on November 18, 1908, the only daughter of a Spanish/Mexican/Cuban father and an Irish mother, both determined stage parents. By the age of eleven, she was already doing a "single" in the vaudeville houses around her native Philadelphia. At sixteen, she made her Broadway debut in the 1925 musical, *When You Smile*, and worked for almost another ten years before Leonard Sillman's *New Faces of 1934* made her an "overnight" sensation.

Along with such fellow performers as Danny Kaye, Jerome Robbins, and Carol Channing, Ms. Coca spent five summers in the Poconos working for producer Max Leibman. Yet even after she was firmly established as a comedienne, Ms. Coca hit a run of hard times. The ten years beginning in 1939 was her "blue period," an era of desperate unemployment broken only by occasional night-club jobs. Then, in 1949, Max Leibman was given a TV show to produce—the "Admiral Broadway Revue"—and he sent for her. After twenty weeks of working on her own, she teamed up with Sid Caesar; from 1950 to 1954 their combination of talents on "Your Show of Shows," a 90-minute live broadcast, made TV history.

In the years since, Ms. Coca has been reunited with Sid Caesar only a handful of times. In 1967 they appeared in the Emmy award-winning "Sid Caesar-Imogene Coca-Carl Reiner-Howard Morris Show" and six years later, did Neil Simon's *Prisoner of Second Avenue* on the Chicago stage. In 1977, they revived their special chemistry and headlined at the Sahara Hotel in Las Vegas.

On her own, Imogene Coca is certainly a singular performer. She has starred in two TV series, "Grindl" and "It's About Time," has appeared in numerous Broadway shows, including *Billy Rose Concert Revue, The*

Girls in 509, and *Janus*; has acted in the films, *Under the Yum Yum Tree* and *Rabbit Test*; and has toured all over the country in such plays as *Bells are Ringing, Luv, No, No Nanette*, and *Plaza Suite*. In 1962 alone, she traveled 36,000 miles to 120 cities doing *Once Upon a Mattress* and 24,000 miles to 90 cities with *The Thurber Carnival*. And though she had lost an eye and injured a leg in a 1973 car accident, at the time of this interview, she was appearing on Broadway in *On The Twentieth Century* —singing, dancing, and clowning—and had been nominated for a 1978 Tony award.

Ms. Coca's first husband, Robert Burton, died in 1955; she and her second husband, King Donovan, tour and perform together. They have two residences: a Manhattan apartment and a Dallas townhouse.

This interview was conducted backstage in her dressing-room at the St. James Theatre. Ms. Coca does not act in any way the "star"; rather, she believes her appeal lies in the very fact that she is "ordinary." Impish-looking as ever, she was shy, sweet, and touchingly eager to please.

You've been involved with the theatre almost literally all your life. Your parents worked in vaudeville–your father as an orchestra conductor and your mother, for a brief time, as an assistant to Howard Thurston, the magician.

Yes, my mother happened to read an ad in a Philadelphia paper that said, "Young ladies wanted. . . ." She was sixteen at the time. She applied for the job, got it and was bitten immediately by the show business bug. So she came to New York and then all her sisters followed her. Eventually they all married actors, but on one occasion when my mother played Philadelphia, which was her home town, she met my father who was conducting an orchestra there, and that was that.

You apparently accompanied your father to the vaudeville shows from the time you were about three years old.

Ever since I could walk.

And you spent most of your childhood in theatres.

Yes, I watched my father until I was eleven. That's when I began playing the vaudeville houses myself—the ones around the Philadelphia area. Then when I was thirteen and had graduated from eighth grade, my mother brought me to New York. I've been in the theatre ever since—and I haven't kept track of how long that's been!

Do you think that was an advantage in your later career, having started so young?

I don't particulary think so, no. I think perhaps it would have been wiser to have finished my education. You can obviously learn so much more that way, not only about life in general but also about the theatre itself. If my mother had brought me into New York to play children's parts, perhaps that would have been better for me. But I was actually working as a member of the chorus! I found out only five years ago that one of the theatre producers where I worked was arrested because I was so young. I never even knew it happened.

Was it your own idea to start working in the theatre so young, or was it the will of your parents?

I think my father had a lot to do with it. At eleven, I hadn't even thought of performing. But my father believed I was good and since he was such a good conductor, the theatre managers couldn't turn him down. They couldn't very well say, "We don't think she's ready." But no, I had not particularly wanted to do that work. It terrified me actually; I really wasn't ready for it. Yet by the time I had graduated from the eighth grade and had taken a lot of dancing lessons, then I knew that I wanted a career in the theatre.

Your father wanted you to be a concert pianist, didn't he?

Yes, he was very disappointed that I didn't apply myself to it, and now I realize that it would have been a great thing to have been able to play the piano. You can never learn too many things if you're going to be in the theatre. Even if you say, well, I am not going to be a concert pianist, playing the piano still comes in handy if you're in a musical. You can get the score and practice yourself, or you can play for your own enjoyment and relaxation. Nothing you learn is ever wasted in the theatre.

And once you had begun working, did you ever take time out to study acting?

No, no I didn't. I regret that. I think it would have been most beneficial. All I ever studied was a little singing and dancing.

Were you much of a success in vaudeville?

No, vaudeville in that period was beginning to disintegrate and to tell you the truth, I only worked in the inferior houses around Philadelphia so that I could come home at night. They were not the kind of theatres that had the top acts at all.

Could you give me an idea of what it was like to be working in vaudeville?

I don't really remember it too well, to be honest. I've always been terrified of fireworks and I remember that people were setting them off on the Fourth of July at one theatre we were in. That was the first theatre I had ever worked at, and I was petrified. But my mother was standing in the wings and I realized that she expected me to behave like a professional, so I stayed on in spite of my fear. I remember *that* vividly, and yet it's the only recollection I have of that whole summer. Obviously, I didn't enjoy it much.

In 1925 then, still underage, you were in the chorus of a Broadway show. Do you remember feeling a sense of excitement about being on Broadway?

Well, I didn't know there was anything particular about being on Broadway, that's how unprepared I was. At that age, it didn't mean anything to me; I wasn't particularly thrilled. I don't even remember the New York opening. And the show was not a success. Afterwards, I went to work in a night club.

In 1934 you did a show called **New Faces.**

Yes, now that I remember very well.

And that was the first time you were acknowledged as a comedienne?

That was the first time I did comedy. Actually, I was engaged as a dancer and I accidentally did some pantomimic comedy. A few of us were fooling around backstage, doing absolutely nothing and the producer saw us and said, "That's very funny." We said, "What's very funny?" He had been tickled by something he saw us do, but I had no idea at the time what it was.

One of the boys had been doing a little step, you see; I became intrigued with that and I imitated it a bit and I was vaguely aware we were joined by a couple of other people. The theatre was very cold and one of the boys had given me a polo coat to wear which was very long on me. We were way backstage doing whatever it was we were doing and the producer should have been watching the number that was being rehearsed, but obviously, he wasn't. He was watching *us*. And then he wanted us to repeat it in the show. I said, "What will I wear?" He answered, "What you have on"—which was the polo coat. And so opening night in New York, we came out and were petrified. We filed out in a line and faced the audience with no expression at all; we did these nothing things and walked off. At first there was dead silence. After the second appearance, the audience started to laugh, by the third appearance they applauded, and the fourth appearance was a big triumph. Finally, we were one of the hits of the show. And the press said, "There's a new young comedienne whose name is . . . ." And that's how I started to do comedy.

For the producer of the next show, there were months of discussion as to whether I should talk comedy or just do pantomime. It was decided to include a couple of sketches in which I would talk. And that's how I became a comedienne.

Did you then try to develop your pantomime? Did you practice it and try to improve it?

I never did. I just did it. The dancing teacher with whom I studied the most had been a student of Delsarte. She had us pretend to be flowers that were opening to the sun or a sun shining on the flowers. We did a lot of movements that expressed how a flower would feel in a rainstorm or in a windy field, what its reaction to these different elements would be. Looking back, I realize that whatever pantomime I learned I really learned from her. She never used the word "pantomime" and so I wasn't conscious of it.

I never planned to be a pantomimist, it just happened. I've had a very accidental kind of career.

During your years before television, you spent quite a long time out of work; you had a lot of difficulty getting jobs, and so you must have had a tremendous amount of determination to have kept going as you did.

Well, there again I was lucky. One time I didn't even know I had left the theatre. I went home to Philadelphia to visit my mother and she kept saying, day after day, "When are you going back to New York?" Then suddenly it dawned on me, and I thought, how about that, I'm not going back, I've left the theatre. I find it hard to make any decision, but there I had made one without even knowing it. And that very day Oscar Hammerstein called me from New York and said, "Would you come up here? I'd like to talk to you about a show I'm doing." The show happened to be *Oklahoma*, it happened to be done in *this* theatre, and he wanted me for a part. But at the audition, Richard Rodgers wanted me to sing, and I couldn't think of a single song. They weren't too happy about that so I didn't get the role, but I walked out of this stage door and a man stopped me and said, "You're Imogene Coca," and I said, "Yes," and he said, "I have a place called Green Mansions up in New York State, which is just like where you worked for Max Leibman. Would you work for me this summer?" And I thought, why fight it? From that time on, I've worked steadily.

In 1949, when you did the "Admiral Broadway Revue" on TV, did you have any idea that you were one of TV-comedy's pioneers? Did you realize how enormous television would become?

No, I didn't. I didn't feel like any kind of pioneer. I just had been doing a night club act and couldn't wait to get away from it. When Max Leibman, for whom I had worked up in the Pocono Mountains and on Broadway, called me up and said he wanted me to do a television show with him, I thought, oh, how marvelous, I can get away from this terrible night club! That's all I could think of. I didn't think about television one way or another; to me it was just four weeks' work.

Well, of course, it went on for much longer and turned out to be something altogether different.

How did you begin working with Sid Caesar?

Well, the writers weren't writing for me at all—which was okay because I had a lot of material that I had done in other shows. But after awhile, I began to run out of it. Now, Max Leibman knew everything I had ever done and so I went to him; I suggested that I do "Better Go Now"—a song followed by a pantomime about two people going into a moving picture house. To my amazement, he said, "Why don't you do it with Sid?" I didn't really know Sid. I mean, we would pass each other in the hallway and politely say "Hello," but that was about it. I wanted to say, "I don't want to do it with Sid. I'd rather do it with my husband, with whom I did it in *New Faces*," but I didn't have the nerve—pretty silly, considering that Max was an old friend of mine, and my husband and I had developed this pantomime between the two of us. So I soon found myself in a room with this strange actor, telling him what to do.

I don't like that kind of a situation because actors hate to be told what to do unless it's by the director. Yet I had no choice, so I told Sid the story of the pantomime and he just automatically picked it up. Fortunately, I didn't have to say to him, "Well, that's not the right reaction. Do this instead." I didn't have to say a word. He just did it and did it beautifully and when we performed it on the air, it was a big hit.

The next week I went to Max and said, "I'm running out of material, why don't I do 'Slowly I Turn'?" Here again, I thought he'd ask my husband (who's since passed away) to do it with me, but again he said, "Do it with Sid." I thought, Oh dear. So there we were, alone in a room again. Sid said, "Do you really want to do this old burlesque bit? It's so old, everybody does it." And I said, "I very much want to do it. Burlesque bits are like folklore. Each burlesque comic has his own version of the sketches and this one was given to me as a present by someone I greatly respect. I know exactly what should be done in it, but *if you don't want to do it, that's fine*." To my chagrin, he said, "Ah well, we'll do it."

Well, it was such a sensation that the writers must have done at least thirty different re-writes, varying it so that it could be done again. They would make it two other characters, but always the ending would involve my ripping Sid's clothes off in a frenzy, not all of them, of course, but that's the ending of "Slowly I Turn."

That sketch had traditionally been done with two men, and I was the only female who ever did it. So, as I say, the writers wrote and re-wrote and re-wrote it, and then they started writing for the two of us. That's how Sid and I started working together.

So your teamwork simply happened totally naturally.

It was an accident, really.

Was there any way that you improved your teamwork as you went along?

Not consciously. I think it just happened chemically that we worked well together and the audience accepted us immediately. (To this day, people say, "When are you going back with Sid?") We would begin discussing our sketch on a Monday and by that Saturday, we would be doing the show. So we didn't have much time to say, "How can we be better together?" It was always: "What are we going to do?" But the more we did those characters, the more the characters improved, and the better our teamwork was—just through the process of continuing to work together.

Could you give me an idea of what that process was, how you got those skits together? Did it begin with an idea from the writers, or did the writers furnish the dialogue from an idea of yours? Was it improvised? Was it tightly planned?

Well, it would vary. Sometimes the writers would write a sketch, mostly involving a marital situation, that would be absolutely perfect; we would do it and not a word would be changed. At other times, the idea would be Sid's and mine, and we would supply one hundred percent of the dialogue. So, from week to week, it would change.

I remember one sketch that the writers had prepared for us. The idea was that the husband buys his wife a new dress, and they go out to dinner; she thinks everybody in the restaurant is staring at her and she wants her husband to go over and say, "Stop it!" But, of course, nobody's even looking at her. In desperation he says, "Every time you get a new $200 dress," (and remember this was a long time ago, now it would be a $500, $800, $1,000 dress) "you go crazy and you think everybody's looking at you." Well, Sid objected to the price of the dress, and for three whole days we discussed how much a man like this would spend on a dress for his wife. We really did delve into the characters without saying that that's what we were going to do. We did our own kind of research. There were times when we had long discussions about whether a person's name suited them or not. So you see, those sketches were approached very seriously. It was not just an attempt to make people laugh, although, hopefully, we would do that. Our main concern was that the skits be based on truth.

You had some of the best comedy writers working on that show— Mel Brooks, Woody Allen, Neil Simon for a spell. How important do you think good writing is to comedy? Do you think it's possible to flub a well-written script?

Oh, surely, yes. But keep in mind that it's almost impossible to take a badly written script and make it good. Of course, the people you mention are the ones who have made it big since, and certainly Mel Brooks has had a spectacular success. But Mel was not the kind of writer who wrote; he had ideas, marvelous ideas for situations and such, and secretaries would copy them down. There were others, less famous now, who actually sat down and wrote. We had on that show what I would call the ideal situation: the actors had the freedom to express their feelings, to add what they had to add, and the writers didn't resent that, they worked along with it. I don't mean in any way to put the writers down, but the reason the show was so good was that it was a communal effort. Nobody was out to say, "I want the *most; I* want this, *I* want that." Everyone's concern was how good the *show* was going to be.

Was there ever an occasion when, nearing show-time, a particular skit just wasn't working? How did you handle that? Were there many quick changes made?

Well, there was one time when they were going to have the two of us in a cafe in Paris, and Sid as my husband was going to embarrass me by ordering hotdogs and things like that. And I thought: Oh, this is a dreadful sketch. This is awful. But I never said anything about the sketches because Sid's taste and my own were exactly the same, and since the writers were all male (except for one) I always considered it better for the man to say that he didn't like the material. Well, it got to be Thursday and Max said to the writers, "Why don't you go into the other room and start on next week's show. And Sid and Coca, why don't you get up on your feet and start rehearsing the sketch?" That's when Sid turned to me and asked, "Do you think this is a good sketch?" Now I had in no way indicated that I didn't think it was good. But I told him I thought it was terrible and when he asked Max Leibman, who really *was* "Your Show of Shows," Max agreed. Sid said, "So why are we doing it?" and Max said, "Because it's already Thursday and we're doing the show on Saturday." But Sid insisted that we think of something else. So Max thought and thought and finally suggested that it might be funny if Coca—everybody in those days called me Coca—had wrecked the family automobile; that could be given away by her talking to her mother. . . .

Oh, "Breaking the News," that was a wonderful skit! It was included in the movie, **The Best from Your Show of Shows.**

That's right. Sid walks in in a terrible state of mind because everything's gone wrong at the office and all he wants to do is to get in the car and drive out to the country. And I finally have to admit that there is no car, it's been totalled. Well, we improvised that and Max then called in the writers to take a look at it. He said, "I don't want anyone to say a word. The French sketch is out. I want you to see what we've put in, and find out if you have any suggestions." Now, if you say that to most comedy writers, they'll go crazy, but Max Leibman was marvelous; he really was a great producer and nobody would have thought of screaming or yelling. As a matter of fact, they all laughed; they loved it and even had some jokes to add, some things to change here and there. It was one of the better sketches we did, but only because everybody had the courage, even though we were faced with a performance that was so close, not to do a sketch just because the time limit was on.

The pressure of time must have been enormous in a weekly show like that.

It was, but Max didn't allow us to feel the pressure. Sometimes we would do a dress rehearsal and he'd throw out a segment he didn't like. At dress rehearsal! We would be set to go on the air in two hours! He would replace it with a pantomime that perhaps we'd done another season. He'd bring the kinescopes over, the orchestration would be reworked. One week he actually changed twenty minutes of the show. And it worked beautifully.

Who was your best teacher in preparing the characters for those skits—the audience or the other actors?

I think the audience lets you know whether you're on the right track or not very fast. As for other actors, forget it. Actors don't usually criticize fellow actors; it's considered a director's job. That's why I say I dreaded having to go over that initial skit with Sid. I thought, Oh no, I'm going to have to say to him, "Look aghast here; and here look delighted; and here look a little tentative. . . ." You just don't *do* that with another actor. It's not protocol. But luckily, with Sid it didn't have to be said.

When you did a skit and you felt that you were losing the laugh, the audience wasn't responding, given the limitations of the TV format, was there anything you could do to correct it?

On television there was nothing you could do. We had a different problem. When you are in front of an audience as we were when we did "Show of Shows," you find yourself doing extra things. You suddenly find a piece of business that is really working; it just comes out of you, something you never expected but suddenly it happens, and it gets a *big* laugh. Yet you know you cannot let it go on, you have to cut that laugh because you are facing a commercial or a station break. We had three station breaks in the "Show of Shows," besides all the commercials. If we had been on stage, we could really have let it go—not too long, of course. When they get a laugh, actors sometimes have a tendency to say, oh boy, and then to overdo it. But it was a little frustrating to have to kill the laugh right at its peak.

Did working live in front of an audience ever make you nervous?

Oh, I was always nervous. You see, we froze the show, so to speak; there was no improvisation, no ad-libbing after one o'clock on Friday. That was it. The crew came in and that was the show they were going to put on television on Saturday night unless, of course, something was taken out. But when we were on the air it was all strictly planned out. We were doing the sketch word for word without a teleprompter, without cue cards; I was doing numbers with lyrics that I had had very little time to learn and doing dances with choreography that again, I had had very little time with—so it was just a very nervous thing.

Did you ever find a way to relax?

Sunday was the relaxing day. From Monday to Friday, which was the moment of truth, the tension was building. There was no escaping it.

Do you think the principles of comedy are fundamentally the same, whether you're playing Mel Brooks or Neil Simon or doing a stand-up comedy routine?

Comedy is an extremely variable form. And Mel certainly isn't the same as other comedy writers at all. He uses crazy, improbable situations, whereas someone else, like Neil Simon, will use a normal, true situation and make it comedic. Neil Simon takes the fact that some man has lost his job and the people upstairs are throwing water on him from their terrace, but that is a real man and he's married to a real woman. Mel Brooks will take a situation that has nothing to do with truth, that is based on absolute insanity.

I've always been primarily concerned with comedy through acting—satire, I guess you'd call it. And stand-up comedy is another thing altogether, that's telling jokes. I'm not putting that down because I couldn't tell a joke if you put a gun to my head. And punch lines, I avoid them whenever I can, I hate them. So therefore, I have nothing but awe and admiration for stand-up comics.

I did a lot of satire that was aimed at ballet. But I could dance, so I wasn't really making fun of anything that I couldn't do my-self. I was doing the actual choreography of every ballet I satir-ized—though I would add a few switches here and there. In that sense, I distinguished it from burlesque. A burlesque comic would be someone who couldn't dance, didn't use the actual chor-eography, and yet was dressed as a swan.

How does farce fit into these categories?

I always think of farce connected more with the spoken word, not with pantomime or dancing or singing. Farce is played out in a specific situation. I consider Lucille Ball the best farceur of them all. She based her comedy on truth, yet she went way, *way* be-yond it.

Is there anything one can do to improve one's comic sense?

I can only go by my own experience, and I never did anything consciously; I didn't set out to be a comic and I've never tried to improve myself in any conscious way. I've always tried to be as good as I can be, but I never said, "This will make me funnier." I think the key is to watch people a lot. There is so much funny ma-terial in normal human behavior. For instance, when I first saw "Afternoon of a Faun" performed at the ballet, I was hysterical. I thought I would have to leave the theatre. It struck me as being the funniest ballet I'd ever seen. And yet it's brilliant. But the jumps that they do looked to me like Keystone comedy jumps, like a Mack Sennett silent film, like the kind of hops that those comedians would take before turning a corner.

So you took the truth of the ballet and distorted it just a little.

I took it just a *step* farther. In the ballet, the nymph drops about three stars—well, I dropped about twenty.

Do you think that in comedy there's a more direct connection be-tween the actor and the audience than in serious drama?

I think so—comedy is a more personal thing. You tell the same joke to ten people and you're going to have ten different reactions. Some of them may even be violent—how dare you tell a joke like that! Someone else may be laughing his head off, while another person says, "What does it mean?" Yet if you took the same people and you had somebody with a good voice sing a lovely song, they'd *all* accept it.

I know some people who can't *stand* me and other people who think I'm the greatest. This happens to every comedian. When I was working at a very chic club here in New York, there was a man who would come in every night. Why he'd come, I never knew, because I never saw him laughing. One night he got permission to come back to the dressing room to see me and he said, "I had to come back here to tell you that I can't stand your work! I sit there night after night and hear people laughing and I wonder, why are they laughing? And why is it that I think you're so unfunny?" I told him, "Well, don't be so upset about it. This is comedy and the reactions to it will vary. Just don't let the laughter of the other people upset you. Since you know how long I'm going to be on, why don't you go out, smoke a cigarette and come back when I'm finished?" He was grateful that I had taken it in such a nice way, but the fact was that I understood completely. My husband couldn't stand Bea Lilly, and yet Bea Lilly was one of the funniest.

What do you think the answer is? What is it about you that people have consistently found so funny?

I don't know. Maybe it's because I seem so vulnerable—which I am. It's something I've never quite fathomed, and it still surprises me.

Can you tell me how a person develops a sense of timing for their comedy?

It's mysterious, like having a sense of rhythm. It's really established by the interplay between the comedian and the audience. If an audience is laughing a lot, you have to play your skit a little differently. If they're not laughing a lot, then you play with a little more energy, and a little faster. But as I say, when you're a television comedian, you have to be conscious of the minutes ticking away and you cannot always time your performance the way you'd really like to, and let it go as *far* as it can go.

*Is it important that an audience feel sympathetic towards a come-
dian? Would the comedy suffer if an audience disliked the
person?*

Stand-up comics, for the most part, don't require sympathy.
Their humor is very often abrasive and if it isn't, they may not get
their laugh. They depend upon a shock effect. Someone like Don
Rickles, for example, sets out to irritate. Yet I think the audience
has to know that deep down inside somewhere, the person saying
all those dreadful things is really very nice. It takes a lot of courage for someone like Don to come out and say the insulting things
he does—and yes, underneath it all, I think the audience must
feel a sympathy, even there.

I've heard that most comedians are very serious people.

Oh yes. I used to give a lot of parties during the "Show of
Shows," and all the comics in town would come. You've never
seen a more serious group. Looked more like a bunch of under-
takers. Now, there were the exceptions, like Jackie Leonard, who
was always on. Jack was a dear sweet sensitive man, and he
would say the most terrible things to people for a laugh, not realizing that he could easily have hurt their feelings. But on the other
hand, if you didn't say hello in a proper tone of voice to Jackie
Leonard, he would be near tears. *His* comedy was insulting people, yet he really didn't mean those jokes as insults. But it's true
that of all the comics in the room, he was the only person who was
ever funny. Milton Berle was always there; he was very serious,
very much the gentleman. Red Buttons, Carl Reiner, Sid, of
course—he was the quietest of them all. They would have made a
very good audience—if only they hadn't taken life so seriously.

*Is it very important to your comedy that you like the people that
you work with?*

Oh, it is. It's awful to work with somebody you don't want to work
with. I've been very lucky that way. I've worked with Danny
Kaye, whom I admire very much, with Sid Caesar, Eddie Everett
Horton, and my husband, King Donovan. If I don't like somebody, if I can't get along with them, I avoid ever working with
them again.

Is that purely for your own enjoyment—or would your comedy suffer as well?

Oh, it would suffer terribly. You've got to work *with* your partners. If somebody isn't working *with* you, if they're jealous of every laugh you get and they won't accept what you want to give them, it's like playing tennis with somebody who's not trying to bat the ball back to you. It's impossible.

Are there any tricks of technique that you have learned to use in order to make an audience laugh?

I try to stay away from such things. If I become too conscious of what I'm doing, I stop doing it. After *On the Twentieth Century* opened in Boston, a couple of people came to me and said, "That's so funny what you're doing with your hips when you say that one line. . . ." And you know, I never got that laugh back. I had suddenly become conscious of my hips and that was the end of that. It's much better for me to play the moment, to let my body do what it's going to do, my face do what it's going to do, my hands. . . . If I analyze too much, I'm finished. Because of that one comment, which I'm sure was meant as a compliment, I lost two laughs in the show, and I can ill afford to lose them. I had had no idea my hips were even moving. Now, that is not necessarily the way to do comedy, but it's the only approach I know.

I've always been interested to know how a comedian keeps a certain kind of sketch from becoming pathetic. For instance, if you're portraying somebody who's terrified of spiders, there must be a thin line between its being funny and its being kind of a sorry mess.

Well, that's hard to answer. I think all you can do is immerse yourself in the material and hope for the best. It sounds silly, but there were so many occasions when Sid and I would act out a skit and we were not trying to get laughs—we were so far into the characters themselves—and yet we were getting laughs all the same. Now explain that. I can't explain it.

The first movie satire we did was of *An American Tragedy—A*

Place in the Sun, the film was called. We did the scene in which the boy (Sid) takes the girl (me) out in the boat to kill her. Carl Reiner was the alter ego; he was on a mike saying all the things that Sid was supposedly thinking. Max Leibman had a whole bunch of singers on a mike making all sorts of wonderful crazy sounds of birds and things. I remember that I got really cold, and I was really scared. There was something very eerie about it all. I was talking and talking and talking and Sid's voice, his alter-ego voice, was saying, "I'm going to kill her, I've got to kill her," and every time he attempted to, it would never work. And I just went right on talking through the whole thing, not conscious of the fact that he had a rope around my neck and was pulling it, or that he had an ax at one point. I was really playing the character in the movie, and both Sid and I got so engrossed in it that we couldn't even remember if anybody had laughed or not.

Do you think the characters that you play and the kind of person that you are are very closely related?

I think so, yes. Some part of yourself goes into anything that you do.

And when you would do your sketches, for instance, the one about breaking the news, about smashing the family car, would you ever use your own personal memories as a way of getting closer to the character and her predicament?

Not in that one, no. That character was quite different than what I would be. There were little things that crept in that were closer to myself, like when she was talking to her mother on the phone, she was speaking more or less in the same way I'd talk. I have a habit of talking around things rather than getting to the point, without even realizing that I'm doing it. Sometimes, when I would see a sketch in the kinescope, I'd notice that I had been doing myself. But if I had wrecked a car, and had to tell *my* husband, I can't *imagine* what I'd do. I've never learned to drive, so the situation is pretty far from my experience. But I'd probably have left the house and moved to another city. I would run away from a situation like that rather than face it full on.

Do you think audiences react differently to a woman comic than to a male?

I think it's much easier for a man. Much easier. Maybe it's not that way anymore, now that the lib movement is on, but when I was working in night clubs, an audience could get pretty abusive to a woman when they were a little drunk. Boy, you could get it. And it's very, very hard for a woman to answer them. I always ignored it myself. I'm sure that Joan Rivers or Phyllis Diller wouldn't be like that. I promise you, they could take care of anybody. They could probably murder a rude audience and I would love to see it happen. But I don't have that kind of a wit; I think of a good reply about two years later. So I used to go right on as if nobody had said anything to me. It was especially difficult because I did not do jokes, I was doing satires, and it's very hard to come out of a character and say to somebody, "Why don't you drop dead, buster?" and then go right back to work. If only a witty reply had not been beyond me. I think a man automatically answers faster, and he's less likely to get trouble from a tipsy crowd.

Do audiences more readily accept certain kinds of comic routines from women—like a feather-brained type of character?

No, I wouldn't say that's true. The wife I did with Sid wasn't exactly a feather-brain; she may have expressed herself in a rather peculiar manner, but he never got the best of her. Ever. And I think that's what people liked about it—the fact that here's this big guy with a little woman, almost like a mouse looking at an elephant and telling him where to go. Not that she was aggressive about it, but in her own way she managed to be, if not the head of the household, at least on equal terms with him.

Do you think there's any such thing as national humor?

I think it becomes national only when you use certain slang phrases. There are language barriers, but no, I don't think there's anything particularly American in humor. Basic, basic comedy is the same all over the world. If a man slips on a banana peel, or if a man drops a $100 bill through a grate and is trying to get it out, that's funny no matter where you come from. Truthful comedy, I have always found, is the same all around the world.

I've never understood why anyone laughs when they see a person slipping on a banana peel. That's something I personally have never found funny.

I haven't either, but most people do. It's probably the way the person falls that is funny. To me, it would be funnier if the person didn't fall, if their foot lowered onto the banana peel and something distracted their attention so the banana peel was never stepped on.

We did a sketch on "Your Show of Shows" about a cake; it was a birthday party for kids (we were all acting as the kids) and the audience was positive Sid was going to get the cake right in his face. But the cake was never touched. It was the anticipation that made it a very funny sketch.

So, in that case, the comedy had to do with the reversal of people's expectations?

Oh yes, you can get a lot of laughs that way. And you can also get them by throwing the cake. It's your choice. The same audience will laugh differently at each one.

Do you think there's any such thing as bad taste in comedy?

Oh, there can be. When people go too far to get a laugh I think that's bad taste. When a comedian is too obvious, and doesn't let the audience use some imagination, but instead hits them on the head with something, that kind of very broad comedy always offends me. The comic is making you feel stupid by having to be so explicit.

I don't particularly like to watch comics who do too much pornography. It's not that I'm prudish, nothing shocks me; but I think that it's an easy way to get a laugh. It's the easiest way in the whole world, to come out in a night club where people are drinking, and to tell a dirty story or to use four-letter words. But what does that prove? It gets somebody a salary at the end of the week but that's about all. I don't think there exists a word I haven't heard and probably used at some time or other, but in a comedy act I just find it unfunny.

Is there anything audiences are finding funny today that they didn't used to?

I think pornographic humor is much more on the loose, in Vegas, for instance. But the old style still works, too. I was wondering how Sid and I would do in Vegas because we have never used a four-letter word or any other questionable material. Yet we did beautifully. I thought we would bomb there; I thought that if you didn't come out and say, "Good evening, ladies and gentlemen, welcome, why don't you all go umph yourselves," you know, just for openers, that we would be hooted off the stage. But not at all; we were very successful in Vegas.

Who are some of the younger comedians that you admire today?

Well, dear, I see so little television, I miss most of prime time, and so I haven't seen any new comedians in ages.

"Your Show of Shows" paved the way for such television as "Saturday Night Live" with its repertory of actors and its live format. Have you seen that program?

No. Everybody tells me I should and I keep saying I will, but I never get to it. You see, my husband and I work a lot together, we've been on the road now for the better part of ten years and we've gotten into a habit: after we do a show, we run home as fast as possible and turn on the television to see what movie is on. We've stuck with that same habit now that we're in New York City. He'll say, "You know what movie's on tonight?—*All about Eve.*" We've seen it about a hundred times, but every time you see that film there's one more wonderful line to remember, one more wonderful performance to savor, and so we're hooked. We have yet to see "Saturday Night Live." Isn't that terrible? I don't consciously avoid it, but whenever I see a television set, I think "movies," which I know is kind of strange.

Do you find working in television today to be much different than it was back in the early days?

Oh yes. I don't like being a guest on TV shows at all. You don't feel part of the proceedings and no matter how nice they are to you, you're always an outsider. Videotape is something I don't like either. Once I start with a sketch, I like to finish it. When they decide to stop the tape for an hour, the whole momentum is gone. And they have very small studio audiences on TV shows these days—maybe a hundred people or even seventy-five. On "Your Show of Shows," we had an audience of about nine hundred people. It was a big, big theatre. So if one group in the audience didn't like one of the skits, another group might. But the people who come into the studios to see tapings nowadays are so self-conscious, and they don't laugh easily. I don't like it. If I did television now, I would hopefully do a series that was filmed, with no audience at all.

Why is that?

I love cameras. The camera becomes your audience and you're not disturbed by people liking you or not. Performing to a handful of people is like performing in your living room, which I wouldn't do in a million years. A camera becomes an intimate thing; you work to the camera or else the camera is on you and you're working to the other actors, and I just love that.

And you don't miss the responsiveness of having an audience at all?

Not at all. In "Grindl," a series I did for television, it was all on camera and I loved it. The show was mostly dialogue which led up to a dangerous situation, like the "Perils of Pauline." Grindl was always doing the wrong thing and no matter how much the villains were after her, they never got her because, very innocently, she never stepped on the banana peel.

What advice would you give to someone who wanted to be a comedian today?

First of all, learn everything. Take acting lessons and dancing lessons and singing and piano. Don't just go out and say, "I'm going
to be funny." Let the audience tell you. Try all different kinds of
parts. Get some good material from a good writer, or write it yourself, and go up to these places like Green Mansions. Just get up
on a Saturday night and face an audience.

*How do you feel being back on Broadway now, in this same the-
eatre that you worked in so many years ago?*

I love it, but I have a very hard part in this show. It's so small, I
can't get *hold* of anything. I'm used to doing roles where you go
on stage and you *stay* on stage. Here, my character goes back
and forth, and it just used to drive me crazy. I fought the part at
first, I tried to get out, desperately, but I have begun to like the
character, to understand her better, and the cast is wonderful.
It's a very happy cast. I've gotten to the point where I like doing it
now.

What would you like to do in the future?

Well, Max Leibman has an option on a straight play and that
would be interesting.

A serious play, you say?

Yes, it's a Gothic murder mystery, actually. It would be the most
serious thing I've ever done. Of course, there are serious parts to
some comedies. In *Plaza Suite*, the first act is really not all comedy. A woman is losing her husband, she's making jokes, but it's
the end of a long relationship. That's about as serious, though, as
I've ever gotten.

Do you feel confident that you can do serious drama?

Well, to be truthful, I'm afraid I might not be able to. It's funny
that after all these years as an actress, I'm still just trying my
wings.

SAM WATERSTON

Sam Waterston was born in Cambridge, Massachusetts on November 15, 1940. He attended Brook School, where his father taught languages, Groton Academy, and Yale University. As an undergraduate, he joined the Yale Dramat, an extra-curricular group, and the experience of playing Lucky in their production of *Waiting For Godot* confirmed his desire to become a professional actor. He spent a season in summer stock with the Wellesley 20 Group, which included Rosemary Harris and Ellis Rabb, and during a junior year in Paris, he became involved with the American Actors Workshop headed by John Berry (who left this country due to blacklisting in the McCarthy era).

Not long after graduating from college, Mr. Waterston made his New York stage debut when he took over the role of Jonathan in Arthur Kopit's *Oh Dad, Poor Dad, Mama's Hung You in the Closet and I'm Feelin' so Sad*. He played Silvius in *As You Like It*, replaced Roddy Maude-Roxby as Colin in *The Knack*, played Prince Hal in *Henry IV*, Tom Lewis in *The Trial of the Catonsville Nine*, and Laertes in *Hamlet* with Stacy Keach in the title role. During this period, he played a wide range of characters, including a pregnant homosexual in *Spitting Image*, but his breakthrough as a leading man came in 1972 when he appeared as Benedick in *Much Ado about Nothing*.

As Mr. Waterston explains it, he had just come back from California after working in a few short-running plays, was broke, and had no prospects. A telephone call from Joseph Papp reversed his luck and led to the role which Mel Gussow of *The New York Times* would call "a superb comic performance," and which would win him the Drama Critics Circle Award, the Drama Desk Award, and an Obie.

Among the stage roles which followed have been those of Prospero in *The Tempest*; Torvald Helmer in *A Doll's House* (with Liv Ullmann in the role of Nora); Vladimir in *Waiting for Godot*; and *Hamlet* himself. He received an Emmy nomination as Tom Wingfield opposite Katherine

Hepburn as Amanda in the television production of *The Glass Menagerie*. In films, he has played Nick Carraway, the narrator of *The Great Gatsby*; a comic Indian in Frank Perry's contemporary Western, *Rancho Deluxe*; and has appeared in Woody Allen's first serious drama, *Interiors*.

Mr. Waterston is tall and angular, resembling somewhat of a cross between Tony Perkins and Jean-Pierre Léaud. He has bemused, sometimes quizzical dark eyes and a gentlemanly manner.

For this talk, which was held at my home, Mr. Waterston arrived formally dressed in a tie and jacket, but he soon removed the jacket, loosened the tie—and looked relieved to do so. As we talked, he was sitting in a large armchair, alternately leaning forward on the edge of the seat, and sinking back with his legs up, drawing his knees to his chest when he laughed. He was anxious to avoid too much abstract analysis of acting, and though the more specific technical processes, he admitted, are endlessly fascinating to him, he was puzzled why anyone else, particularly a non-actor, would find them even interesting. Rather than inflate his accomplishments, his impulses—and quite sincerely—were consistently to cut them to scale.

Mr. Waterston has one son from a previous marriage. His present wife, Lynn Woodruff, is a model, and the two live in an apartment in Manhattan.

I understand that your father was an English and foreign-language teacher with an interest in the theatre. In fact, your first stage appearance was as a page in a production of Antigone that he directed. Do you think his interest in drama had much to do with your motivations to become an actor?

I'm sure it did. He is English and was an amateur actor when he was in college at Oxford. He was a contemporary of a lot of people who are growing old in the theatre in England now—like Gielgud and Redgrave—and he knew some of them. So, he's had a life-long interest in the theatre, and I'm sure that had something to do with my own. As you say, the first play I was ever in was a play that he directed.

What was it about your earliest experiences with acting that excited you? Do you remember?

That's a hard question to answer, because I think that your reasons for being in a business or a craft or an art change over the years. And then when you look at them in retrospect, you apply your more recent thinking to the distant past. I know that when I was in high school, I liked acting *very* much but I was in a school that didn't particularly encourage it. They prepared people for business or public service or the clergy more than the theatre, and they put on just one play a year. But the basic motivation to become an actor—for me and maybe for others—is partly a love of fantasy worlds, and partly a kind of ego reinforcement that you don't find elsewhere. I don't know which of those motivations matters most, but I think the impulse to act alternates between those two things, and one is more respectable, I suppose, than the other.

*You played Lucky in **Waiting for Godot** at Yale, didn't you? I understand that was a turning-point experience for you.*

Yes, it was. There were two things about it that were wonderful. One was that I had a revelation such as Stanislavsky describes coming to people when they are doing a play. I had a revelation in the last performance of that play that ignited the whole character and illuminated it in a great flash right while I was standing on the stage. And then that illumination *worked* . . . instantaneously! That was the first thing that was very exciting. The other aspect of it was the way it worked, which was. . .

. . . that it got a response from your audience?

Yes, but it was more than that. It was like an ecstatic experience. I'm not sure that I'm using that word right, but the only other time I've had an experience like that was when I was skiing once, a year or so later. I'd skied all my life, but never for a long time at a stretch. And then I went skiing when I was a student in Europe. I went to Austria for three weeks, and I skied every day, all day long. I actually began to get pretty good. Towards the end of the time, I was skiing parallel down the mountain, and I was going about sixty miles an hour. (I was probably going twelve, but it felt like sixty.) Everything was just working perfectly, and I wasn't thinking about it any more and suddenly, I had a sense of taking off. It was like flight. And the same thing happened when I was doing that play.

As I was doing the speech, I was thinking things that were

brand new. I had never thought of the character in the way that it came to me to think of it at that moment. All the thought processes were changed, and I had the sensation that every single one of them was being communicated explicitly to the audience. Now, I realize you could delude yourself about that one, but I had some corroboration. When I wanted the audience to laugh, they laughed; when I wanted them to be silent, they were absolutely silent; they interrupted the speech in the middle at the point where I had designed a break, and applauded. So, I had reason to believe that what I felt was real. I felt that I had finger-tip control over the audience. And that's the ego trip of it. But then there was another sensation of incredible communication, which neither I nor they were really responsible for. It was just taking place in the air between us. It wasn't really my fault, or to my credit, that I had figured out what to do—it just came to me! It was like a group experience . . . with me standing there, of course, and everybody watching.

It's interesting that you compare that acting experience to athletics. I can see where they would be very similar in seeking a coordination between the body and the mind. But, could you tell me what the nature of your revelation was? What was it that connected you to your character?

Oh, it was very simple, and I'm not sure it would ever work again. In fact, I just redid *Waiting for Godot. . .*

. . . and you played another character.

Yes, I played another character. And I never told anyone. I sort of *hinted* to the guy who was playing the part of Lucky that I had had this idea, but you know, it's another person. And I was also afraid that I would tell it to him, and he'd try it and then he'd say, "Oh, that's no good; it doesn't really work; it's not exactly right."

But it was really quite simple: we were only scheduled to do five performances of the play, and I had had a very hard time learning the part. It was specifically mapped out, though I wasn't responsible for all the mapping by any means. It was very much given to me by the director. I would sing it here, and go fast there, and make this a unit, and take a break there, and not breathe after this word. . .

Very technical points?

Yes. And I got very good at that. But I always felt that there was
some essence that I hadn't gotten yet. The review in the Yale
Daily News had said I was too smart for the part, and that bugged
the hell out of me. So I was thinking about all these things when I
was on the stage carrying the bags, waiting for my turn to speak. I
kept thinking over and over again that this was the last performance, that I wasn't going to get another chance to do it again,
that I hadn't gotten it right yet, and would I ever get it right, and if
I didn't get it right tonight, I'd never get another opportunity. . . .
Over and over, round and round, the same thoughts. And just
then as Pozzo said, "Speak, pig," I thought: I never am going to
say this again, I am never, I am never going to speak again, I'm
never going to speak again, I, Lucky, am never going to speak
again, so I have to say everything that I know right now! And, of
course, that's exactly the situation of the character. Lucky never
does speak again. And it fits very neatly. So it just took off.

Your experience exactly coincided with the character's. . . .

Yes! And the flash of light was that it coincided. It was exciting!

And it verified the observations of Stanislavsky.

Yes, he says that happens every so often. But, you know, it
doesn't happen so very often.

*Did you study at the Actors Studio where the teaching, as I under-
stand it, draws very much upon Stanislavsky?*

I was an observer at the Actors Studio for a while. But I didn't
study there. I did a couple of plays there once, yet I never
became a member. I did an audition from the play that I had performed and they said, "That's fine, but now you have to do something from another piece of material." I thought, who needs this?
It was very small-minded of me, really. I'm sorry I didn't, in a
way. I think it's probably the best gym in town.

*You think that's the value of it—to have a place where you can
work out, act out and experiment?*

Well, I do know that when people aren't working in the theatre, they have an opportunity there to exercise with very good people. And that has to be good.

What do you think about the value of drama school in general?

Just any old drama school? I think it would very much depend on who it was, and what the school was.

What I'm asking, really, is whether it's important to know the history of the theatre, the literature of the theatre, to have some intellectual terms for thinking and talking about what you do.

I, myself, never went to drama school. I took some courses at the Yale Drama School, but I don't know what it would be like to spend three or four years studying theatre. Acting is a function, however, and the risk that you run by just going out into the world and getting jobs without any training is that you don't have any foundation. Someday, inspiration is bound to fail you, and then so will your body and your voice and your technique for approaching a part. You have to acquire those skills solidly and a drama school sounds like a good place to do it. But I think that carries a liability, too. Because it's a school situation, you're not actually putting the ideas you learn to work, and the possibility arises of applying your intelligence in the wrong way. Just as when you go to college, the possibility arises of learning an absolutely specious and completely invalid way of looking at any given subject. Now, I don't know how you get around that problem, but the facility of analysis and the kind of arrogant attitude which you learn in school are just bankrupt when you have to actually stand on the stage and represent somebody.

Knowing what you know now about the profession of acting, would you go about your training any differently than you have done?

Well, the best teaching I ever had, in any discipline at all, has always been from a great teacher, not from a great place. I went to Yale and in all the disciplines that I studied, there were only three or four teachers in my whole experience there that really enlightened me at all about what we were reading, or studying, or talking about. I think that you have to go look for teachers, whatever you study, because a great teacher for one person is a lousy teacher for another.

You've said that John Berry, whom you worked with in Paris at the American Cultural Center, was a very good teacher.

Yes, he is a great teacher. And he was teaching a course because he had an interest in doing it. He wasn't making any money from it. He was energetic, colorful, tough, and extremely generous emotionally. He was always experimenting with us. But he also taught me the rudiments of approaching a part.

Which were . . . ?

. . . which were based on Stanislavsky and [Michael] Chekhov: dividing your work up into beats; figuring out what your intentions are; getting on a rail and riding it; having little checkpoints so that if you're off the rail, you can get back on; and throwing away all the work when you perform.

What do you mean by checkpoints?

If your own feelings get awakened while you're working, they could lead you anywhere, and so you need to have little landmarks for yourself so that the monitor inside you can say, "Oh, yeah. That's all right. Keep on doing what you want, you just passed the third-mile marker and you're still on the right street." But if you get to the place where the third-mile marker is supposed to be, and you're not where you're supposed to be, then you know that you've got to find it.

You mean where you're supposed to be in terms of the internal emotions?

Well, I'm not talking about blocking, which would be the physical positioning; I am really talking about internal sign posts. For instance, if you get to a certain point in a scene where you're supposed to be ragingly angry at the person who's on stage with you, and you find yourself feeling other things, then that doesn't necessarily mean that anything's wrong because you may be able to justify it; but you've got to make sense out of it somehow.

What would be your first step in the preparation of a role? What's the first thing you do upon being cast?

It's something that I wish I could avoid doing, but that I do automatically, and that is, I figure it out. Then I spend a long time correcting all the mistakes that I made by going ahead and figuring it out.

Figuring it out?

It's the facile analysis that I was talking about before. It's easy to figure things out, and it may be perfectly valid, but it doesn't have anything to do with acting. You can give a very intelligent reading that way without busting it open, without having it breathe. But you find out that you're wrong soon enough; the director tells you so; scenes don't work. And then if you're lucky, things get radically corrected. Finally, with all you've absorbed from what you've figured out and from what's been pouring into you during the rehearsals, you achieve a third state—just doing it without thinking about it.

Rosemary Harris said that it took her four years to forget the things she learned in drama school, but that she was very glad to have gone there, because now that she had forgotten them, she could put them easily and readily to use. So I think that I do that in a sort of mini-way. When I do a part, I work it out the way you would work out a thesis. And then, since that is demonstrably inadequate, I throw it out. But some things remain. And then, of course, I do all the detail work: figuring out what I intend to achieve by everything that I say and do. I try to find verbs for all the things that I'm doing and avoid adjectives.

Why avoid adjectives?

This is a technical point, but it's a useful tool. The nice thing about verbs is that they are not qualities, they're actions—as opposed to adjectives, which are not actions, but qualities. For instance, if I say to myself, "I must get you to allow me to take that chair home with me," and if I make those stakes very high, and if you continued to refuse and I have a whole set of circumstances about who you are and what I have been led to believe you are going to do, then that may make me mad. If that's what I'm trying to achieve, that will be good. But if I say to myself, "I am now going to be mad," or "I'm going to do this angrily," then it doesn't lead inside anywhere—it just stays superficial.

So you root your emotions in actions rather than conjuring them from thin air.

Yeah, but insofar as any of this becomes an intellectual crutch, insofar as this leads you to say, "I am now doing the correct thing, I am doing this methodically," then I think it's bad. What you really want it to do ultimately is to release you into simple behavior. This last time that we did *Waiting for Godot*, Walter Asmus, the director, didn't want to hear, think, or talk about these things. He occasionally accommodated us by talking when he realized that we were just paralyzed without it. He attempted then, in a spirit of international accord, to make us feel better about ourselves by saying, "Sure, we could talk about these things if you want to." But, in fact, what he wanted to do was to have us stand in certain places, talk in certain ways, go faster or slower, and really, that was it. There wasn't anything secret behind it. There was something in the form of the play that he thought was absolutely communicative, and it was plenty, more than enough, better without anything else. Once we got over our automatic resistance to it, the dread of going out on stage bare, then it flipped into the ultimate state that we wanted. Because what you aim for, no matter how you get to it, is to be out there naked, doing something well-formed, in which you are just there.

So this method of not talking about the play and not analyzing its meaning did, in fact, work?

I don't know if it worked for other people, but it worked for me. I felt like it was some of the best work I had ever done. It was certainly very good for me as an actor at this point in my life to have somebody tell me that all the things that I held dear were not important, and that I would still be all right without them. Because along with all the certitudes you acquire, you carry along a lot of junk. It makes you think: "I can't do this unless . . . and unless this, unless that. . . ." And maybe the truth is that you can do with a lot less than you think.

So you're saying that what the actor really strives for is to have all his analysis and technique seep into his subconscious or unconscious mind?

Yeah, and then I think it depends on who the person is. All this stuff would apply not at all to somebody who responded viscerally from the start, who responded in an unfiltered way without the interference of thinking. That person might find the encouragement to think and analyze very useful. But since it's my automatic response, it's also my enemy. Being analytical is the capacity that one learns in school, but it's important to remember that what you are doing to impress the professors, you are ultimately doing to yourself, because it becomes a habit. If you're writing a paper on the history of art, for example, you have the capacity to make talk about the structure and emotional content of Picasso, and to make it sound very good, and for it to be on a certain level, perfectly adequate—but it doesn't have anything to do with the making of the painting.

It has to do with the appreciation of the painting.

Well, it does have something to do with the appreciation of a painting, yes, and that's why professors like to see people write that way. But it won't help you paint. And when I work on a part, all that analysis tends to lead me away; it blinds me to the character.

For instance, when I was working on the role of Torvald, the male-chauvinist husband of *A Doll's House,* I completely figured the guy out. But it took an audience to tell me that I didn't like him and that I was standing away from him and saying: "I don't want any of you to be confused about this. I am actually not at all like this, so let's all participate in stomping all over this guy." I walked on the stage in Philadelphia, and the audience saw that I thought Torvald was a figure of fun, and they made fun of him. Then within five or ten minutes, they began to wonder what the hell they were doing in the theatre. If he was so ridiculous, why did Nora marry him in the first place? What was the price? So then, I inched closer; I made him like people in my family. Finally, I had to say: I am he, he is me. I see how I could do what he does and now I'm going to do it. Dislike me, but believe that it's a real person that you're looking at and not just a piece of cardboard. And when his wife Nora leaves him, it costs him like it would cost you or me. Not: "Ah, finally! The first seeds of Women's Liberation have been planted. The men are going to get it." I had seen all the implications of the play, the historical context of the drama and all of that, but it was leading me off into brain-food. It's satisfying to an audience to see something clearly structured, but what they really want to know is *you*. All they really want to see is *you*. Because you and they are all people and they want to see people.

You're showing them aspects of themselves.

"A mirror up to nature."

Speaking of **Hamlet,** *I was wondering if we could talk a little about the Joseph Papp production that you did in Central Park. That's the role, I suppose, that every actor yearns to do. Did you consciously try to bring something unique to it? Did you make an effort to interpret the role in any new way?*

No, because my entire theory about Shakespeare is that it's right there and that you should do it simply. Now, I don't think that my Hamlet was very simple, but then I don't think that the material is simple. I think that Shakespeare is most satisfying when a context is found that makes the material accessible and that makes it possible to just do it. I'm not sure we ever really did successfully find a context that made him accessible. The one that we did in the Park was done as a military state and everybody was in uniform, very buttoned up. It did make it accessible, but it also had an unfortunate effect of burying a lot of personalities in monochromatic uniforms so that the individuality of these people, like Polonius, for example, was a little bit lost. Hamlet's problem was also a little plain: he's in a repressive state, so naturally he'd be very upset. Everybody was dressed in grey, and every male had a version of the same uniform. It was very, very severe. But that's the production. The pleasure of doing it is something else entirely, and I think it would be just as pleasant to do it in a trash can.

Does the context of a Shakespearean play greatly affect your conception of the character, or is the context more for the benefit of the audience?

The context is just as important, if not more so, to the audience because an actor's got to make a context for himself whether there is one or not. Two contexts that I thought worked very well and in favor of the plays were the contexts of *Much Ado about Nothing* and *The Tempest*. *Much Ado* was set in turn-of-the-century America, and so it certainly couldn't have been anything that Shakespeare ever thought of, but the minute the audience saw where they were, they knew something about the play. They understood what the people were doing in a way that no behavior on the part of the actors could have communicated. So the context fed the actors, but it fed the audience, too. And it was very nice because the circuit kept going on and reinforcing itself.

Do you think then, that Shakespeare is best done for Americans in an American context?

I don't know. *The Tempest* was done on a beach. The whole stage was filled with sand. It had a little hill on one side and another little hill going across the back. Then there was a scrim. It was like a set for *Waiting for Godot* almost. Prospero and Miranda and Caliban and Ariel were barefoot; Prospero had on a pair of tattered old pants and a Sufi jacket; Miranda wore a dress that had seen better times; and Caliban was a mess. But they were all perfectly at home on this sand. Then the people who were shipwrecked came on stage in their gigantic Italian Renaissance costumes, with huge sleeves and big high-heeled shoes and they couldn't walk. Well, it spoke volumes. And as they became used to the island (those that eventually did), they shed some of their clothes and began to be able to navigate better. It reinforced one of the threads of the play very nicely. There was nothing about it that said it was in an American context, but there was also nothing about it that said, "These clothes are being worn so that you will understand that the setting is long ago and far away and

that you are having a cultural experience as opposed to an immediate one." The people who were wearing the distancing clothes
were deliberately made to be seen as incapable of functioning
properly there, so there was a relationship that the audience
could have to those clothes that *wasn't* distancing.

*When Stacy Keach played Hamlet, he apparently studied a great
deal of the criticism that had been written by Shakespearean
scholars. Did you find it helpful to do the same?*

I read a lot of criticism, yes, but I never read anything that talked
about the part in the way that I conceived it. But the most en-
lightening stuff came from people saying, "This is what this sentence means." I got that habit from one of those three or four terrific professors that I had at Yale, who used to have fun telling us
about productions of various Shakespeare plays that he had seen
where interpretations of parts had been founded on the misinter-
pretations of sentences. Whole scenes were done wrong because
somebody thought that a word meant "angry" when it really
meant "blessed."

*I think it was Shaw who said, with Shakespeare, one should "play
on the lines and within the lines, but never between the lines."*

Yes, I think that's true. Because of the experience of working
with Walter Asmus on *Waiting for Godot,* I would like to do
some Shakespeare that is *very* strictly conceived, with very, very
strict attention to the structures that are in the play. I think
Shaw's statement is absolutely correct, because the life of the
play is in the lines. If you stop to act in between them, everybody
loses the thread; they don't get carried on the words. But the audience has to get used to listening in that way, listening without
always checking with themselves to see if they're keeping up;
they have to get used to just letting the words flow the way they
let images flow when they watch a movie. They don't go, "Am I
seeing all that's there?"

*I once read something by Gielgud where he said that classics don't
demand the same imagination of the actor because, for instance,
there is no such thing as the life of the character before the play*

*begins; there is no life except in the play. Do you find that you cre-
ate Shakespearean characters differently than more contemporary
ones for that reason?*

My professor used to say that all the time, too. He used to say,
"Iago is just bad. He's bad, that's it! You can't go asking yourself
what his mother did to him." Yet, you have to be rooted in something. You have to find a door into the heart and mind of the character so that you can come out on stage and just be bad. But it
can't just be hot air, because that way, you can't get in it. How
can you get in—being bad? You can't. And so I think that interpreting Shakespearean characters is somewhat the same as in
other plays where you have to find something that ignites you and
yet will be appropriate to the text. The off-stage life of other plays
is of no use unless it enlightens what's happening on the stage.
You can't figure out little, tricky revelations that you do with behavior, that don't have a textual base, and try to slide an interpretation of the part past the lines.

Is that something you can do with more contemporary material?

You can, but I don't think it would be desirable there either. But
you can, because contemporary plays lean more heavily on
behavior, that kind of how-does-he-pick-up-the-glass kind of
behavior.

*What part does personal experience play in the creation of a
Shakespearean role? Do you draw on that?*

You draw on what you've got. Lots of people have said that everything that you're ever going to be able to use creatively in your
life, you've experienced by the age of six, or the age of three, or
the age of eleven. But those early experiences in your life are the
food for your work. They are.

*Is it a matter of consciously trying to link your psyche to
Hamlet's?*

It's what we were talking about before. Being able to safely fly—
that's what you try to get. As opposed to flying something, you

want to fly! It's not flying a toy plane and saying, "Look at the wonderful way in which I manipulate the controls," although there is a whole school of acting that is epitomized by Olivier, which is largely admiration for the magnificent employment of techniques that he uses. But, in the end, what makes that kind of acting exciting is that Olivier is personally exciting, and with all that jazz on another person, it wouldn't be half as interesting. Because he has a dynamic presence, the flying of this toy plane that he does becomes very interesting. His performance is something that you actively admire. I do think that the reason he is thought, among his contemporaries, to be the greatest actor in England, has much to do with the fact that you can look at his performance and do to it what you can do, as we were discussing before, with a Picasso painting. You can say, "He drew this line here, and look how he did it. Then he balanced it with that there, and look how he did that. Lo and behold, this is how he constructed it, and isn't it admirable!"

Do you think that English actors, in general, are still more outwardly mannered than inwardly motivated?

That may be true, but I'm not sure whether we should talk about acting in these ways at all. These things that we are discussing are just the tools of the trade. You can't really talk about acting because acting is a person. There is no such thing, maybe, as acting; there are only actors, and they all devise techniques that they hope will make it easier for them to get God's gift out. Sometimes their techniques work against them and sometimes they work for them; but they're God-given gifts nonetheless.

The thing that everybody wants to see is an actual person going through an actual experience, and whether his voice has a sixteen-note range or a two-note range doesn't matter a damn because he communicates how he communicates. So it's an intellectual exercise to talk about it at all. You do it, that's it.

Do you think that acting then is a matter of inspiration?

No, I think it's even simpler. I think it has to do with some kind of visibility. People can see you. Part of it is just given to you by the fact that all the lights are turned out, and there is nothing else to look at. Then there are obviously grades of difference between people; some you want to watch more than others. And the actor's visibility can be focused by tricks and devices and techniques and staging and close-ups and editing and all kinds of things. It can be made to seem much stronger than it is. You can do a lot with a little and so on. But ultimately, it is either there or not.

Do you find that your creation of a role is different if it's for the stage rather than for film?

Yes, I guess that it is different in myriad ways, but not fundamentally. Basically, I think that you've got to get into the character, try to understand him, figure out what he means by everything he says, and try to make it all matter a lot. Trying to make it matter a lot is terribly important. Everybody's visibility is increased greatly in proportion to how much their work matters to them. You see that happen all the time in life. There's a crowd of totally anonymous people, and somebody wants something very badly; that person doesn't have to raise his voice, but he starts to glow, and he becomes interesting. This is a factor in films and theatre equally. You don't have to be so concerned about focus and communication and being seen in a film, however, because the director will either take care of it or he won't.

Personality, I suppose, is another word for this quality of "being visible." Yet it's the reason many actors object to doing film work; they say movies call more for being a personality than for being an actor.

Personal mannerisms don't work any better in the movies than they do in the theatre. But the person, the person-ness or personality of the actor is what makes people want to go to see him. Audiences wanted to see Barbra Streisand in the theatre for the same reasons that they want to see Barbra Streisand in the movies. Because, "By golly, there's somebody!"

Which of the two—movies or theatre—do you prefer?

Hmmm. Well, I do prefer them equally. I'm sure that my life would be very different if they both paid equal amounts of money. I'm sure that the theatre would be very different, and it might be both better and worse. When you talk about the theatre and the movies, you have to talk about them as they are today in the United States, and that has to do with economics. The theatre is pathetically underfunded. Pathetically! Because of that, it makes it unfairly difficult to do good work. I mean, a competitive atmosphere is very good for all artists. Not having it come easy is good too; it makes for "muscle." But I think that it's gone too far. The economics of handiwork in this country, of all kinds of handiwork, is under a terrible strain. There's just totally unfair competition from mechanized things, and some balance has to be found if the quality of the handiwork is going to be maintained.

But I love acting in the theatre; I love it. And I love acting in the movies, too. Of course, the pleasures of acting in the movies are very odd, like doing the same thing twenty-three times in a row and altering it not at all, or only a teeny-weeny bit. And as Alan Bates said, "Movies photograph thought." I loved that; I think that it's true. And total release from any concern about pitching your performance, projecting it, is nice. It has forced the theatre to change, too, because people want to be able to see directly in the theatre now as well.

What makes a director a good director for you to work with?

Having a very particular vision.

Are movies entirely a director's medium?

I don't know if I mean that. Even today, the actors that you see in films stick in your head much more powerfully than the directors or the screenwriters do. Their image is before you; they are the vessel that communicates. So it's an actor's medium, because you can't do without them; but I think finally, it's a collaborative medium. In terms of will, the will belongs to the director. But then I think acting's a passive thing anyway. When you get completely high from it, and it is the best that it is, you are in the grips of passion. I don't mean scenery-eating passion; I mean that things are passing through you. You are a pipe in a channel.

Does it bother your sense of a character to shoot out of sequence?

I think that it depends on the material. I've never done a film that was like a play (where the emotional tension is built verbally) that wasn't really shot in continuity. If I had I'm sure my performance would have suffered. *The Glass Menagerie,* for instance, was pretty much shot in sequence. You need to know what you did before; you need to know what temperature was reached in the scene that preceded so the one that follows can follow. *The Great Gatsby* was shot entirely out of sequence and the only thing that was dislocating about that was one situation where the prelude to a scene was shot in Newport, and then months later, a scene that took place on the other side of the door was shot. When a unit like that one is not filmed together, that's bad. As long as you're shooting the whole lump, however, it's not too bad. It's not bad at all, in fact, because it releases you from another thing that you imagine is needed when it's not. Playwrights do an awful lot for you: they structure things. Some actors think that they have to do all the structuring or else they haven't done their job. Yet in a very important sense, a lot of it is already done; and an actor just does as he's told.

So shooting out of sequence does have the advantage of leaving you with just the moment?

Yes. This is a time when the director has to be the judge. He has to see the picture as a conductor hears the music; he has to know if on this given day, when you are shooting the scene, you're talking too fast or too slow, or your motor's not running at the speed that's going to be needed when it gets put in the context of the entire film. Obviously, not everything can be remedied by cutting.

We were talking before about the economics of movies. For **The Great Gatsby,** *David Merrick invested about seven million dollars in the production. Did acting in such a huge Hollywood enterprise make you feel pressured?*

It wasn't a pressure on me! I felt delighted. I thought: "They're doing all this for us! They're building this house just for me!" It was the most expensive film that I had ever worked on before or since. And it was wonderful, it really was. Very impressive how good these people are in all their various little, tiny jobs: the guy that makes the walls look old, for instance. There are so many tremendously able people. When they have that much money, they are all there and it's quite awesome. It was fun, it was exciting. It was like being a little boy and thinking, "I better stay awake and be good."

Do you enjoy watching your performances in the movies or on TV?

When I first saw myself on film, I was just horrified and now when I see myself, it's like watching home movies; it reminds me of where we were when we shot it. But I can't watch a film and tell if it's any good or not because I can't focus on what's actually happening on the screen. I keep having tangential thoughts— about what the weather was like, for instance. I can't tell whether I'm doing a good job or not, because what I really register is whether I thought so when I shot it. I always remember that explicitly. If I thought I did it well at the time, I almost invariably think it is good when I see it. And if I wasn't pleased, I almost invariably think it is bad. But all this has no relation to the truth of whether it is, in fact, good or bad.

Do you generally feel a little bit of dissatisfaction with your work?

Yes, it is kind of chronic . . . and a waste of time for me. If it weren't so chronic, maybe it wouldn't be such a waste of time.

Maybe it's the thing that keeps you going, that keeps you aspiring for a better performance.

Maybe, but I think that it's not worth much. It gives me lots of adrenalin and it makes me want to work hard out of fear, but it's something that I don't think the audience is interested in. They want you in the most direct serving that you can give them, and your preoccupation with whether or not you played it right is absolutely, totally a boring subject to them; it's an interference in terms of communication.

So your self-consciousness as an actor . . .

. . . is totally useless, except sometimes it fits the character and then you luck out. What usually happens to me is that I go through the rehearsal period and I get to the dress rehearsal, and

I say, "This is absolutely hopeless and we're all going to be destroyed by this. It's all your fault. I don't know why I'm here tonight. I think I should quit." Then somebody says, "Pull yourself together," and I say, "All right, I'll go on, but it's going to be terrible," and from then on, I'm fine. I've released myself from all that worry.

Do you find comedy more difficult than serious drama?

I guess the serious stuff is more difficult. For the experience of something serious in the theatre to be really satisfying, the hold on the audience can never be let go. So it requires a much more perfect collaboration amongst all the people who are doing it, and a more thorough wholeness of the concept.

There's more freedom for you in comedy?

No, but it's easier to be bad in something serious than it is in a comedy. You often see in reviews, for example, that people say, "This is not an entirely satisfying evening, but there are some very funny things in it." You don't see that written about a serious play: "This is not an entirely satisfying evening but there are some very sad things in it." A serious drama has bitten off something bigger.

Comedy can be taken in parts and you can enjoy the parts without necessarily enjoying the whole.

Yes, because you laugh. You can't laugh and then tell yourself, "I had an awful time." But serious things require more focus. Of course, comedies can fall apart on a lot of laughs, too, and the audience can come out feeling sort of stale, as if they smoked too much, or as if they've been had. But in terms of difficulty, I think it's probably harder to do serious things.

Do you find then that serious things are ultimately more satisfying to do?

No, because acting is a lot of fun. It's game-playing, that's what it is. And when I say that serious things are harder than comedies, it's balanced equally by the fact that the details of comedy are a lot more difficult than the details of serious work. In comedy, if the details don't work, they don't work, and there's a real accurate way of telling if they're failing. So timing and playing the exact right note that releases the laugh, all that's tremendously tricky. When I replaced an actor in *The Knack*, I had an awful time. There were certain laughs which came absolutely naturally to him; his control over them was very smooth. Yet I couldn't get them at all; the harder I tried, the more impossible it became.

Did you work out a happy ending? Did you finally get "the knack"?

I got different laughs. I was a different person. So, it was bound to work out that way. But at the time, I thought I was terrible.

Is acting ever easy for you, or do you feel that each part is sort of a struggle?

There's an interesting struggle and a wasted struggle. But that's part of the fun because the struggle is to get your imagination around somebody else. The character is like you, but different from you—or maybe very different from you. How are you going to bring yourself to bear, bend yourself to fit him? That's the pleasure of it. In fact, a great portion of the pleasure of acting is rehearsing.

Is that the point in the whole process of a performance that you most enjoy—the rehearsal?

The experiences vary, but I would say I most enjoy the first two-thirds of the rehearsal, and then the run after the first two or three weeks. They are the greatest fun. The last third of the rehearsal is the most painful, but it's often the most productive; the pressure's on and things sometimes come very fast. I had a wonderful time rehearsing a play in seven days once. We did *Rosencrantz and Guildenstern Are Dead* at Williamstown and the pressure was on the whole time. There wasn't a second to indulge in any of this stupid struggle because solutions *had* to be found. And I loved it.

When you're performing, do you find that you have new and

deeper insights into the character; does your conception keep growing, or does it reach a sort of plateau?

New and different insights. The play changes, the shape of things changes. If it's a comedy, the laughs move around, the scenes shift. I don't think the audience notices too much. The surprises and the differences that are fascinating to us are, in reality, quite small. Again, one forgets that the playwright has done an awful lot of work. After a certain performance, you may think, "Aw, the whole thing went out the window." But the play still said all the same words, the structure was still there, it still presented the same characters, and was played by the same actors.

Do you find yourself getting bored after a long run?

Yes, but it goes in cycles. I think this is true for a lot of people. The play sags and then you think, "I can't face this any more," and then something new comes along, the thing changes, you change a little bit, and everything seems to pick up—at least for a while.

Is there any particular method you have to make a performance seem very fresh, when in fact you're a bit tired?

Fear is a good tool!

Are you nervous before you go on?

Not always. Critics bother me a lot. I don't like them. I don't think that they apply the right criteria, and again I think it's this business of analysis. I don't know how there could be a good critic because I really think that a good critic would be an appreciator. And I don't know how anybody could be expected to appreciate the things that they see when they have to see so much. No one should be obliged to go to the theatre that often. Once you do, your ability to respond changes. More and more of your visceral and intuitive responses get put to sleep, and your brain gets fancier.

How about good reviews—do they increase your self-consciousness?

Oh, the truth about reviews is that you hate the bad ones and you love the good ones. That's the truth for me. There's not too much point, in my own life, in looking any further than that. I don't think that critics are interested in the same things. Criticism, at least over the period that I have witnessed it, has always been preoccupied with everything except what was going on. It's either preoccupied with the past or terrified of missing the innovative. Critics are not able to just look. That's why it took such a long time for criticism to catch up with the movies.

Yes, in the old days, movies were not considered worthy of a critic's attention.

The cinema was so plainly just something that was going on, that people were going to see, that they were loving, and that was making buckets of money. There was no history of movie acting to compare people's performances to, so they just said, "This is not art." Movie criticism, when the movies were booming, was like TV criticism is today. The general attitude goes, "It's pleasant, but we know the whole medium is sort of polluted anyway, so we're only talking about different varieties of garbage." And now the critics look back at all those films they ignored and they say, "Oh my, *auteurs*, cinema this, cinema that." They apply fancy words to it, and they make themselves great. It's all very classic. I dislike critics. I know some people that don't read them at all, but I can't bring myself to do that. I want to be flattered.

You are at the point in your career where you can choose your roles. Is there anything specific that you look for in a part?

I think it is an exaggeration to say that I can choose my roles. I am a working actor now just as I always was. In the sense that I can choose my roles now, I've always chosen them. I haven't done anything that was absolutely awful unless I had to. I was on a television interview with Henry Fonda and he said that he was always worried about what he was going to do next. One would think that he was in a position to choose his roles. But it's not so. There's one important dividing line in the profession of acting, and that is between those who can generate work on their own, who can find financing for their own projects, and those who can't. Those who can, get to choose; and those who can't, choose among either a large or small number of possibilities.

Let's say you were offered several roles for the same set period of time. What would it be that would make you want to do one over the other? Is there anything in particular that you look for?

There are three elements. One is trying to guess whether it will be good, bad, or indifferent as far as your career is concerned. There's the money, and then there's the intrinsic interest of the thing itself. I have been lucky throughout my career in that if something has been very, very interesting, I've been able to do it somehow. I've escaped by the hair of my chin not having to turn something interesting down because I had to make money, because I had to drive a taxicab just to pay the bills; that's never quite happened.

*I imagine that playing Prince Hal in **Henry IV, Part I** would be fun because he's rather a guiltless character. Do you tend to take on the characteristics of a role you play?*

I think that's one of the good-bad things, the sugar-coated nasties about being in the theatre. You delude yourself into thinking that you possess the qualities of the person that you're portraying, but you can't go very far without finding that you're kidding yourself.

The best example of that was when we did *The Trial of the Catonsville Nine*. It's a play about the Berrigan brothers and others who were on trial for protesting the war in Vietnam. We held discussions after the play was over with the audience, and they were frequently skeptical or hostile toward the position of the people in the play. The characters, of course, are real historical figures, they were contemporaries of ours, and we all developed strong sympathies for them. Soon, we began talking to the audience as if we had their credentials! There was a period there where we would actually say to the audience, "How can you sit there doing nothing?" Yet, in fact, we were being paid perfectly handsome salaries for performing on Broadway in a play for which we were receiving critical acclaim, making a decent living, and furthering our careers. And the characters we portrayed were out paying with their lives for what they felt! When I did

Hamlet, a similar delusion occurred. I started saying to myself, "Boy, how smart I am! Look at what I'm thinking!"

When you did **The Trial of the Catonsville Nine,** *though, did you feel it was important to make a political statement against the war? Do you care if what you do has a social message?*

By the time we did that play in New York, I knew hardly anybody who was in favor of the continuation of the war in Vietnam, so I have to say that it was not a difficult position for any of us to take, although we were all certain that we were being watched. It was a lot less "real" than it was "theatre." However, it doesn't much matter what we thought because the play remained. The fact that we were for it or against it didn't matter because the play did its good by itself. But your question is, do I think the theatre should have social significance?

Not whether the theatre should or should not, but whether that's important to you in terms of the particular work you choose to do.

The theatre's social impact is contained within what it is; it shows people to themselves and that is its social impact—period. That's not the only thing that it does, of course; it has a lot to do with the world of the imagination and opening people's horizons and getting people to think and feel about things. The theatre has certainly been the instrument of a number of different social institutions and it works well as a support for religion or for a political system or for different social consciousnesses; it's a good propagandizing instrument. But I don't think that's what it's fundamentally about. The importance that the theatre has in our culture now has a lot to do with the fact that it's a handicraft. And it isn't about things, it's about people. It's something that people are doing in front of people, and I think that is a gigantic social service in itself. We're finding this out in the way that these cities of ours are going to pieces—solutions to social problems require *personal* engagement; they cannot be even benevolently designed.

Systems don't work without a lot of personal involvement. That's why we were wrong when we were doing *The Trial of the Catonsville Nine* to feel as we did. The most eloquent person in that play was the guy who spoke the least. He was a priest who had returned from South America where he'd been thrown out for helping some poor peons try to organize a little cooperative somewhere in the mountains to feed themselves. He went to a dinner party soon thereafter and some people said, "We're going to pour blood on some draft- files in Catonsville, Maryland tomorrow. Who's for this and who's against it? It's about the war in Vietnam." Well, he hadn't had anything to do with the war in Vietnam, but at the time, it was just a yes or no situation. He did not do terribly much analysis, but he committed very much of his life. And if my work has any social value, it will be because I have devoted my life to something that is humane. I don't do it with the same motive that he did, so I'm not saying that we're comparable in any way, but he was willing to act, to commit himself personally, whatever it brought. To me, he was the most powerful personality of all those in the play.

So the existence of theatre is a great social benefit in itself, and you don't feel it's necessary to make explicit political messages.

I think that the things Norman Lear has put on television have probably had some good impact. It's very difficult to figure out what their impact has been, but it certainly has been something. And it is not idle of him to have thought that, with this gigantically powerful instrument, he might be able, while he was entertaining people and making his own living and giving lots of other people jobs, to do something positive about major problems that face our society—like racism and prejudice, the liberation of women and all the other issues that he has said it's okay to talk about on TV. He certainly does that and television is certainly a great place to open a forum. But whether you could directly, with a play, create a revolution—I just don't think so. On the other hand, I don't think that it makes the theatre impure to espouse such a position.

You've called yourself a "fact actor." What do you mean by that?

I mean that I try to exercise a certain amount of restraint; I try to remember that the play speaks, and that my job is to let the play speak for itself. What I'd like to do in the future is be more clear, more blunt. I have more to do in terms of the simplicity and directness of my acting. The great thing about the theatre is doing it.

STEPHANIE MILLS

Stephanie Mills began singing in the choir of the Cornerstone Baptist Church in Brooklyn when she was three years old. At nine, this daughter of a New York City Housing Department construction worker was performing on Broadway in *Maggie Flynn*, a musical which starred Shirley Jones and the late Jack Cassidy. At the time of this interview, Ms. Mills was nineteen; she had played for nearly four years the leading role in a hit Broadway show—that of Dorothy in *The Wiz*; had been able to buy herself a full-length mink coat; and had purchased a 27-room mansion for her parents in Mt. Vernon, New York.

What was most amazing then about this 4'9" performer was that she seemed in every way to be a typical teenager—except perhaps more happy and well-adjusted. She had brought a cousin along to lend her moral support during the interview, which was held in the office of her public relations firm, and though she spoke of wanting independence, it was clear that she was rooted in the love of a close-knit family. She had a great deal of warmth and energy, and seemed most herself when we began swapping stories about bite plates and braces.

Still, Stephanie is a child star; she has grown up in the theatre. She has the unique combination of a child's-eye view and the stage sense of an old hand. Now, at nineteen, she is just about to leave that childhood behind and step into the spotlight as an adult.

(Several months after this interview, Stephanie was invited by President Carter to sing "Amazing Grace" at a birthday tribute to Martin Luther King, Jr. at Ebenezer Baptist Church in Atlanta.)

How did it happen that you became involved in show business?

I never really said that I wanted to be on Broadway or anything, but I always wanted to sing. Since my sister was an actress [she was in *Claudine*], and my brother used to sing, my family was always involved in that kind of show-business atmosphere. So my career wasn't anything that we planned, it just sort of happened.

And you were about nine years old when you first got into it?

Yeah, my first Broadway show was *Maggie Flynn* when I was nine. After that I did some Off-Broadway things, I won the Amateur Hour at the Apollo Theatre and that whole trip. But my whole life changed at the age of nine.

What was it like being a nine-year-old on Broadway?

Well, I didn't have a stage mother, so to me, Broadway was nothing. I was up there with nine other kids, we were playing nine black orphans, and as far as we were concerned, we were having fun and getting paid for it! Getting paid to sing and dance and act crazy.

Were you going to a public school at that time?

Yeah, I was put into a private school in seventh grade, but before that I went to the public school. We'd put on plays and I'd be the director. I sang in the Glee Club and all that, too.

Did being on Broadway make it difficult for you to relate to kids your own age?

I always thought that I was more mature than anybody else so it wasn't that hard. And most of my friends were very mature, too.

Were the other kids jealous?

There were a few who were, but they weren't my friends so I just blinked them right out.

You don't feel that you lost out on any kind of adolescence?

No, because I had a side of both worlds. I lived in Brooklyn till I was sixteen and then we moved to Westchester. And I had time to go to public school; I used to hang out and stuff, so I know what that's all about. I know what it's like both ways.

Do you think you'd be essentially the same person today if you hadn't gone on stage as a child? Is your character different because of the experience?

I think I'd be the same person, but *The Wiz* educated me a lot, personally and professionally. I'm sure I'd be much more naive about a lot of things if I hadn't had this experience. In the beginning I was very naive about dealing with people in the theatre, like producers and gay people, for example. I had never been around gay people before. I'm a much calmer person now, more intelligent about business, too.

Are you calmer because you have a sense of confidence in your own abilities?

Yeah, but also just because I'm more independent now than I used to be. I like to go places by myself, which I don't often get a chance to do; I like to be alone, away from my family sometimes.

Do you feel that since you play a child in **The Wiz** *that people then treat you as a child?*

Yes. When I first played the role of Dorothy, I was fifteen going on sixteen and when it opened I was sixteen. But people don't realize that now I'm older. I'm not a little girl anymore, you know, I'm a young adult now. People tend to want to keep you a little girl; people want me to stay being Dorothy. Even in my family there's this whole Dorothy-little-girl image that they want to keep.

How do you like being a public person, a famous person?

That can get kind of obnoxious at times. Sometimes I read something that someone has said about me and it's really not true; I mean, it's just press. That can bother me. Or, like, I went to an amusement park Sunday and I couldn't enjoy myself because there were so many people there. I'm just like they are, you know, I just want to enjoy myself—but I couldn't.

Is that because they recognized you?

Yeah, and they'll be all over you—you have to watch it. You want to act crazy and stupid and stuff, just as if no one was paying you any mind. Yet you can't. Imagine how it would feel if you went to a restaurant and someone was watching you eat the whole time. Yet, except for people recognizing me, I never think about it. I don't sit in front of a mirror and say, "Oh, I'm a star." I just do what I have to do and let people accept it.

Do you think that you and Dorothy still have a lot in common?

Yes. Dorothy's very insecure at the beginning and I was very insecure—still am in a lot of ways. The only one who really listens to her is Toto. She's a very loving person, a very giving person, but it takes that whole transition to Oz, meeting the Lion, the Tin Man, the Scarecrow, and the Wiz to let her know that she is very attractive, very kind—that she does have something to offer. I identify with that in Dorothy: I think everybody can.

What kind of training have you had?

I never had any training. I never took singing, dancing, or acting. I take classes now—ballet, African, and modern dance classes— but I never had any training.

Is there a reason why you don't take singing lessons? Do you feel they would somehow impede your natural talent, your natural singing?

I never had the desire to and I didn't think I needed to. I don't want anybody to tell me where to place my voice or what note to sing. I know how to reach certain notes and I never had any problems. If I was always hoarse, then I'd know that I was definitely singing wrong, but I've been singing a long time now and haven't had any problems so I must be doing something right. Sometimes I sing at home and work on my breathing. I hear a lot of people

that have been trained formally, I mean they've been trained forever, and to me, they still don't sing correctly. So it's all a matter
of how you want to sound—whether you want to sound very
trained or very free.

*And do you feel that your acting comes from the same place? That
it's instinctual, natural?*

Yes. Yes. I do. I think it's better to follow your instincts. I mean,
if I had to do a movie, I'd have somebody coach me on the script,
but I wouldn't go and study acting, make it my business to go to a
class every day—no.

*Who do you feel has been your best teacher—the other actors, the
audience, the director? Who gives you the most feedback about
what you do right and what you do wrong?*

My family. If I do something, I ask them: "Well, how did you like
that?" and they'll say: "Well, I thought you could have done that
better." I question them about certain things. I always try to do
my best but sometimes you try and it's just not there.

*How did you prepare yourself for Dorothy? Did you study Judy
Garland's version or try to stay away from it?*

I didn't study Judy Garland; I didn't read any books; every day,
I'd just work on it. And I thought a lot about how I wanted to portray her, searching for things inside myself that I could bring. But
our version, you know, is not just a take-off on *The Wizard of Oz*;
we're not imitating it, we're doing it totally different and just using the same story.

*So you think that the character of Dorothy is very much affected
by whoever brings her to life?*

Right. One person can take the role a certain step and then another person will pick it up and take it somewhere else, another
direction in which they think it should go.

*Now that you look back on it, what in particular do you think
your version does differently with Dorothy?*

I don't think our version just deals differently with Dorothy. I think all the characters have really changed. In the original story you saw the Wizard as this big man, a monster almost, but then he turned out to be really an old man. In our version, he's a slick, jive sort of Wiz. So all the characters grow and change. And we have a message in our play, like the songs "Believe in Yourself," and "Home," and "Be a Lion." All of it is very positive, very universal. There's no heavy black thing in it at all—it's just purely entertainment. It doesn't have a heavy message—it has a very positive message, and that's what I like.

Before you perform each night, do you have to rest up, be by yourself? There's so much exuberance, such a terrific force needed on stage. How do you turn that on night after night? Is there any particular ritual you go through?

Not really. Sometimes I like to be by myself just before I go on but that's kind of difficult. And, also, I like being around my friends. I like being around people that I like and who like me. That's where I get my energy.

Do you find that it's difficult to keep a performance fresh when you've been doing it so long?

It is very difficult. Sometimes it gets stale and I get bored and I find myself walking through the performance. I have to go away and do other things. I'm working on a new album now. I just signed a record contract; that's something new for me to do. And I take a lot of vacations. I've been doing *The Wiz* for four years. I can't stay there for even a month straight now it seems—that's just too long, it's too hard. I mean, *The Wiz* is that kind of show—you have to be right on it.

When you find that you're up on stage and you're feeling kind of bored, is there any technique that you have to pick yourself back up?

We play around on stage a lot. We'll pinch each other, for example, just really goof off.

Do you feel that you've come to the end of your line with Dorothy, that there's nothing new you can bring?

Yeah, it's just like with anything else. You get tired of it, and you can only take it so far. If you worked at a job and were there for five or six or eight years, you might feel that it was time to move on. You've taken the job and done everything you can with it. Especially in creating and entertaining; you can only stay in one place so long because you grow as a person and you want to do something else.

I think that I've reached my peak as Dorothy. I've gone as far as I can go with her and now I have to leave and do other things. I've outgrown her, physically and mentally. It's just time to separate, leave her behind and let someone else take the role somewhere new.

Did you used to get nervous before you went on—do you ever still?

I did in the beginning, but not now. After doing it for so long, being in front of people doesn't bother me anymore. It's second nature.

Are some audiences more responsive than others; do they vary from performance to performance?

Oh, yes. Yes. We can have a fabulous audience Tuesday, Wednesday matinee, Wednesday night, and then have a dull audience on the weekend. It's funny because you'd think the weekend audiences would be more responsive.

What do you do to enliven an audience when they're not responding as you would like?

You can't really do anything. They're going to do what they want to do. You just have to keep singing, dancing, acting, and if they appreciate it, they'll show it. If they don't, they won't.

You don't find yourself broadening your gestures or putting more "umph" into it?

No, because that would tire you, and you'd lose your pacing. You know, when you're doing a show that's two and a half hours, you have to pace yourself. You want your energy to be *up* the whole time, but there are moments when you level off so that you can peak at the end. You can't overdo something because of the audience. They have to accept what you give them. You know what I'm saying? It sounds cold, but it's not—because *you* know technically what you're doing, you know how to give them a good performance.

At a specific point in the show, do you take it easy and relax?

Sometimes in "Ease on Down the Road" I take it easy. I don't sing as much. The dance parts I try to stay up on because I love to dance—I'm really into dancing.

When you feel that you've been bored or tired for a particular performance and haven't done as well as you could have, do you feel a sense of dissatisfaction with yourself?

Yes, I do. I'm very critical of myself so I feel bad. Giving a bad performance is very bad for me and for the show. So I think about it. Sometimes it can't be helped, because not everybody feels good every day; everybody has those times when their energy is just not there. But you learn to work with it. I say to myself, "Okay, I can't go on worrying about this, I can't let it ruin my whole evening." I just make sure that the next day I'm really ready for it.

It's a big responsibility to be the center of the show, as you are.

It is. So many other people depend on my energy—they all count on me. And no matter how energetic the other characters are, if Dorothy's energy is not up there, the show seems like it's dragging. If I'm walking through my performance, then everybody else in the cast is going to look at me and say, "Well, if she can do it, why can't we?" and then they all fall into that feeling. It's a psychological thing. Dorothy's just the center of the show. Sometimes I don't know if I like being in that position. Being in a Broadway show is *so* wear-and-tear; you have to be there, right there, right on it, all the time.

Are you distracted by things when you're up there on stage?

I'm only distracted when someone in the front rows is snapping a camera. People don't realize how much that bothers a performer. It flashes and really, for that minute, you can't see. Sometimes people are talking upstairs, fighting over a scene or something and that's distracting. Or when big men come and stand down front, that bothers me. But you can't stop in the middle of a performance and say, "Hey, you, sit down." You just have to blink it out, pretend they're not even there.

What is it about your role that particularly satisfies you?

I like the kind of character she is. She's a clean character, she's decent. And the little kids can really relate to her, they look up to her—and they really believe that I'm Dorothy, that I dress like her every day. I like that even though it's a responsibility. I'm getting older now, you know, and I'm not their age, even though they think I am. But it's nice. I like the whole prestigious thing about Dorothy. It's a role that anybody in the world would want to play, if only for one day. It's a fairy tale—it's the world's most famous fairy tale. It even beats *Alice in Wonderland*. Dorothy has this . . . magic. People believe that she has all kinds of powers and can get them things. I really can't explain it, but when a person plays her, that magic rubs off a little. People remember you as Dorothy, they never forget and so you never quite lose her powers.

Do you feel that the Dorothy you were at the beginning has changed, that the character you play now is different?

Oh, yes. Very much. She's grown now and she's slicker. I know the stage very well now, I know how to project and do different things, how to work the stage. I'm much better able to deal with people now, so Dorothy is, too. She deals better with the Tin Man, the Lion, and all. In the ways that I've changed, I just relate all that back into her. But it's funny, I think I act more little girl-ish *now* on stage than I did before.

Is it because you're trying to be a little girl now, whereas you don't feel such a little girl?

No, because I play her like I feel. I sing the way I feel. I don't try to put something in there that's not.

How do you feel now about musical comedy work—would you want to come back to the Broadway theatre and do it all again?

Well, I don't think I could do a straight drama, even though I would love to do one. But there's nothing about musical comedy that I don't like. I like it all. I don't think I would come back and do another Broadway show for a while, though, not for three or four years. Even then, I would only do a very *limited* engagement. But this is where I grew up. The theatre's where my roots are. I started off on Broadway, and to me, the theatre's wonderful. It's where you can create, and once you're up on stage, you can just keep on creating. When you're out there, you're out there. Whatever mistakes you make, that's you, you've got to keep going. And you can dance, you can get it all out, because you're there—it's live, it's not taped, it's not filmed. It's there.

I know that I couldn't do or be anything else. This is my life. I love it. You have to love it to deal with it, to go through all the stuff you have to go through, because it's not all glitter and glamour the way people think it is. You have to love it. And I do.

Do you feel that because you're a black performer, the roles available to you will be more limited?

No, because I think there's politics in every field, whatever you do, whether you're black or white or green or yellow. I don't think the fact that I'm black matters at all.

Is it important to you that the work you do reflect some kind of positive image?

Yes, it is important. I wouldn't do anything that didn't represent *me* because I want my personal self to be involved in it. I've been offered a lot of films that I didn't think were right because I don't want to do anything that's black exploitative. I'm not into that. I mean, say you've seen me play Dorothy and then you go to the movies and you see me in a black-exploitation film—that just doesn't jell. That's going from one extreme to another. You say,

"What is she doing? Is she just out there to make money?" I'm not. Whatever I do has to make a step in my career.

Do you feel that since you've played Dorothy, you can't take a lesser role?

It doesn't necessarily have to be a big role, but it has to have a certain prominence. Even if the character I played came on for one minute it could be a good role, as long as the importance of her being there was such that you'd remember it.

Would you want to do a TV series?

I'd like to have a special once a year or something, but not a series. That's just like Broadway. You can get really tired of it.

Who do you consider to be the greats in musical theatre?

I would have to say Liza Minnelli, Barbra Streisand, Ethel Merman. Those are people who really have roots in Broadway, too.

Beyond being a wonderful singer and dancer, what is the quality that makes someone a great musical star?

It's a magic that they have. People really believe in them. And that's what it's all about—the public. They have to believe that you are really sincere about what you do. No matter how much money you have put behind you or how much press they give you, if people don't believe in you, you're not going to be a star. When I look at Barbra Streisand or Diana Ross, there's magic there. They have something that no one else has; it's unique, and it's a giving thing. It's strength. You look for that strength in them. That's what people come to see; they leave their frustrations and their problems at home and they look to the star for strength. That's what I do. It inspires you to keep going, keep dreaming, keep living.

BRUCE DERN

Bruce Dern is the black sheep of one of the Midwest's most distinguished families. His father was a law partner of Adlai Stevenson, his grandfather was governor of Utah and Secretary of War under Franklin D. Roosevelt, and his great-uncle is the Pulitzer Prize-winning poet, Archibald MacLeish. Yet Dern, who was born on June 4, 1936 and raised in the Chicago suburb of Winnetka, found himself consistently at odds with his family. He was sent to the exclusive prep school Choate, but was too miserable to remain there for long, and when he quit the University of Pennsylvania over a difference with his track coach, he permanently dashed his parents' hopes that he would follow in the family tradition and become a lawyer.

Dern studied acting in Philadelphia at the American Foundation of Dramatic Art and later in New York at the Actors Studio. He made his Broadway debut in 1958 in Sean O'Casey's *The Shadow of a Gunman* and the following year he had eight lines in Tennessee Williams' *Sweet Bird of Youth*. He later toured as Tom Junior (the character Rip Torn created on Broadway), but shortly thereafter, the momentum of his career came to a halt. For about a year he supported himself as a cab driver in New York and in 1962, he decided to move West.

After a number of performances as a TV villain, most notably on "Alfred Hitchcock Presents," where, as he says, he played a "hillbilly psychotic peach-picker," Dern became typecast. When he wasn't playing a corpse (his head and hands were cut off in *Hush, Hush, Sweet Charlotte* and he was beaten to death with a poker in *Marnie*), Dern was cast as a biker, doper, or crazed killer in a run of B-movies. (Witness *The Incredible Two-Headed Transplant* where, as a diabolical scientist, he ripped into a baby's arm with his teeth.) Even as late as 1972, Dern was cast as the Bad Guy: in *The Cowboys*, he became the first actor ever to kill John Wayne on screen. He's not without a sense of humor about his career, however, and when Wayne told him, "You're gonna be hated everywhere in the world for this one," Dern reportedly shot back, "Yeah, but in Berkeley they're gonna give me a standing ovation."

There were, of course, a few respectable assignments. In *They Shoot Horses, Don't They?*, Dern played an Okie who enters a dance marathon with his pregnant wife, and as the obsessively clean-living basketball coach in *Drive, He Said*, he won the National Society of Film Critics Best Supporting Actor award. But it wasn't until he appeared as a gentle humanist in the science-fiction film, *Silent Running*, that he was able to fully break from his mold.

Since then, he has appeared in such films as *The King of Marvin Gardens, The Laughing Policeman, The Great Gatsby* (as Tom Buchanan), *Smile, Family Plot, Black Sunday*, and as Marine Captain Hyde in *Coming Home*. For the latter, he has received an Academy Award nomination as Best Supporting Actor of the year.

Bruce Dern lives in a beachfront house in Malibu with his third wife, Andrea Beckett. They met while he was a teacher and she a student at the Actors and Directors Lab in Los Angeles. They are known to avoid Hollywood social life, though Dern counts as his close friends Jack Nicholson and Robert Redford. Still a disciplined runner, he competes in amateur events and neither drinks nor smokes.

There are a few curious background details to this interview which should be explained. . . . After nineteen years spent exclusively on movie roles, Mr. Dern returned to the Broadway stage in early 1979 in *Strangers*, a play about the life of Sinclair Lewis. Opening night reviews were mixed and a closing notice soon posted, but with the play increasingly successful at the box office, the notice had been taken down. Yet such a posting automatically releases an actor from his contract, and Mr. Dern elected not to continue with the play—though he had spent a full year in preparation and it had run in New York only a week. The morning after the final curtain, he flew back to his home in California.

The first part of this interview was held on the day *before* the play closed, when it was clear that the experience had physically and emotionally exhausted him, and the second part was held a few days *after*, when Mr. Dern was more rested and relaxed, when the trying disappointments were fully behind him, and when he was, as an actor always is, "hungry for more."

Part I

It must be discouraging to have your play close in a week when you've been working on it for so long.

I've been working on *Strangers* for a year now; there's a terrible feeling of loss, but at the same time, the role of Sinclair Lewis was a very painful one for me to play.

You felt that there was a certain commonality of experience between his life and your own.

Yes, absolutely. His family background was very similar to mine; both of our families were totally against having their sons go into the arts. His father was a doctor, mine was a lawyer; he was from Minnesota, I'm from Illinois. He wanted to be a writer and I wanted to be an actor; neither of our families ever understood those ambitions.

When did you first become interested in acting?

It was in 1956, '57, when I quit college.

You were a track star at the University of Pennsylvania. I've heard that you quit the team when the coach insisted you trim your sideburns.

Yeah. He said to me, "Cut your sideburns and conform to the image of an Ivy League athlete, or quit the team." I protested and refused to do it, but the University upheld him—and so did my father, who was one of the trustees. A week later I was out of college and in a dramatic school. My parents wouldn't help me out at that point, so I drove an ice-cream truck to support myself.

But you weren't interested in acting until that time?

When I was young I was never a big movie-buff or play-goer; I didn't know anything about it. But around that time, I saw James Dean act in *Rebel Without a Cause*. He was really communicating to the audience and for the first time I became aware that an actor could have such power. I decided I wanted to communicate that way, too.

In another interview I read, you said that as a child you had a tendency to be a liar. Could that show a leaning toward acting that you weren't aware of at the time?

I wasn't a liar, really, I was a fabricator. I told stories, but they weren't what you would call outright lies. I painted pictures for people and described things in their entirety. But my family didn't like that. I think that was why I was sent off to camp and to prep school at a young age. They didn't want to hear stories; they just wanted the facts: it's either raining or it's not raining. They didn't care how hard it was raining or how the rain made you feel.

Once you did quit school and decided to be an actor, did you know right away that it was a profession you'd be good at?

I knew it was the right thing to do. I knew immediately it was all I ever wanted to do with my life, and I knew I would spend the rest of my life doing it.

And that was just intuition?

Yup. It was suddenly, the first time in my life that I had a sense of direction. I was no longer being programmed by my parents.

Do you regret not having finished college?

No. If you've already decided that you want to be an actor, unless you're getting a tremendously well-rounded and complete acting background when you are in college, I think it's a waste of time.

You don't think that general book knowledge adds to your capacities as an actor?

Well, it's good, but it costs you four years, doesn't it? Meanwhile, everybody else is out getting work and learning how to act. Then, when you're twenty-two, you come out with an education, which is fine, but you've got to start at the beginning. Suddenly you're twenty-six and you're where the other people were when they were twenty-two; you're still four years behind.

Your first acting training was with a man named Gordon Phillips at the American Foundation of Dramatic Art . . .

. . . and he gave me the best foundation you could get as an actor. He taught me to be succinct and to be publicly private—those are the keys to acting. You have to be able to look in the mirror in front of a thousand people and tell them exactly what you see: what your fears are, what your hopes are, your joys, your dissappointments.

You studied at the Actors Studio with Lee Strasberg; I assume you're in favor of Method acting?

Yes. Method acting enables you to find the things which will relax you, unlock you, and let all of that private emotion come out. It has to do with being able to recall the emotions and sensations of a particular incident, but it takes about five years of total concentration to learn how to do it.

Do you feel a difference when you work with people who have had the same training as you've had?

Yes. Enormously. The two films in which I worked with people who were trained the way I was trained were two of the most spontaneous movies that I've been in—*The King of Marvin Gardens* and *Coming Home*. Those were all Method-trained actors— Jon Voight, Jane Fonda, Jack Nicholson, Ellen Burstyn, and myself. Yet, I would say definitely less than a third of the actors and actresses who work in America are Method-trained.

Can you say what it is that makes the difference?

Yeah, reality, honesty, truth. You're saying real things to each other. You may be portraying another person, but the lines you're speaking have meaning for yourself as well. There are a lot of actors who just act *per se*. English actors, for instance, are trained in a totally different way; they work on a character from the outside-in, and it's much more mechanical.

Have you ever felt so affected by another actor's style that you tried to imitate it?

Absolutely not! That's the most suicidal thing possible. I may look at someone's work and like what they do, but I never study it or copy. When I saw James Dean perform, I admired his power to communicate, but I would never have said, "The next time I do a scene in a car, I'm going to drive the car the way he did." No way. That would cut off everything I've been trained to do. It's the most destructive thing that could possibly happen to any artist on any level.

Do you feel it was a mistake to go off to Hollywood so early in your career?

The mistake was that I waited so long. It was a mistake to drive a cab for a year trying to get a two-line part in an Off-Broadway play when I'd already done two Broadway plays and one Off-Broadway, and nothing had happened. I couldn't get auditions and in the few auditions I did go to, I didn't get the part. There was no TV or film work to be had here anymore—the days of live television were over. So what do you do? You go where the work is.

*You acted in lots of Roger Corman B-movies, like **The Incredible Two-Headed Transplant**. Do you feel that was worthwhile as a training ground?*

Yes. We were acting in movies and whether they were grade-B or not...I've never believed in a "B"-movie. The only thing that makes a movie a B-movie is the size of the budget and therefore the trappings that go into making it—what's available to you and what isn't. But when they start rolling the cameras, whether it's with ten thousand dollars or ten million, you have a chance to act. And if you're real and honest and basic, the scene is going to come out real and honest and basic. It's only the director who is handicapped by the size of the budget; the actor is never handicapped by it. Good actors survive low budgets; they always have and they always will.

You've said something which fascinated me: you didn't realize acting was as much a business as it is. You thought that as a tal-

ented actor, you could play these small-budget parts, play them well, and then in getting recognition for them, get progressively bigger, better parts. But it didn't work out that way.

Well, so many actors just train, train, train. When they know they can really do good work, they wonder why people aren't hiring them. But they're not being hired because they're not being represented. You have to have an agent who believes in you, who loves you, who will fight for you—and I didn't have that for a long time. My agents fought for me, but on such a small level that it really didn't matter. It's all a question of the way you are—and this is a terrible word—but it's the way you are *sold*. How are you being presented to the buyer? That's the most important thing; it's not more important than training, but it's the most important thing about succeeding in the industry.

Everyone talks about the training of an actor, but no one talks about the marketing of one, and it's a fascinating area: why some make it, why some don't; how some make it, how some don't. We all know that people who are extremely talented often don't get the opportunities that people who aren't as talented do get. Why? And why did it take me twenty-three years while it took Warren Beatty a year and a half?

Well, now, if I were a talented actress starting out, how would I go about getting somebody to present me well? Is there a way to avoid getting stuck going nowhere?

You would just get *Equity* magazine or *Screen Actors Guild* magazine, look at a list of all the franchised agents in town, get a picture and a resume, and start knocking on doors. Everyone else does it and you'd have to do it the same way. When I tried, nobody would see me. I finally got one little woman to be my very first agent in 1958. She represented me for about a year and a half, and then I went on to somebody else, then on to somebody else. She was a very sweet lady, you see, but she was on such a small level; she couldn't get me any movies, she didn't know any movie people, and there was no live television being done. It was tough, yet you have to do that. And then you've got to progress from one agent to the next, unless that agent is really doing a good job for you. I've been with my present agent now for almost nine years, and he turned my career around.

How did he do that?

He made sure that I was presented in a different way than I had
ever been presented before. We went eighteen months with no
work at all.

*He made sure that you waited for a role which would significantly
expand your opportunities?*

That's right.

*You must have gone quietly crazy there during the time when you
were waiting for the right part to come along.*

I did. I don't like not working. I don't want to work on a movie or
a play every day, but I would like to be working many more weeks
in a year than not working.

*What did you do during that time? How did you manage to sup-
port yourself?*

My agent was paying me—my wife and I—giving us a certain
amount of money every month to hang in there.

And then the role you finally got was . . . ?

Silent Running.

Did you, during that time, doubt your talents?

No, but I wasn't sure that other people knew I was as capable of
as great a range as I knew I was. I think that's true of most actors;
people feel, "He can do that but he can't do this." About me, for
a while they used to say, "He can do everything but comedy."
Then *Smile* came out, and they said, "Well, all he can do is comedy." If you are a hot commodity as an actor, if your films make
money, then you can do anything; otherwise, you can hardly do
anything. It's as simple as that.

*And you think that principle of you're-only-as-good-as-your-last-
movie holds?*

No, I think you're only as good as your next movie. People like George Segal, Jimmy Caan, and Redford have built up a reputation and a following and a bankability that lets them go on and on. They certainly have abilities, but they've also been built up through magnificent marketing by their representatives.

Your problem was one of being typecast. You were always the hateful, violent psycho.

I've been typecast three times in my career. When a movie you do is hugely successful on a certain level, and a lot of people see it, they never forget that image you've created. For me, there were three times when that visual experience was never forgotten. The first time was in 1963 in an "Alfred Hitchcock Presents" episode; I played a very frightening itinerant worker and it got a lot of recognition. The second was *The Cowboys* in which I had to shoot John Wayne, and the third was *Black Sunday.*

What does a role have to have to lure you into playing it now?

Dimension, multi-dimension.

Do you actively look for roles to play? How does that work?

My agent does. I read anything that he sends me. If somebody sends him a script that they want me to do, and if they have money and if it's really going to be done, then I read it. I do not read scripts just to read scripts that aren't going to be filmed. It's too heartbreaking. I just can't do it anymore. I fall in love with something that will never come to be, and that's *extremely* cruel. I can understand that people who write scripts are eager and ambitious to get their pieces of material put on, but to send an actor something just to excite him, thinking that maybe then he can get it produced, is just heartless. And I object to that adamantly.

Are there only certain actors who are in a position to do that? To have their weight get the financing?

I am in a position to do that on a certain level, yes, but I am not really the person who can make it happen. I don't have two million dollars to put into a movie. I'm just trying to scrape together enough money to make my house payment.

Are there some types of roles that you feel you couldn't play?

Oh, I'm sure there are. There are certain performances I've seen, and once I've seen them, I realize I could never have gotten that far. For example, Bill Devane's portrayal of JFK on television was very real, because he sounded just like the guy, and I could never have done that; I could never have gotten that particular accent down the way he did.

And I don't know if I could ever do Shakespeare. I certainly don't think I'd be very good at it. I'd rather read Shakespeare than see it done or try doing it myself, and I'm not even thrilled about reading it. It's just not something that's ever turned me on.

But I do go through real bad periods of fear that someday they're gonna say, "Stop, you're finished, we don't have a part for Bruce Dern anymore," and that's real scary.

Part II

Returning to the stage after having spent nineteen years exclusively in movies, did you find there was a great difference in the acting requirements?

Yes, the overall discipline was greatly different. In the theatre, you need more strength, more energy. . . .

More courage?

No, I don't know that you do need more courage. I think that it's just as difficult to have a lens a foot from your face and maybe, in most instances, that's the more terrifying experience. But if that's what you've been doing for nineteen years and then suddenly you have a thousand faces ten feet away, it's equally frightening. Everybody says how courageous it was for me to have come back to the stage; only Jack Lemmon and Al Pacino, Bob Duvall, Stacy Keach and maybe one or two others have ever returned after having done film work. But to me, that's what acting is all about. I'd like to go back again before another twenty years are up, that's for sure.

What does a film assignment give a theatre actor, and what does a film actor get out of doing a play on stage?

Well, the theatre makes a film actor aware of his instrument which is something he hasn't been forced to use—his voice projection and all that. There's a sense of a line not being able to be repeated. On stage, an actor just has to go on living the life of his character straight through; he isn't able to cut and say, "Let's do it again, I did that wrong." That's the biggest thing. For a stage actor adjusting to film, it's learning the intricacies of letting the small things stand for themselves. In other words, having the confidence to do something on a small level and let it be seen by the camera. I think you can get away with things in the theatre that you can't in movies. You can cover up certain deficiencies with a kind of theatricality, you can be flamboyant, you can take off in different directions, you can hide certain faults, and yet you can't do that in film because the camera picks up *everything*.

People who work in one medium to the exclusion of the other are going to have trouble making the adjustment. But if they're really good actors, they can survive it. The bottom line is that if you're good, you're good.

Some people criticize film by saying it's more of a personality medium than an acting medium.

For certain actors and actresses it is. I don't think we're going to see John Wayne playing Sinclair Lewis, not that I'm better than he is, but just that he plays John Wayne. And thank God he does. He does it very well. There's a whole talent to being a personality on the screen. Bob Redford is a perfect example of a guy who started out as a personality and yet he's fought desperately in every film he's been in to be other than a personality, to be a character. There is an unfortunate charisma about him (not unfortunate for the audience, of course) that has built him into such a bonanza in the picture business. People say, "I just want to see Redford," but he's really a much better actor than that.

Many stage actors tell me they feel very much out of control in films because it's the director who decides which takes will go in and how the characterization will be built.

Well, it's true. But when that switch is turned on and the director yells, "Action!" you are in total control. And if the story is about your character, the editor will ultimately have to use what you do. So you just better never dog it, you better never have take two be worse than take one or take three—they've all got to be the best possible work you can do.

Do you have any difficulty doing take after take?

I do if the director is not specific about what he wants changed. That's tough. If he just says, "Well, let's try another," hell, I can try it twenty different ways, but if he doesn't tell me what he's looking for specifically, then it's difficult.

Do you like to work very closely with a director or do you like to work things out on your own?

I like to work closely.

And what makes a director a good director for you?

I suppose there are three things. I like someone who is constantly suggesting ideas and making me come up with things on my own, challenging me and allowing me to arrive at my own conclusions. I also like a director to embrace me, to embrace what it is that I do. By that I mean saying, "That's it, that's it; now just try this." And the key to it all, of course, is being verbally specific. Any director who is specific with me I love; anyone who isn't is a struggle.

So many actors today want to be directors. Why is that?

I myself would never want to direct a movie, but I can't blame them. It's out of the frustration of not getting enough work as actors. It's grinding down for movies, you know. The end is in sight.

You mean there are less and less movies made for higher and higher budgets?

Yup. And that pattern is going to continue. It's because of the box. People don't want to leave their homes to see movies and those who finance them aren't going to keep at it. In 1961 they made about 600 movies; in 1978, they made about fifty.

Are you under a lot of pressure when you're acting in a film?

There's definitely a lot less time to rehearse than there would be in a play, but a film is pressurized only because it has to be shot in a certain number of days. And some films are much more pressure than others. In *Coming Home* there was no pressure, *Black Sunday* and *Family Plot*, no pressure. With *Smile* there was enormous pressure.

Because it was a lower budget?

Yup. And *Silent Running* was the greatest pressure I ever worked under in my life.

Do you miss the sense of an audience when you're acting in films? Is there some sort of vitality that an audience gives you?

Well, you do have an audience to an extent. You've got forty or fifty workers around you all the time. They're a different kind of audience, but they're an audience.

Should an actor try to treat the camera as if it were another person?

No. I think the key to working in films is to be unaware of the camera. Only be aware of where it is—and then be unaware of it.

Does it bother you to act out of sequence?

Sometimes, but that's just something you have to put up with. There's no way that's going to change. I've never shot a movie completely in sequence, and I don't think anyone ever has, although people always try, or say they'll try, at the beginning. We tried, for instance, in *The King of Marvin Gardens*, but it never worked out.

When your performance in a film is good do you generally know it before you see the rushes?

You generally know it on the first day of shooting. You know from the script. If it's not there on the paper, it's not going to be there on the film. It can get better pictorially, or in certain small ways, but if it's not written well, it will never make a good film. The writing is the thing in the theatre and the writing's the thing in the movies. It's got to be there.

Do you enjoy watching your own performances on film?

I never believe those people who say they don't go to see their films. If it's so, then I don't know why they're actors. How can they learn or grow if they don't watch their mistakes? And if they can't stand to see themselves, why do they make *us* put up with it?

How would you compare the satisfactions of acting in the two mediums—stage and film?

I think, all things included, I get more from film. I had an unfortunate experience with this play in that it just didn't make it, so that, no doubt, colors my opinion. As the months go by, you get more out of a play; but ultimately, as a sum total, you get the most out of a film.

Why is it that movie actors so rarely do come back to the stage?

Fear. Economics. The crap-shoot of it. What I went through last week. I got what I would call unanimous rave reviews, with the exception of one critic, and yet, it's over. At least in a movie it's there forever. This play isn't there forever. After thirty-eight performances in New York and in Boston, only about 38,000 people will have seen it. You wish more could have seen it. I mean, you want to be seen. The rehearsal period is fine; you get a long time to do that in the theatre, but when the run is over, there's no more to it. I've grown as an actor from this experience with *Strangers* and I did just about all that I feel I would like to have done with the role. I'm sure if I played it a lot, I'd have found some new aspects to it, but under the circumstances it was an impossibility, so I've just got to let it go.

You can have the experience of working on a movie and not having many people see it, either.

That's the story of my life. I've never been in a movie that's made a profit. The greatest disappointment, of course, is *Coming Home*.

That's a disappointment?

Well, it's lost more money than almost any movie I ever made. No one went to see it; they did in New York and in L.A., but in San Francisco, where so much of the Vietnam protest movement began, it ran one week. The kids that went through it, who went to Vietnam or Sweden or Canada or burned their draft cards, the girls who had guys that went and came back wrecked, none of them want to see it; they don't want to see *The Deer Hunter*, either. That's why it's a disappointment. Not on the level of what we achieved—it's a cornerstone in my career, but. . .

Perhaps the Academy Awards will give that film another push?

I doubt it. I mean, I think Jon Voight will probably win as Best Actor, Jane Fonda might win as Best Actress*, but I certainly don't think I'll win.

Why not?

Well, because it's my first time out. I'm above the title in the movie and I think a lot of people are turned off by voting for someone in the supporting category who's above the title.

So you think there are unwritten rules that govern the voting?

There are no rules, but there should be. It *is* an injustice that I am in that category, but when there are two male performances in a film, and one guy appears in the movie much more than

*Jon and Jane did, in fact, win.

the other, then the second person automatically becomes the supporter.

*I've heard that you could have continued with **Strangers**, but decided not to. Was that because of your partially collapsed lung, or were there other factors?*

It was a number of things. When they put the closing notice up, I took it literally. No one told me it was a tradition in the theatre, no one told me it was provisional. The notice is very clear, and it said last Tuesday when we came to the theatre that we were closing on Sunday night, period; even though the notice was taken down, it gave me the option to leave. And that's what I took. I've been away too long from the movie business. It's been twenty-one months since I've worked on a film. And it was my feeling that the play wasn't going to get any better than it was.

You know, you were telling me how painful the character of Sinclair Lewis was for you to play—he goes through such a devastating breakdown in the course of the play that he ends up in a straitjacket. And I've been wondering: why do you do it then? What is it that makes you put yourself through that kind of turmoil?

That also, finally, took its toll on me and was another reason why I took advantage of the posting. I do it hoping to find a technique that will allow me to act but that won't tax me so much. In films you can do that because you don't have to act a traumatic part any more times than it takes to get the scene done; you can get it over with. But on stage, it's much more taxing. You have to become a wreck every night. I'm not cut out for that. For a short period of time, I can do it, but I certainly couldn't do it for six months.

In the theatre, though, there is a possibility that the role will be constantly changing—you may see something in the part on one night that you never saw before. Some actors have told me the audience has a great deal to do with that.

Absolutely. Some of the audiences knew who Sinclair Lewis was and some of them didn't. In the scene where he's giving his acceptance speech at the Nobel Prize ceremony, there were times when I felt, as I should have, that I was giving the speech to a room of 1,200 Swedes, but there were other times when I felt I was giving it to the audience at the Golden Theatre. And that's the difference between film and stage. In film, you're always giving it to the 1,200 Swedes, but in the theatre, sometimes those Swedes are a long way away, and you better give it to the people in the theatre or you'll never get to sleep.

But yes, new things do happen when you're playing a role night after night. And it was the slowing down of that process which made me disenchanted enough to stop. What I felt was that new things were not happening on a regular basis, and I . . . it frightened me.

What specifically did you learn from the experience of playing Sinclair Lewis?

The more I played it, the more tragic his life became to me. I learned much more about him than I learned about myself, but in learning about him, I opened up gaping chasms in my own personality, and I am trying to address myself to those in the future—the ways I deal with people, with my own work, with other people's work, and with criticism.

*Sinclair Lewis's family always felt that in his books—**Main Street, Elmer Gantry, Arrowsmith**—he was making fun of the kind of Midwestern, small-town people that they were. And you identified with his attempt to get his parents' approval. Was it cathartic to act out those experiences—even though they were painful to do? Did it purge you of those feelings in yourself?*

No, the pain is still there. I always wish that my Mom and Dad could see what it is that I've done, though they're both gone now. Whether it was my first performance or my ninth or my thirty-eighth, the feeling was just as strong. There's not a kid in America that isn't stuck with making somebody proud, you know. Including you.

Yes, but you're lucky as an artist to be able to transform those feelings into something very beautiful.

Everybody, I think, can do it in their own way, whether they're actors, or whether they're street vendors. It's all a matter of having pride in your work, of being a total professional at what you do. How much effort do you put into your work? Do you try every single day? I was doing all those performances with a partial collapse of my right lung, and I don't think the audience was even aware of it; it wasn't easy. I couldn't get my breath.

I'd like to talk to you about how you prepare for your roles— whether they be for the screen or the stage. What is generally the first thing you do upon being cast in a role?

The first thing is to read the script a number of times, yet I always work on putting the person together before I work on the piece itself. I start at the very beginning and build the character from the inside-out. I do extensive research and I make notes.

What kind of notes do you make? Do you ask yourself questions about the character's background?

There are certain questions I always start out with: Who am I? Where am I from? Where am I going? What do I want? What do other people think I want? What am I? And what do other people think I am? If I can answer every single one of those questions, I've usually got the basic skeleton of the person I'm trying to do.

I then compare myself to the character. I see what I have that fits him and what I don't have. And after I've decided what I don't have, I address myself to getting those things.

In the case of Robert Hyde, the character you played in **Coming Home**, *how did those comparisons stack up?*

Well, I said to myself, he is a man, he is 6'2" and weighs 172 pounds. There's no way I could change that. He's got blue eyes, a certain color hair. . . . And at this point in his life he's in the United States Marine Corps. That's where my experience began to fall short of his. I haven't been in the service or gone to Vietnam, so I had to do some research.

Did you talk to people who had fought in Vietnam?

Yes, I did, but I talked more to men and women who had gone through similar kinds of emotional breakdowns as Robert Hyde goes through, from mediums other than war. They were people who, whatever the cause, had felt that they didn't want to go on. And that was a big help to me.

The research, though, is just a doorway into the character, isn't it? You're still left with the problem of stepping through.

Absolutely. And Robert Hyde was one of the most difficult people for me to do that with, because I don't have particularly rigid morals or mores or convictions, which he certainly did.

How then do you go about duplicating those qualities when they're not normally a part of your personality?

You look for them somewhere inside yourself. You find, in this case, the inner rigidity that you feel toward certain things, even though they're other than what he felt rigid about. When I'm making the comparisons between us, I'm asking myself: what does the Marine Corps mean to him? And what does the Marine Corps mean to me? And then how do I bridge that gap? You see, the Marine Corps means nothing to me and it means something very strong and idealistic and rigid to him; so I must find something that evokes an equal response in me and then put that in the structure of his body. Therefore, we will both be talking about the same rigidity only it will have been arrived at in different ways.

And what was it that you felt you had a similar kind of feeling towards?

My feeling was that a lot of guys joined the Marine Corps in those years because they had a chip on their shoulder and an anger about something that had happened to them. They wanted to join an elite corps and be part of a winning team, a proud tradition, they wanted to be great Americans. There was a pride in the Marine Corps that made these guys feel they were part of something very, very special. And I feel that it's very, very special to get to the point where you have overcome difficulties in your life, where you can stand up and be counted, can look in the mirror everyday and say, "Goddamn it, I'm an actor and I really believe in what I'm doing. And no matter how hard you try to keep me from doing it, no matter how many different directions you send me in"—and this is in terms of my family—"I made it, and I'm here."

So you had a similar feeling towards the profession of acting as he did towards the Marines?

Yes, absolutely. But more than just acting, it was a commitment to the principles of truth: I am me, I am honest, I am honorable, I have integrity. This is who I am; when I cry, I cry; when I laugh, I laugh; when I get angry, I get angry. And yes, it's all those things put together.

Do you think that no matter what the gaps between you and the character are, you'll find something that will fill them from inside yourself?

You go as long and as hard as you can until it's time to do it. By then, they're either there or they're not. When it's time to roll the cameras or it's opening night, you can't say, hey, I'm not ready. Sometimes you get them all and sometimes you don't.

You've said that you work from the inside-out. But do certain external details sometimes help fill in a character for you? For instance, when your skin was made up to look as pitted and scarred as Sinclair Lewis's, did that give you a better sense of his physical awkwardness?

Yes, but all physical external things come from the inside anyway. I mean, my face as Sinclair Lewis is a perfect example. The guy had terrible acne, and that's an external thing, but how did he get the acne? He got it because of all his internal problems. He got it from his Mom and Dad, which is where we all get everything.

Do you feel sometimes that you're working from your subconscious?

Yeah, I'm not sure what it is that's in my subconscious, but I'm sure that I'm working with it all the time. Emotions take over sometimes and I'm not sure how I've come up with them.

What might an example of that be?

Well, during certain sections of the play, I'd start crying without knowing why. I knew why in the sense that it came out of the lines I was speaking, but I didn't know why I would cry at one performance and not at another, or in one situation and not in another. During the last two or three performances of the play, I found myself getting very weepy and teary when Sinclair Lewis picked up that book on American literature and started reading those criticisms of himself.

Do you ever learn much from reviews of your work?

I learn to have my heart broken again and again because I take them very personally.

That's something that I admire tremendously, the ability to stand up and be so vulnerable and risk such rejection as actors do. I wonder how an actor copes with that.

You never do. It cracks more than it doesn't. It's very tough. Not only are they saying "no" to you personally in bad reviews, but they're also saying "no" to you in the market place, and that's much tougher because it affects your ability to get that next job. The critic is just saying, "We don't like you," but the effect of it is to say, "We don't want you." Still, I've won a great many more than I've lost.

And there's no way to harden yourself against the bad ones? It never gets any easier?

It doesn't for me. I realize it's one man's opinion, but I got jumped on by a lot of reviewers for my performance in *Coming Home*, for example, and that hurt. I picked up a gun and pointed it at Jane [Fonda] in one scene, and since the last film they'd seen me do was *Black Sunday*, they thought, "Oh, there's Dern doing his thing again." It wasn't at all the same thing and that scene would not have worked if I hadn't done that. Very simple. They'd have loved it if any other actor had done it. Most people loved it anyway, but I'm just saying that there were a couple who nailed me. Nobody in this world can tell me that they aren't affected by criticism, negative and positive. I used to save reviews a few years ago, and I'd save the good ones with the bad ones—I'd save the *outrageously* bad ones with the good ones, that is. Now I don't save either. I guess that means I've matured.

Is there anything you do in between roles to be prepared? Do you find yourself creating a fund of references from various observations of people around you? From memories which surface?

Yes, yes absolutely. I'm a people-watcher. I'm an observer, an astute student of the human condition. Not sociologically, but individually. I would say Jane Fonda, for example, is a sociological observer. She looks at things in groups and in classes and in bunches: this group of people, that group, them, their. I'm never concerned with anything but him or her.

Do you find that other arts feed you—going to museums and concerts and. . .

Boring, boring. I can't get through a museum. A natural history museum I can, but not an art museum. I like things that come direct from reality.

Do you do any kind of acting exercises to keep yourself from getting rusty between roles?

Sure. I may take the part of a character and play him for two or three hours during a day, just out in my general life. I'll go to the store or drive my car in town as somebody else. Different things like that.

When you're feeling some sort of strong emotion in your private life, do you ever find yourself taking note of it, and saying, "I have to remember how this feels"?

No. I'm just a bottle of emotions; I'm a great romantic, and I get emotional over absolutely everything, so. . .

Does the process of acting drain any of that off?

Acting doesn't use it up, no. With me, there's always more emotion.

Is acting generally easy for you, or is each role a struggle?

Acting is easy and each role is a struggle. Acting itself is the easiest thing in the world, but learning to act is the hardest. Learning how to be a Method actor, learning how to do it well and correctly, is very, very hard. Doing it, once you know how, is easy because you're just behaving a real life.

You've trained as an athlete and you still do a lot of running. Is there a relationship between acting and sports?

No, I don't think so. There is for me only in my own head, only in the way I go after goals and the terms I use when speaking—I look upon my career as you would look upon a ball player's career. But otherwise, there's no real correlation. In sports, your productivity as a growing athlete—in terms of bettering your scores and your time—is quite limited by age. I am now forty-two and I look forward to getting better and better; there's no such thing as being over the hill for an actor as there is for an athlete.

What is your goal as an actor? What would you consider an ultimate achievement?

I think that I'm still in the constant struggle to become a pure artist as an actor. I probably will never accomplish that in my lifetime, no one ever has, to my knowledge, because to be a pure actor in a play, one hundred percent of the time, you have to do two-and-a-half hours of absolute moment-to-moment behavior. That means that every moment, every breath is absolutely real, nothing is calculated, and nothing is put forth for the audience. You are really the character, you are really the person.

How close do you feel you've come?

I would say that in my work I am up to the forty-percent level, yes, I would say that four out of ten moments are pure. I've never

seen more than about fifty or sixty percent ever. That's not a
knock, it's just the state of the art. I mean, what artist ever says,
"That's one hundred percent"?

Is acting a creative or an interpretive art?

Creative.

*That's interesting because most people I've talked to have said it
was interpretive.*

No way. Not for me. I'm not interpreting, I'm creating—a life.
I'm not sitting back and looking at a life. My feeling is that when
it becomes interpretive, you're not really doing it. Then you're
doing what the word says, you're "interpreting" what you feel
about something, and you're a step removed. The character of
Robert Hyde in *Coming Home* is a creation. He's nothing until
he's brought to life by me—or by whoever plays him. So isn't that
creation, when something is nonexistent and then suddenly it's
alive? Moving?

*And you're saying that if another person had acted that part, it
would have been an entirely different part?*

Absolutely.

*A lot of people say their first responsibility is to the writer and
that they're only interpreting his or her creation.*

All the scriptwriter is doing is giving you the words and the circumstances. He's not bringing the character to life; he's only
bringing him to life on the paper. If what you're saying is true,
then why was *The Great Gatsby* not a successful film? There's
never been a book that's been more widely read by a certain
kind of culture in America, and yet it can never become a film
and work successfully because everybody has his own interpretation of the title character. The poor actor that is saddled with
playing Jay Gatsby is stuck with 220 million ideas of who he was
and what he did. He can never fulfill all those; he has to find the
character for himself—he has to create the role. But Fitzgerald

never intended that role to be anything but interpreted. When it was created, it suffered. And that's not a knock at Robert Redford, because he did a good job at it. But it's an almost impossible hurdle for an actor to handle. And it's an illustration of the difference between creation and interpretation.

You consider what the scriptwriter gives you to be just a sketch, a suggestion of the character.

That's right. I have to think about what makes him do all the things that he does which the writer never gets into. That way, you get a full embodiment of the person. When you get a script, all you have are words and a description of the physical characteristics of the person—that he's so tall, he looks baggy, whatever. And the rest is up to you. If an actor just played what was on the paper, then we would basically get John Wayne, Clint Eastwood, Clark Gable—we would get the personality of the star and not the human being. The star is a human being, too, of course, but his personality doesn't vary a lot from role to role.

This is not to say that you can do without the writer, because the screenplay—the structure, the story, the dialogue—is monumental. But at the same time, the writer should never overdescribe what the actor is to do in terms of behavior. The actor must arrive at that himself.

One last question: when you sign for your next role, will you be nervous? Do you generally worry about how you'll do?

Get nervous to do a role? No way, José. I'm nervous when they don't sign me. I've never once in my life been nervous acting.

How wonderful to find that thing in life that you just want to do so much.

Well, that's what it's all about.

ESTELLE PARSONS

Estelle Parsons is an agent's nightmare. The winner of an Academy Award, two Off-Broadway Obies and two Tony nominations, Ms. Parsons could easily have had a glamorous career in the spotlight of show business. Instead, she has consistently chosen those roles which interest and challenge her over those more lucrative and prestigious offers.

She was born on November 20, 1927 in Marblehead, Massachusetts. From the age of about eight, Ms. Parsons wanted to be an actress, but her family, which traces its Puritan ancestry back to the *Mayflower*, felt that a life in the theatre would be too troubled and difficult. And although she acted with the local community theatre throughout her childhood, her father (a lawyer) and mother (a court stenographer) steered her into the more traditional academic fields. In 1949 she graduated from the Connecticut College for Women with a degree in political science and spent a summer harvesting crops in England with the Women's Land Army. She returned to attend Boston University Law School, but quit in dissatisfaction after the first year. When she ran for a seat on the Marblehead Planning Board, she became the first woman and youngest person ever elected to it. Still not quite happy, however, she struck out for New York City to try her luck singing with bands.

She was hired to sing with Jerry Herman's first revue and with several others offered by Julius Monk. During the day she worked at NBC as the original *Today Show* "girl" alongside then-host Dave Garroway and a chimpanzee known as J. Fred Muggs. It was there she met her husband, Richard Gehman, a magazine writer; but several years after the birth of her twin daughters, the marriage ended in divorce.

Ms. Parsons left NBC, and appeared a short time later on Broadway as a reporter in the musical, *Happy Hunting*, which starred Ethel Merman. She went on to a number of other musicals, yet it wasn't until she appeared in her first serious stage drama, *Mrs. Dally has a Lover*, that she received major recognition. For her work in the title role of that two-character play, Estelle Parsons received a Theatre World Award;

and the following season, in the Absurdist drama, *Next Time I'll Sing to You*, she won her first Obie as the Best Actress in an Off-Broadway play. Since then she has appeared Off-Broadway in *The Threepenny Opera*, *The Automobile Graveyard*, *In the Summer House*; with the Lincoln Center Repertory Company in *East Wind, Galileo, People Are Living There*; and on Broadway in, among others, *Malcolm, Seven Descents of Myrtle, A Way of Life, And Miss Reardon Drinks a Little*, and *Miss Margarida's Way* (for which she won the Drama Desk Award). She has recently directed a theatre piece, *Voices*, about the thoughts and emotions of five women who differ in age and circumstance.

For the film *Bonnie and Clyde*, Ms. Parsons won an Oscar as the year's Best Supporting Actress, playing Blanche Barrow, Clyde's sister-in-law and the grudging member of his outlaw gang. She received an Oscar nomination for her portrayal of Calla, the repressed lesbian schoolteacher who befriends Joanne Woodward in *Rachel, Rachel*, and has appeared in films such as *I Never Sang for My Father, Watermelon Man*, and others.

Estelle Parsons lives at the same unfashionable Upper West Side Manhattan address that she did before becoming well known; it's a building with no doorman and a mailbox labeled simply "E. Gehman." Her small living room is cluttered with books and plants and obviously lived in by someone with a taste for comfort and simplicity. Her daughters now grown, she shares the premises with a lawyer-boyfriend, fourteen years her junior.

On the day of this interview, Ms. Parsons was suffering from jet lag, having just flown in from Hawaii where she had acted in an amateur production of *Macbeth*. ("I'll do Shakespeare for cab fare," she has said.) Though obviously exhausted, her voice slow and nasal, she was nonetheless clear in her thinking, emphatic, and had a quick, warm grin. At first worried about over-cooking the chicken soup she had simmering, she finally decided it was under control, and flopped onto the couch, pulled up her knees and began to talk. It soon became clear why Estelle Parsons has been called "the female Harry Truman."

I understand that you first started in a community theatre at the tender age of four. Do you remember the first time that you experienced your power as an actress?

Yes, that happened when I was about eight or nine and I was doing a play called *The Bird's Christmas Carol*. The girl is crippled and she dies at the end—on Christmas.

That's a surefire way to move an audience!

I could hear the pocketbooks opening and the handkerchiefs coming out for all the people to do their crying at the matinee. It was a revelation to me.

It seems unlikely that with your New England background and your parents in law and the courts, you would go into something as emotional as acting.

I didn't really start professionally until I was in my thirties. I started in musicals in 1957, when I was just thirty, so you see, it took a long time for me to really get around to it. And then I actually began acting in 1962. I was thirty-four when I played my first role.

Does being a commentator and reporter for television have anything in common with being an actress? Did it prepare you in any way?

No, it's completely different. In television you develop yourself as a personality, and in acting, I think that's precisely what you *don't* want to do. You don't want to set any boundaries, and that way, you can express a wide range of qualities. I think people who set boundaries don't tend to be the best actors. They decide they're a certain personality, they wear their hair a certain way, have a particular locket, and a certain style of clothes. But that sort of person isn't very adaptable as an actress; she tends to continue to play herself. Most very good or great actors, I think, are sort of indefinable as people; they don't have very hard edges.

When you worked in musicals, you apparently got a lot of encouragement to continue. Why did you decide against it?

Broadway musicals aren't awfully interesting. I guess they would be if you really were interested in singing or dancing and you got a chance to do solos. But for a person who basically *acts*, who deals with the emotions, they're very stylized and constricting and not ultimately very rewarding. They have no great depth.

So you don't think that musicals contributed at all to your later work as an actress?

Well, it's an entirely different form, but everything helps. When you get to the classics or verse drama, which are, so to say, musicals without music, you have to have a very good sense of external work: of rhythms, of being loud and soft, and all that. It tends to get in the way when you're doing naturalistic drama, but it's good to be able to do, and it's valuable to know how to exploit all the aspects of the theatre.

What attracted you to the fields of singing and acting? Why did you choose those over another career, like law, which you started to pursue?

Acting seemed to be more interesting than anything else. I'm not sure it's true right now, but if one had to make a living at all, it seemed to be the more interesting way to do it. And I didn't have anything else that I particularly liked doing. There aren't an awful lot of areas open in which a woman competes with women and not men. I never had any desire to compete with men, as in law, since, you know, it's a losing battle. Acting seemed to be the one thing which was both absorbing and where the competition would be only with other women. And I never had anything to say on my own. I would have preferred to be a writer, would have preferred something I could have done at home. But there wasn't anything accessible that I really wanted to do. For a woman anyway, jobs are bounded by the hours spent, and I had worked in various menial jobs where everything seemed to revolve around hours. Acting just made the hours pass more quickly than anything else.

You seem to be expressing a certain dissatisfaction. Do you feel you made the wrong choice?

Well, I genuinely liked it when I was very young. I liked singing and expressing myself that way because I didn't find real life and social activities very interesting. But ideally, I would have preferred to do a lot more than act. I was never really that interested in acting *per se*; I was interested in the theatre, in the whole process, the group activity, actors working together. And since I was interested in more of a peer-group process than exists in the theatre, I have never found it ultimately satisfying. I've never been able to create the conditions in which it would be. But I'm always working on that, trying to figure out what really would be satisfying and how to achieve it.

Getting back to those days of decision, then, how did you get involved with the Actors Studio? Were you attracted to the particular kind of training that was being offered there?

Well, I read in the paper that all of the best people were working there, and so I thought that would be the best place to go. At that time, all the directors and the actors were there; this was before everybody went to California. And there was TV in New York and more work in the commercial theatre, so I decided to try to get in. I just started auditioning and eventually was accepted. But no, I wasn't looking to pursue any particular kind of training.

Do you think good acting is a matter of good teaching?

No, I don't think you can really teach anyone to be a creative artist. You're either born with some talent or you're not, and training does not necessarily have anything to do with making you better. If you look at creativity in writers, actors, any kind of artist, their final product is not necessarily better than their first. I mean, Marlon Brando in *A Streetcar Named Desire* was probably as good as he'll ever be. Certainly, after four years of training, you don't become a better actor. Training, to an artist, is just irrelevant. It's a personal process—you want to develop yourself in certain ways and you pinpoint your problem areas. But to say that you are going to be taught to do good work is absurd. It's all a matter of creativity, time, and place.

Is there no reason to go to a school at all?

The whole purpose behind all that professional training is to be with the people who are doing the hiring and get yourself seen and known. At the time that I went to the Actors Studio, there was no way to meet people except through taking classes, and I think that's why most people took them. It was just to keep working out, keep your hand in, your stuff fresh.

This is something new where people think they can go to school to learn to be an actor. And even so, I don't know that it's any different now; I think that people go to Yale because they think that's where the good playwrights are, that's where the real biggies have slid into professional situations, where they've gotten a lot of attention both in the press and commercially. So the schools are probably still just a way to be seen and known.

Then you don't consider yourself a Method actress as Lee Strasberg teaches it at the Actors Studio? You don't make use of Stanislavsky's observations on acting?

I've never been able to read any of those Stanislavsky books, so I don't know. Acting to me is a living. I was trained in the theatre as a kid, doing amateur productions, so by the time I got around to Lee. . . .

But do you try to make an inner connection between the character that you play and the person that you are, do you make use of your memories to find feelings that are similar to your character's?

No, no; I don't try to do that. I just try to interpret the character that the playwright has written and then in repeating the role over and over, certain emotional experiences come to mind which make it more personal. But that's a process that happens by itself.

Then if a character has a particularly grievous moment, let's say, you wouldn't reflect back on your own experiences to try to relate that emotion to one you might have felt?

Usually, it's not necessary. For a person like me—and I suspect for anyone who is any good—the material itself is inspiring enough to create its own emotions. In doing it, your own life will filter into it and you'll have both. I think if you're insecure as an actor, or if the material is not too good, you rush for something familiar in order to be sure you'll be able to function. But as soon as you've worked a little while and you lose that insecurity, as soon as you have some faith in your own talent, then I don't think you need to do those things.

And if a character had experiences entirely different than your own, you wouldn't feel there was a problem in playing her?

No-o. It doesn't come naturally to play characters that are far removed from you so it's good to try. Sometimes you succeed and sometimes you don't. But it's all a matter of working at the material in the style of the production.

Is psychoanalysis an important tool for an actor?

Yes, I think therapy is more important than training. More than anything else, you should be aware of yourself and be able to function physically and emotionally in some free way. The general run of actors is bound to be neurotic in this day and age, particularly in this country where the profession is not very highly regarded or esteemed. It's all right to be an English actor, but if you're an American, it's not really accepted. So it's important to gain as much self-awareness as you can. Training will probably only cover up your problems, your faults, your insecurities, and that never is any good for ultimate interpretation or creation. You want to be able to invest more and more of yourself in the work, not use it to cover yourself up.

What would you do if you were presented now with a good play and decided to accept a part in it; what would your first piece of business be?

The best thing to do is to read it aloud. Usually, I get a good sense from reading it. I try to question or refine my responses and then go where they lead. If it's an historical character, I do a lot of reading. I get more inspired by that than by the text itself—in the text, it's the character who provides the inspiration, not the words. If there are technical, physical things that are required, I'd work on those; if the part is very demanding vocally, I would work on that; if an accent is needed, I would start preparing for it. So you see, I don't have any set pattern that I follow.

Do you make notes about the character?

No, I don't. Sometimes I try to get a visual image of the character, but I am never really able to do that either.

You were saying that you stick with the text and the emotions which arise out of the character's particular situation. But do you ever extrapolate from the text and try to imagine what sort of parents the character had, what kind of childhood or whatever?

I just go wherever the material leads me. If I start thinking about those things during the rehearsal period, they probably have something to do with the creating of the character and I'll pursue them. But it's only certain kinds of material that require an understanding of an earlier life. Some plays are involved with what goes on before and after the events on stage, and others are involved only with the events themselves.

*Could you tell me how you prepared the character of Blanche Barrow in **Bonnie and Clyde**?*

Since that was a movie role, it was altogether different. There is no real creation of characters in a movie because a movie script, if it's any good, is just so accessible that the acting of it will happen spontaneously. A play is different in that way; you can't just pick up a good play and act it the same night. But I had a lot of time before I did that film. I did a lot of research in the library about the people, the time, the real events, the Bonnie-and-Clyde story. I don't know if it was beneficial, but it gave me a good deal of confidence. Knowledge like that may be useful in choosing clothes and working out customs, but there is no real preparation for movie work except to just be spontaneous. That's really the most important thing for an actor: to invest himself in the moment. There's an awful lot of real behavior, individual behavior in films, a great freedom in the moment, and that's the essential thing for an actor to cultivate.

Does that "real behavior" have much to do with the way we be-
have in real life?

It's just the opposite of real life where we attempt not to be too
terribly involved in momentary activities. For instance, whether I
like you or don't like you, whether I like that photographer sitting
there or not—is more or less unimportant. But if we were in a play
or a movie, those feelings are the feelings that would be important
to the audience. In real life there's no need to give them freedom—they're irrelevant; but in a play, one has to be acutely involved in them.

So the best preparation is to achieve a state of mental "pre-
paredness," an ability to be spontaneous. Is that a matter of re-
laxation?

Preparedness is more a matter of openness and concentration
than relaxation, I think. It's being receptive, being prepared to
accept anything. If you are a closed person, you have to get rid of
the blocks. To me, relaxation means a certain lethargy, a lax-
ity—I would think you can be very relaxed and very blocked at
the same time.

But if you're relaxed, your blocks, or your defenses, are supposed
to melt away.

People keep trying to put it into words, but it's all an enigma.

Yes, these words like "openness" and "receptivity"—these are
things one associates with religion or mysticism.

It has to do with inspiration, I think. If a piece of material inspires
you, then you're prepared to play it. Many times when you begin
analyzing what inspires you, you wring it dry. It turns into an intellectual exercise. To function out of inspiration is the best kind
of functioning. Frankly, if you have to take a lot of jobs that have
no inspiration, I think you should give it up. However, you do
have to take jobs to earn a living so that you *can* do the work that
inspires you. But to plan a life without inspiration, that's another
language entirely; I don't see why anyone would want to do it. For

starters, it's too difficult a life. If you're not going to get the ultimate rewards from doing brilliant, inspired work, then I don't
know what the point is. I suppose the alternative is to work purely
for money; that's what television is about and that's a whole different world.

*You once said something that really intrigued me: when you're
working on a character, the aspects that give you the most difficulty eventually give you the greatest thrust into the character.*

Yes, there always seem to be textual things, lines that the character expresses that don't seem to come out of her mouth as
you've envisioned her. I find myself wondering, "How am I ever
supposed to get to that line and how does that fit into this whole
being?" There are always parts of the personality that are less accessible than others.

*And you find that something out of character is generally a clue to
a greater complexity of character?*

Very often. I always hate to cut material early on. I think there's a
very definite scheme of working that should be utilized but never
is. I think actors should have an opportunity to do their work before a director directs, before the director even appears, because
a director is always an inhibiting figure. Sometimes he's inhibiting in a good way, but acting is a painful process and actors are
always willing to let the director make the decisions—that's bad.
Good directors don't make the decisions and then, of course,
actors start complaining because the director *hasn't* made them.
Ideally speaking, actors should do a lot of work with the material
before the director steps in. That way, the director has only to fit
all these characters into the proper environment. Chances are, if
the actors have got their work properly done, he probably won't
even have to do much of that. But we don't really have an opportunity to work that way in the theatre; very often, I work on characters that I'm interested in at the Actors Studio and have them
more or less ready when the rehearsal period arrives.

*But you do look to the director to edit your work then, to decide
which of the many possibilities of playing the character fits in best
with the whole scheme?*

For me, a good director is someone who leaves me alone; I think I can ultimately judge by the audience and by the situation of a performance what is best to use. I like extremely fluid situations in performance. I don't understand people who want to set every single aspect and then execute it; that's not my idea of fun. I like everything to be fluid and fresh and new and spontaneous—an occurrence of the moment. I like to try new things every night; sometimes they succeed and sometimes they don't, but I can *tell* what is right or not right for myself. That certainly is the best way for an actor to work: to just try everything. It's so rare to find these situations except perhaps on a very small scale in amateur productions. It's hard to do, and it often needs encouragement— that's where a director should step in. Because acting is a painful and exposing experience, actors tend to want to do very little; they really need a lot of pushing and stimulation to go further; it's just reflexive to want to stop when it gets hard. So I think the role of a director is to be encouraging in that way. These days, the kind of directors we have in the theatre are not awfully important or useful to a production. And I, for one, don't like directors.

There is, however, a need for some kind of leadership in piecing the parts of a play together. Without a director how would you arrive, peacefully, at a unified concept?

If we had a theatre where actors got together and worked on the text, a natural sort of leadership would evolve out of the characterizations themselves; what was required for the play would develop on its own. It's something different from what we know of now as the director-actor relationship, but if that sort of work could be done, we would come out with a better result for the audience. Now, with the union setting rules of rehearsal time— seven hours here, eight hours there, *one* director and a bunch of actors—you just go in and present yourself to the director. But the director can't do your work for you, and what you end up with lots of times is the director's performance. I really balk at that, but it seems to be what occurs more often than not.

*When you directed your own theatre piece, **Voices**, did you try to just provide encouragement, and stand aside to let the actors do their work?*

I tried to do that, yes. I tried to be the kind of director that I would want, but I frankly didn't find it too successful. I had the impression that they wanted to be directed and were more interested in their next job than in creating the ultimate character in the work we had. With jobs being what they are and lack of security being what it is, that's probably inevitable and true of everybody in the American theatre. But I felt they had their eye on themselves in the acting profession and were dedicated to creating the character that was written, as you would in an ideal circumstance. I was surprised at their unwillingness to move away from themselves into strong characterizations. We were all just very much involved with where we were going to get the next job and hopefully it would be a movie job and anyway, if you play yourself, you're a lot better off than if you play a character. There's not a lot of work for people who want to play characters; they tend to stay at a very low-income level and low-profile level. So, if you play yourself, you're going to get further ahead and ultimately be much more successful.

Do you think it's that cult of personality which makes the climate for acting in this country particularly bad?

I think that, yes. Also it's because we don't have the opportunity to do really good *theatre* work. Almost everything is naturalistic, so when you ask an American actor to move away from him- or herself, to really make a leap into another character, it's something we don't have the facility to do. We just don't have a wide experience. If you could play a Restoration comedy one month and Shakespeare another month and T.S. Eliot another month and Arthur Miller another month, you would have a much greater facility to handle a larger scope of material. The fact is that this month you're going to have to do a TV commercial, next month you're going to have to play a part on a TV show, the third month you're hoping to get a job in a movie, and in the fourth month you may get a routine Broadway job.

So to get back to the idea of training, being a good actor is not a matter of schooling, it's actual work in front of an audience?

That's right; it's life experience on a stage in various styles of theatre. You can have all the training in the world in those classics at a college but it isn't going to really broaden you; what you need is an opportunity to play these things over and over, and play them with some confidence and some freedom.

It must be difficult to feel that freedom, though, in a professional situation with a rehearsal period set at four weeks—as it so often is in the theatre.

There's no way a group of people can get together and get to know each other and come out with a good product in four weeks. Unless it's Neil Simon or something that's just so accessible and superficial, and even then, I don't know.

The longest workshop period seems now to be settled at eight weeks, and that's good; it's twice better than four weeks. But if you're going to have a good product, you shouldn't have that pressure; you should have the pressure of the piece itself and not the day-to-day countdown toward opening night. American Conservatory Theatre has a workshop program where they tried to do *Miss Margarida's Way*. I rehearsed that play for seven weeks. They were given four; they weren't ready but they had to do it anyway. I mean, how is that a workshop?

A young actor's freedom is necessarily limited too, I imagine, by having an eye on what the critic is going to say.

It's very bad that critics now go to regional theatres and regional theatre reviews end up in *The New York Times*. I mean, everything is just encroaching on the actor's ability to function. The actor can only really function in a situation where he feels he can be free to *find out* what the piece is all about. Given the time to do that, and a director who can encourage him, and a facility in dealing with various kinds of material, you'd have a much better theatre than you have today.

You tend to play very emotionally confused, tense, hysterical women. Why do you like those particular parts?

I don't particularly like them, you see, but I have trouble getting cast in the things I really do like. The roles I've played have not been terribly interesting to me, but they were the best that was offered; I just had to be satisfied with them. I attempt to peddle things that I'm interested in, but I've had no success with that whatsoever because I guess I'm not particularly commercial. I end up doing pieces that seem to have some validity to me— which probably means that they have the seeds of their own failure—but at least they're interesting. Broadway fare is not interesting to me. So many of the things I read I have no interest in, and yet they turn out to be quite successful.

I'm surprised that winning the Oscar didn't give you greater opportunities in terms of roles.

I don't think I've turned down any roles that would have been terrific for me. Whenever a part comes along on Broadway, if it's something interesting, I get to do it, but there is no classical theatre, and I hardly ever see anything money-making that I want to do. I'm not terribly interested in the theatre as it is. I mean, I don't go an awful lot. I'm interested more in music, concerts, individual performers.

As a spectator, what would make you feel satisfied coming out of a theatre? What should the theatre be giving the audience that it isn't now doing?

I think the essential ingredient is that it should be alive. It should be a communion of souls in the same way as religion. Nowadays, you go to church and you're turned into a zombie by a sermon or service; the same thing is happening in the theatre.

For instance, the theatre today is full of microphones. In *The Act*, Liza Minnelli decides she wants to get up and do a nightclub routine which is beyond human endurance, so she lip-syncs the songs in order to get through the evening eight times a week. That's got nothing to do with a sense of human communication— nothing to do with theatre. The minute you're miked you've lost theatre because there's no way to have communication if someone's voice is coming out of a box and you're sitting there watching. More and more theatres have mike systems now. They are so big that you've definitely lost the sense of soul-to-soul contact. A theatre has to be a space that is capable of human activity; and more and more theatres, even at the universities, even on tour, have twelve hundred, fourteen hundred seats. Pack them all in, get as much money as possible, and give them a lesser product. But that's the commercial theatre and I suppose that any good work is always done in a smaller space with less financial remuneration. That's where you have a theatrical experience—in a small space.

Would you say there's a dearth of good writing and an excess of actors?

No, I think that there's a dearth of material that would weed out the good from the bad. If we had some kind of classical tradition we would have better work. If we had actors who had to come up with something other than their street activities; if they had to really play serious stuff on the stage; if the epitome of our theatre was great classical performances, we'd have something by which to judge, and we'd have a different respect for actors. Dancers and opera singers have to be able to do what they do. But we have this naturalistic theatre where if you can do something in the street, you can do it on stage. Look at Liz Swados with her bunch of nontalented teenagers in *Runaways*. Everybody gets up and applauds them because they are kids on Broadway. I mean, we are just going from non-theatre to non-non-theatre, to the point of absurdity.

Acting is the kind of thing that people have a fling at, which is why nobody can make a living at it. It's just the pits. I think it's terrible that there's no responsibility to talent in this country. Anyone who's acting as an indulgent diversion is just as acceptable as somebody who's making a life work of it. I don't know what can be done about that, but what it means is that people who want to dedicate their lives to it don't have the opportunity to do so. There is not a living to be made by being a really good interpretive theatrical artist. There just isn't.

Have you always felt this discouraged about the acting profession? Is this a matter of today's mood, or is it something you've felt for a long, long time?

I'm not discouraged about the theatre, but it's gone steadily down—it's in a down phase now. I think it will go up again. There

are times in history when there is a need for it, and as far as opportunities for actors are concerned, it's all a matter of fate,
luck—the time, the place, the rhythms of society.

*Are there any films being done today which give you that sense of
"communion" you were referring to?*

I get that experience, and I don't really know why, from Euro-
pean movies—French movies. For two or three days afterwards,
I'll walk around with a sense of being part of something, a sense
of identification. They're just made that way. They tend to be
more involved with human problems; they combine a certain artistry with their commercialism.

What particular movies are you thinking of?

Oh, *Hiroshima*, *Mon Amour*, the movies directed by Chabrol and
by Lelouch. They're not, I suppose, terribly deep, but they do
tend to expand a human horizon. The takes are longer; there are
more frames in the close-ups. (What made Marlene Dietrich a
legend, for example, was that her close-ups lasted longer.) That
allows you a more profound relationship with the people in the
films. It's not what is generally felt to be a proper attention span
in this country, where everything is just glossed over so quickly.

And your main interest now is in doing classical parts?

Yes, what I really love is Shakespeare and the classics and if I
could spend a life involved with them, I would do it. But there's
simply no opportunity in this country to earn a living and do the
classics.

I just went to Hawaii and did *Macbeth* with an amateur group.
They asked me to come but if I'm going to do more of that, I'm going to have to solicit all of these minor festivals where I may or
may not earn any money, where they may or may not take me,
and where the union may or may not let me work. The union
denied me permission to do *Macbeth*; they said I was taking a job
away from an amateur, and there's a big brouhaha about it now.
I went to this island of forty thousand people that has no professional theatre and never had a Shakespeare production . . . the

union's objection was ludicrous, you see. It was very meaningful for these people that I was there; the attendance was three times greater than it had ever been. They had never seen Shakespeare before. Besides, I have asked every director that I can get in touch with to do the classics. I've not had any offers. At the same time, I'm told that a theatre in Long Beach is staging *Antony and Cleopatra*—which is the play I particularly want to do—with Diana Rigg and Alan Bates. Every single available job here is given to some English actor. You see, in terms of personal artistic achievement, it's just a dead end.

Don't you feel limited working with an amateur production? Can you get much satisfaction from that?

Oh, yeah. With certain kinds of material I couldn't, but Shakespeare is so full and the characters are so big that they just can't help but respond to one another. I might be happy doing anything with an amateur group, but really, they were dreadful. They couldn't do it. Yet it didn't inhibit my work. There is just so much to be done in the classics; it's such a challenge that the people around you don't matter that much.

What do you look for in a role? What makes you say yes to a particular script that's presented to you?

A psychological soundness, I think, is the most important thing. I'm not very good at contrived characters, or characters who are merely devices for the plot. Shakespeare is terribly sound psychologically, although that's actually irrelevant there because it's so theatrical and story-fied that all that psychological stuff is really just intellectual rumination. It's not necessary to be involved psychologically with Shakespeare's characters because they just work: if you offer yourself to them, they call themselves forth.

How do you feel generally about the parts that are available to women? There seems to be a flock of new movies with women characters who are actually friends with each other.

Well, *The Turning Point* with Anne Bancroft and Shirley

MacLaine is the only one I saw, and all it showed was that women were as big fools as men have always written about them. That seemed to me like Hollywood hokum with no insights into anyone. I mean, both those characters were absolutely addlepated, and I don't think they are fooling anyone but themselves and *The New York Times*. No, there is certainly not enough deep thought and writing done about the lives of women, and while there's all this talk about new, creative female roles—where are they?

I read an interview with you several years ago where you described yourself as an artistic revolutionary.

Really? Oh, my God. I said that?

It was in reference to a Che Guevara poster you had up. Someone asked you why you had a picture of Che.

Yes, well, I had posters of Bob Dylan and Che Guevara here but I took those down quite a while ago. When my children reached their teens I thought I should really provide them with a sort of conventional home atmosphere. So I called in a friend who was a decorator and tried to make this place look like a home instead of where I lived. But what I meant by that phrase was that I don't like to create a formula and then live by it or function out of it. And in the commercial theatre I think that's what's essential. It's like in anything else that's commercial—you have a product and that's what you sell. I am not interested in that. As a person I am always looking for new experiences and always trying to keep the doors open to new things.

At the time I said that, I was having a great deal of trouble finding my own way of expressing myself. It's very hard in the theatre when you are working in a group. It gets so much more complicated than if you are one person doing something alone; in a group process you never know how much is you and how much is the pressure of the group. How much of your ideas are you getting from the group or from the material you are working with; what is inhibiting your behavior and what is furthering it. It's all so complex and that was at a time when I was very much trying to find myself. Without my knowing it, however, my problem really involved the material I was working on which did not in any way inspire my expression. As I say, it was always the best of a bad lot.

What I'm inspired by are the classics and there's no way to do them if you've got to support yourself at the same time.

I was not brought up in an atmosphere that nurtured art for it-self. I had a need to earn a living. Perhaps I didn't. I mean, maybe I could have said to my family, "Look, I want to be this artist and I will need to be supported all my life." For all I know, they might have said, "Well, let's find a way to do that." But, of course, I did not wish to be supported by my family. I wanted to make my own way. So, I always had to temper what I wanted to do with what was available and what would earn a living for me— and then I had two kids to support. Now, I probably could have said to my parents or my sister, "Take my children," but I didn't want to do that either. So, you see, there's always been a struggle to maintain some kind of artistic standards in the midst of all this.

Do you feel that your approach to acting and the theatre has changed over the years?

No. As a matter of fact, I don't think so at all. I was really ap-palled when I directed this piece that I seemed to be instinctively wanting to function in a way that my director had functioned when I was a little kid. It really surprised me a lot that I hadn't developed more sophisticated instincts. I don't think my ap-proach to acting has changed, either. From the time I was a kid I think I had the same concerns: to speak loud enough, to under-stand what the writer was attempting to say, and then to try to execute it. Sometimes I feel that I don't involve enough of myself in the work; I'm involved in the character yet I'm not bringing enough of my own self into the character's inner life. But I wouldn't say that I've changed at all. There's just been a process of trying to make my abilities more readily available.

When I was starting out, I couldn't count on my emotions to be there. If I had to cry, for instance, I couldn't be sure that I would be able to. But there too, I realize it wasn't that I didn't have the ability to cry, it was that the material didn't excite me. Now, it doesn't matter whether I can cry or not because I know so many other ways to do it, and, frankly, I don't care. If I don't cry, then I don't. In the old days, if the script called for it, I would feel com-pelled to produce the tears. But sometimes you cry and people don't even know you're crying and it's all so complicated—the re-lation of the audience to what's happening on the stage. And in the movies, they are so much happier if they can shoot glycerine into your eyes; it gives them something to do instead of sitting around. So I don't know whether it's that I function better or just that I no longer worry about it. There's not so much pressure to prove myself to myself.

When you're performing a part, do you tend to lose yourself in the character and "shed real tears," or are you always aware of the difference between you and the character?

Oh, I'm always aware of it. Oh, yeah! I think you'd be crazy if you weren't. An actress is someone who's able to use herself, not just lose control. That would be self-indulgence; that wouldn't be acting.

And so you don't ever have trouble turning off a character when you're done performing?

I'm never involved in a role after the moment is over. I don't think you could be really. It's not a pleasant experience to be very deeply, emotionally involved; it goes against the reflexes of the human instrument. Nobody wants to be involved in profound or passionate things ultimately; people are always sliding away from those experiences when they're thrust into them. And as an actress, it's tiring and painful to do, so you really don't want to continue it for any longer than you have to.

Do you find yourself getting bored with a play after you've been in it for awhile?

Oh, I've gotten to a point where it absolutely became an endurance contest, where I have counted the days, marked them off on three calendars instead of one! I find that doing the same thing every day is deadly. Even when I had work that I really liked, I have never stayed in anything more than four months; that's about as long as I can take without going cuckoo. Even in a period of a week, I think it would be so much better if you had two things to do instead of one. That's one of the great advantages of repertory work to me. But you know, when you have to do something for a period of time and you know you have to do it, it's like when you're in a flop show: you can't treat it realistically. You have an

investment in it, and so you just create the performance technically and the fact that it's a dry, uninspiring time for you as a person does not show to the audience.

But I like to repeat a good character in the sense that I like to
play her every year or every two years. That way, I can grow in
the work in a way that I can't grow when I just have a rehearsal
period with a director and then a production period. It's simply
not possible to get the best results that way. But, of course, I
don't know that anyone's interested in the best results except the
actors themselves. I mean, very often you may do very good
work, satisfying to the audience and enough for the production,
but you would still like to get more out of it; it becomes purely a
personal thing.

*Ideally, what do you think the relationship between the audience
and the actress should be?*

I think the audience, if you're going to have good theatre, has to
be much more directly involved. I think they should boo when
they don't like it. I think they should complain if they can't hear. I
think they have to be a part of the experience. The theatre is so
dull in a vital, humanistic way because the audience doesn't have
the freedom to express itself. You know, if you get angry at something, you say, "Oh, my God, I want to boo, but I won't because I
don't want to make a fool of myself in front of these other people.
I don't want to be an exhibitionist." But the fact is that you can't
really have alive acting unless you have an alive audience. When
they sit there and settle for something half-good, then the producers, the directors, and the actors go on giving them something
half-good; it's such an organic thing that they don't know the difference. You think you're doing great work up there on stage, but
if someone isn't pushing you to do better, then you don't do
better.

I think it's partly because as an actor you can't see your product. If you're a painter, for instance, you can see what you've
done; you can look at it one morning and say, "Jesus Christ"—
you have a flash of insight and it impels you on. It's the same with
writing. Along with the idea that you *can't* judge your own work,
at the same time you have an external opportunity to be objective
which you don't have with acting. The audience should really
supply that. Not the director—because that's a one-to-one rela-

tionship; the additional pressure should come from the audience, but it's something that doesn't happen these days.

In Miss Margarida's Way you had a particularly interesting relationship with the audience. You were a teacher and the whole theatre became your classroom.

But that's very different from a regular play. That's another whole dimension. As an actor, you can't really cultivate that aspect of yourself because that would mean that *you* get directly involved with the audience, and, in a regular play, that isn't what should happen. You should be playing the play and the audience should be involved with your playing the play; in most cases, it's dissipatory for an actor to be involved with the audience.

For instance, when an actor complains about an audience, and starts thinking that the audience is no good, that's another key—as difficult parts of a text are a key. When I start thinking that way, it means to me that I'm not doing good enough work. If a part of me is involved in whether the audience is responding properly to my work, then I *know* I haven't got one hundred percent concentration on the matter at hand, that I am just diverting myself from my principal task—which is to fulfill a character to the point where the audience will be transported into my world.

Do you have any problems making the transition from stage acting to film acting when you need to?

No, not usually, because movie and TV scripts are so excessively written. The only time I had difficulty was with Robert Anderson's *I Never Sang for My Father*, where we used the stage script. I rehearsed as I would for a play—all day and all night, nonstop—because it was clear that the material was *not* accessible, the feelings were not accessible. But a script that's written for movies or TV is just written differently—everything is right on the surface.

Does it disturb your sense of the development of a character to act out of sequence?

Well, it doesn't because in a movie there's no need to get a grasp of a role. When you're rehearsing a play, you've got to play it, so you need to get a hold and an orchestration of the character; but in a film none of that is necessary. The director is going to do what he wants so all you really have to do is satisfy the director. I don't see anything else to do in a film.

You don't get much satisfaction out of doing movie acting then?

I might say none. Money. You mean personal satisfaction, in the sense of day-to-day work? Like if I go to the studio and do some really good work, will I come home feeling great about it? Not great enough—no. I enjoy films as a vacation and I enjoy the work just because I enjoy acting on any level, but satisfaction in terms of a lifestyle, no. The work is too superficial. You can be satisfied with what you did, pleased or proud of it, but you can't find any kind of keep fulfillment.

Do you enjoy watching your performances in the movies?

I don't care much; once I've done a role, I've done it. I've seen most of them, but I don't have much interest in it, really. I try to see them once in a theatre to see how the audiences respond, and after time goes by, I like to see them because then I can look at what I've done objectively, but I don't even care much about the rushes. Once I've done the acting, it's just done and over with and I tend to lose interest in something that I've already achieved. I think that's why I'm always looking for new challenges: once I've accomplished something, it just goes out of my mind, I'm no longer the least bit interested in it and I'm looking for something new.

On which side of the debate do you come down—is acting a creative or interpretive art?

Interpretive, because you are dealing with somebody else's creation. And true, you may create a character out of somebody else's created play, but I am very aware that if I tried to write a play, a novel, or music, I would have to have something to say, and as an actor, I only have to agree or disagree. I am only putting forward what the playwright has to say and that, of course, fig-

ures in my choosing of a role. If the message of a piece is repug-
nant to me, I won't do it. I wouldn't want to be a part of it. So in
that way, it's obviously an interpretive art. And interpretive art
is, of course, extremely creative, but it's a secondary part of the
process. Now, a creative artist cannot act necessarily any more
than an actor can create, but they are definitely two different
things.

*Having known and created so many characters in the plays and
movies that you've done, do you feel that you're a good judge of
character in real life?*

No, I don't think so because I'm very self-involved. I don't tend to
be interested in other people. I don't really look carefully and ra-
tionally at those around me. I'm only interested in my responses
to them and in how they respond to me. If they like me, that's
good. If they don't, forget it. I'm really very subjective.

What do you generally do in between roles?

I spend so much time reading—all the plays and scripts that are
sent to me—that's what I do principally. And then I've never had
much time between roles because I used to go from a show that
would close Friday to another job on Monday. I don't do that as
much now because I've tried to become more careful in my selec-
tions. I'm trying to put a great deal more thought into deciding
what will really be meaningful to me. I feel that I *waste* a lot of
time in pursuits that are not terribly significant.

*How about your cabaret singing? Are you planning to put to-
gether another act?*

There again, I found the level of material had to be so superficial
that I didn't find it awfully satisfying. But when I have time I do
go over to the Actors Studio and work on roles that are challenging to me. I may or may not ever do them commercially, but I'm
always working like that, just because I'm interested in the characters.

BARNARD HUGHES

As his producer Grant Tinker once observed to a reporter from *TV Guide*, Barnard Hughes is "the final proof that Leo Durocher was wrong about nice guys finishing last." Indeed, not only is he one of the nicest, but after forty-five years as a professional character actor, Mr. Hughes has finally stepped stage center: for his portrayal of *Da*, the feisty Irish Archie Bunker, he has won the Tony, Drama Desk, and Outer Critics Circle Awards as Best Actor of the 1978 Broadway season.

Born on July 16, 1915, the sixth of seven children, Barnard Hughes grew up on an estate in Bedford Hills, New York, where his father, an Irish immigrant, worked as chauffeur. He dropped out of school after one year at Manhattan College and shortly thereafter was hired by the Shakespeare Fellowship, a group that rehearsed nights and performed weekends at schools around New York. During this time, Mr. Hughes supported himself with odd jobs—as a runner and proofreader on Wall Street, a checker on the docks, and later a salesman at Macy's. Though he has had no formal training, his early stock work led him from one job to the next, and he has consistently found employment in television, films, and the theatre.

It would be impossible to list here even the majority of his credits (Mr. Hughes has played more than 400 roles on the stage alone), but a representative sampling would include mention of films such as *Rage*, *Hospital*, *Where's Poppa?*, *Cold Turkey*, *Sisters*, and *Midnight Cowboy* (in which he played the aging homosexual, "Townie"). He has appeared on TV as the Polish priest on "All in the Family" and his own prime-time series, "Doc," in which he was a friendly neighborhood physician. His wide range of theatre work includes Polonius (to Stacy Keach's *Hamlet*), Chief Constable Dogberry in *Much Ado about Nothing* (for which he received a Tony nomination and the Clair Bayfield award), *Abelard and Heloise*, *How Now Dow Jones*, *Hogan's Goat*, *Line*, *The Three Sisters*, and *The Devil's Disciple*.

Mr. Hughes is married to the actress Helen Stenborg whom he met while performing in veterans' hospitals following World War II. They live on the Upper West Side of Manhattan and have two children: their son Douglas, a Harvard graduate, had, at the time of this interview, produced and directed a revue which was being performed in South Carolina, and their daughter Laura, an aspiring actress, was doing her second season of apprenticeship at Williamstown Theatre Festival.

Though Mr. Hughes has a bald crown and only a sparse tuft of grey hair, a rolling belly and steel-rimmed spectacles, there is an unmistakable brightness about him. He subways each day to his dressing room at the Morosco Theatre where, on the afternoon of this interview, he came padding in, perfectly punctual, in his tennis shoes. Around him in the tiny room was a blizzard of notes and telegrams from theatre-goers—a sign not only of the numbers of people who wish him well, but of how much those wishes mean to him. As he spoke, Mr. Hughes was alternately cheerful and pensive, but always there was a lively sparkle in his grey-blue eyes and a radiant bonhomie. He had clearly given some thought to what he would like to say and took evident pleasure in saying it. "I probably sound like a pompous fool," he told me, "but I just *love* to talk about acting."

*Mr. Hughes, I understand that you got involved in the theatre al-
most as a fluke—you took a friend up on a dare. Could you tell me
about that?*

Indeed I could. As I recall, I went with my friend Arthur Nesbitt,
who has since become a writer, to a production of *Hamlet* at the
Brooklyn Academy of Music. We enjoyed it very much and
thought most of the company was superb; but there were some
young actors playing the minor parts, and I took exception to
their performances. On the way home, I said to Arthur that if I
couldn't do better than that, I'd give up. I was not an actor at the
time (I had left school and was working on Wall Street). About a
week later I got a letter saying that my audition was set up for five
o'clock on Tuesday afternoon, and that I should bring something
I'd memorized. Well, I had no idea what this was all about.

Since Art was my best friend, I told him about it and he admitted that he had sent the letter requesting an audition. He'd read
in *The New York Times* that a repertory company was being
formed to play schools and colleges around New York, and since
I'd shot off my big mouth, he thought I should see whether or not
I could in fact make it as an actor.

So I memorized a part and went down at the specified time to
audition. I think the old man there was so staggered that anybody
had the gall to come down and present himself when he was as
unprepared as I was that he gave me the job. It was a bit part, of
course, playing the haberdasher in *The Taming of the Shrew*. All I
had was one line: "Here is the cap your worship did bespeak."
But it got me into the company . . . and I've lived happily ever
after.

Do you remember your first performance?

Oh, I do. I remember getting into costume, putting on my make-
up—all the while looking around me to see how it was done—
holding the cap and standing in the wings with the actor who was
playing the tailor. From that moment on, I had a total blackout; I
wound up five minutes later back in the dressing room with no
idea whether I'd even been out on stage. I just kept mumbling,
"Did I do it? Did I do it?" And finally I heard a glum voice answer
me, "Yes, you did. But do it better the next time."

*Was that dare just a catalyst for you? Would you have made a
stab at acting sooner or later? Certainly, you must have had a
great interest in the theatre at the time.*

I did. I was an enthusiastic spectator and I suppose that I always
nursed the fantasy of trying my hand at it. Art's calling my bluff
just precipitated the whole thing, really. But I don't know how I
would ever have had the courage to do it, knowing as little as I did
about acting, without that stupid dare to prod me on. I needed
something to make me forget all my inadequacies, to allow me to
just jump right in. I've been grateful for his push ever since.

*Did you decide right then and there that acting would be your
career, that you'd stick with it? Was it love at first sight?*

I started then and never stopped until I went into the Army, but I
hadn't really made my mind up as to whether it would be my
career. One job had just followed another and I got caught up in
the life of the theatre. The Army was a great relief in a way because it was a chance to *change*, to step back and take a look at
what I had been doing. Spending those years in the service allowed me to give long and deep thought to it all; and I realized
then how much I wanted the theatre, loved it, and needed it.

As soon as I had discovered how terribly important acting was
to me, of course, it became much more difficult to find jobs.
When I didn't care, I'd gotten all the parts I wanted. But I did
hold on and the work finally started coming my way. Outside of
that one hiatus, I've rarely been unemployed since. I may have
wanted for *pay* occasionally, but I've never wanted for jobs. I
always considered the work more important than the money,
anyway.

*During that brief time when you had difficulty getting roles, and
in the time since, when you may not have been cast in a role you
wanted, did you ever doubt your abilities as an actor?*

Never, never, never. Ever. When I wouldn't get a job, I would
just say to myself: "My Lord, how stupid can people be! It was so
evident that I was perfectly right for the part, so obvious. Those
poor fools! Oh well, it's their problem, not mine." And of course,

when you have an ego that size, you cover it up with large doses of humility and gentleness. That's how I've gotten this totally unwarranted reputation for being nice!

Can you say what it was that attracted you to the art of acting? What was it that you loved so?

We all have something that we want to say and I've never found a way of saying it other than through acting. I can't write, I'm not terribly articulate, and it's difficult for me to formulate ideas. I used to think that acting was a matter of accents and limps and character quirks, but I've come to understand that acting is a point of view; it's your ideas about the man you're playing, your ideas about the time in which that man is living. A friend of mine wrote a poem about a mockingbird, and I think it expresses a basic truth about acting: "You never saw any mockingbird going around in dark glasses and a trenchcoat," she wrote. "No, it's the *songs* . . . he knows that if you've got a fellow's music right, you've got him by the soul." And that's what I've found out about acting, that's what the essence of the trick really is.

But you've had no formal training in acting?

No, I never had any.

Do you regret that?

Oh, I suppose you regret not having had everything. If anything was there and you haven't had it, you're sorry you didn't. But really I do regret it. I've had to fiddle around and find things out for myself, not quite knowing what I was even after. I've realized that learning to act is a slip-sliding process: you get better and then you get worse, and then you get a little better than you were before, and then you get a little worse. It's three steps forward and two steps back. Each time you advance a bit farther; each time you're slightly on the upgrade.

Did your stock work give you a good footing as an actor; was it training that you found valuable in your later career?

It gave me a great facility. I got a chance to work with some very

good actors, especially in comedy. That was a period in the
American theatre when farce was king, and we did traveling festivals of them: *Baby Mine*, *Getting Gertie's Garter*, *Mrs. Temple's
Telegram*, *Nightie Night*, *Twin Beds*. . . . In those plays, the beat
was all; you could just drive those audiences like a locomotive;
you had total control over them. You could stop them by raising
one finger, let the action pause, and let them all simmer down;
but then you'd turn up the gas again and start them going. Those
audiences literally got sick from laughing—they'd get sore, their
stomach muscles were just exhausted by it. And old actors in
those days would help me and show me the error of my ways.
Mostly they'd say, "Why don't you just stand still while I act,"
but that isn't such a bad idea, either. Repose is a gift which is a
long time coming to a lot of people. When I was a young actor, I
thought it was important always to be *doing*, and no matter where
the moment of the play was, I'd be all shakes and twitches; I
thought the attention of the entire house was riveted on me. It
takes a long time to realize that the man saying, "O, what a rogue
and peasant slave am I" is deserving of all the audience's
attention.

*So in stock you learned pacing and how to control an audience,
and you were able to put all that to use right away.*

Yes. It's difficult to say what the process of learning to act really
is. If a play is well written, you see, an actor's job is seventy-five
percent done. You may want to do a trick with a reading, lighten it
or change the meaning slightly, if you think that would be helpful.
But if the play is well motivated, that's it. Of course, even some
very good plays are not totally motivated as far as the actor is
concerned. They may have some moments where the inner logic
of the character breaks down, and there's a gap that the actor has
to fill. The process involved can be like trying to string pearls onto
a necklace; you want to get them all on and have the necklace
come out in the right shape.

Have you ever found a part to be unplayable?

George Bernard Shaw is one writer whose work I have always
found difficult to play. I just recently did Reverend Anderson in
The Devil's Disciple, and that took a little banging and shoving

and squeezing and pushing to make it come out even. In Shaw's plays, you're not dealing with real characters, you're dealing with ideas, with cut-outs; you stand them up and just make the voice come out. Every character in a Shaw play *is* Shaw, you see, but with a different point of view. I've played Doolittle in *Pygmalion*, however, and I think he's an exception. He's a joy to play, a kind of tap dance.

Is it an enjoyable challenge to work on a role that you find not so well motivated, like Reverend Anderson? Or is it more of an agonizing struggle?

It's always a great satisfaction to finally get it together because the work is the joy, you know, and to be challenged and to find that you've solved your problem is the great pleasure of acting. But with Reverend Anderson, I experienced a lot of agony; it was close to the most unhappy time I had ever had until, all of a sudden, the day came when I began to see light breaking through. I saw a way to string the pearls—it may not have been the right way, but it was the only pattern that made sense to me. And it's great fun to save the whole United States in the last five minutes of a play—which Reverend Anderson, with that great switch of character, actually does. But I admit to you that I spent a good number of hours sitting home wondering whether to put my head in the oven or hang myself in the closet until I finally found a way to make sense of that part.

Do you generally have much time to prepare for these roles?

Oh no. As a matter of fact, I haven't had very much time to prepare for anything in my life except *Da*. And I don't think the fact that I had more time with *Da* has had anything to do with its runaway success. It was just a happy accident. If you have too much time to prepare for a role, you tend to over-intellectualize it and that's bad. What we do in the theatre is *feel*, maybe we think, but we don't want to intellectualize. I think all art is that way. I went with a friend to the opening of his gallery show and he was terrified that people were going to ask him what he meant by his work because he really wasn't sure himself. I feel that way, too.

Do you see yourself as a creative artist?

I think there are opportunities for an actor to be creative, but certainly your first responsibility, after feeding the family, is to the playwright. Sometimes they're not worth the trouble, but when you're working on a good play, your job is only to interpret what has already been created. I've always felt that what the playwright wrote sitting up in his room over a period of a year or longer. is more important than my own on-the-spot ideas. Sometimes you have to substitute your own because the playwright's ideas just don't work. But there are times when you go off on a tack of your own and find yourself coming around again to the playwright's way of seeing things.

I think that when an actor prepares for a part, he should fling himself at it, do everything, try anything, and then edit, sort out, see what works and what is needed. Harold Acton once said, "Talent is the ability to do and character is the ability to refrain." And I think an actor should have large doses of both to get the balance of a role. Acting is craft, you see, and if it isn't art, it at least can be lifted to what closely approximates it.

Is there anything you do in between roles to sharpen your instincts for acting?

I think actors should expose themselves to practically everything under the sun and have an interest in everything. I've always found actors to be the best company in the world, the most fascinating people because they're interested in absolutely everything—in the man across the street, the man across the globe, everyone. My children have been around actors all their lives and they tell me how wonderful it always was to be surrounded by such exciting, excited souls. They'd go over to their friends' houses and everybody would be so drab in comparison, shaking hands, never opening their mouths. With actors, it's a different life.

What is the first thing you do upon being cast in a role? Do you generally learn your lines right away?

Well, there are two schools of thought. I've recently worked with directors who want you to know your lines before you come to rehearsal, but I think that's disastrous, just disastrous. Acting is

cooperation; you're not up there acting by yourself, you're playing *with* somebody and so you want to hear what the other actors
have to say before you go ahead and learn your own part. You
can't be expected to act in a vacuum. If you learn your lines,
you're certainly going to be learning ideas—because that's what
acting is—and if you learn ideas, then when you finally get to the
theatre, the other actors are going to be intruding on what you already set up to do. Why, that way lies madness.

I remember years ago when you got a role, you didn't get the
whole script, you only got your lines with the cues. That's why I
learned to talk my way in and out of situations; I had to learn the
situation and not the lines first in case, God forbid, I forgot them,
at least I would know where the scene was headed. People who
go up on stage knowing their lines first generally don't know what
the play is about and can't talk their way out of it. I've always
been able to do that and, when I was doing soap operas, it made
things much happier for me. I knew that I might disgrace myself
but at least I wasn't going to die of a heart attack right there in
front of all those people.

What is the ideal procedure for you when preparing a role?

I think ideally you go to the theatre and the whole cast sits around
and you just give yourself up to the material. If there is something
that's not obvious from reading the play, the director will point it
out and suggest each actor's responsibility to certain scenes,
what he thinks should come out of it. Then you read, and you
read, and you read, and you feel the whole play shaping around
you. When the cast gets up and begins to work, you let yourself
feel relaxed. I think one of the most important things about preparing a part is to relax so that you can accept what comes. You
hear a lot about people who work well under tension, but there's
plenty of tension when you get to the performance. And the greatest service a director can do—aside from casting a play well—is
to keep the rehearsal period relaxed and joyful so that the give-
and-take of putting it together can proceed happily, easily.

*Aside from having a well-written play, can you say what produced
such good results with* **Da**? *Was there anything about the preparation process of the play that added to its success?*

Well, with *Da*, we originally went downtown to the Hudson Guild Theatre. We all loved the material or we would never have done it in the first place; we certainly weren't going to be making any money out of it. If we had any ulterior motive at all, it was to be seen in a part that we thought we'd be good in, in a play that we had a lot of respect for. And Melvin Bernhardt cast this play impeccably—that had a lot to do with it. I think it created a feeling which permeates the play to this day. Some of the material is very, very intimate, particularly between Brian Murray, who plays my son, and myself; I think our good feeling for each other gives the play its texture and its color. Not only have I admired Brian for a long long time, as both an actor and a director, but through the working of this play, I've come to love him, really. There's nothing he can do out there that I don't understand. Our working together is a very fluid thing; there's a happy looseness between us, and we know if something interesting happens out there we can take advantage of it. Yeah.

Do you find the same satisfactions working in film as you do in the theatre?

I suppose I do, but the satisfactions are very different. In the theatre, I enjoy the physicality of acting; it's enormously satisfying to work hard physically, and there's a stamina that builds with good playing; I'm proud of the fact that I have that energy. In the theatre the pleasures are immediate; you know exactly how you're doing when you're doing it. The biggest difference, though, is that in film somebody else is making the choices for you, while in theatre, your performance is your own; you're making your own cuts, your own two-shots, you're still in control when that curtain goes up.

Have you ever felt that a film director improved your performance with the control he had?

Yes, I've really had very good outings in film, so there's no reason for me to complain. An interesting thing did happen when I played "Townie," one of Joe Buck's clients in *Midnight Cowboy*. John Schlesinger had the whole cast sit down and read the work together, which is something you so rarely do in film. And when it was time to shoot my scene, he said to me, "Why don't you use the script, but try improvising your way into it. Then pick up your lines and improvise your way out again." He said, "Suppose you're 'Townie.' Tell me about yourself." He asked me questions and I answered them as if it were an interview and I were really the character in the script. *Wonderful* things came out of it and we got so much of it on film.

But when I went to a screening of the final version, all of this material that I thought was so wonderful had been cut out of it! I was really upset. Yet I saw the film again after it had opened a few weeks later and I realized that yes, indeed, John knew exactly what he was doing. If there had been more to my part, it could never have erupted into that violence. If there had been more of me, the audience would have felt sympathetic and the violence would have been utterly gratuitous. That would have worked against Joe Buck's character. And I thought, boy, hopefully, I'll always be in the hands of a film director as good as John Schlesinger.

You did a TV series a few years back called "Doc." How do the satisfactions compare there? Did you find a TV series as pressurized as many people say it is?

No, as a matter of fact, I don't get into pressure much. It's amazing what I can discard if I don't want it to get to me. I never allowed TV to affect me that way. My concerns were entirely with the work; all I could do was put out my best effort even when there were things beyond my control. I loved the experience and I enjoyed the responsibility. I wouldn't mind going out there again. And I think the people working in TV are just wonderful people.

But I always feel more comfortable in the theatre. I'm part of the theatre community here in New York. This is my life. I will gladly do film or TV work if I'm not engaged here, but if ever I have a choice, why the theatre is what I want. I just love the routine of it; I love coming into the theatre, I love coming down the alleys, I love curtain calls. I used to love going on the road and I hope to be able to take this play on the road. I just love being an actor. I really do.

How do you feel about seeing yourself act in films or on TV?

You know, this sounds ridiculous, but I'm always surprised that I get so many character parts offered me, because, for some reason, I still have another image of myself. I mean, I look in the mirror and I know that no one is going to ask me to play Laertes next season, but still, I have a picture of myself that is quite different from what I see. And the truth is, I can't bear to watch myself act. When I see myself in a film or on television, I always wonder: how did that guy get the job? I could be so much better than he is.

A sure way to clear the family room where we watch television is to turn on the set when Dad's on. Everybody runs for the tall grass. My daughter always made a point of being out of the house when "Doc" was on the air. My son would watch it occasionally, but he's a director so I suppose he can look at things more clinically than the rest of us can. Sometimes, when the show was on, if people had invited my wife and I to dinner on Saturday night, and if we were all seated at the table, they would wheel in a portable TV or hold off eating until after the show had aired. Oh God, it was just agony for me. It's an embarrassment. I never minded watching myself when I was alone, but watching myself act with strangers around is a humiliating experience. Don't ask me to explain that; I don't understand it at all.

You mentioned that, in preparing to play "Townie" in Midnight Cowboy, *you used improvisation as a way of feeling out the character. Do you generally find improvisation a good tool when you work on a character?*

No, I'm most terrified of improvisation. Some people are awfully good at it, but not me. That was the only time I ever did that and it was helpful, but I wouldn't want to do it again. Sometimes in my own preparation for a part, I take notes on the character, and that's a sort of improvisation on paper. For instance, when I did Jeeter Lester in *Tobacco Road*, I wrote down a whole slew of questions: when did he and Ada get married? What happened to the other children? Where did Jeeter come from? All these things. Some of them are never answered, but it allows me to store information and ideas about the person in the back of my head. An actor is like a computer; data is fed into him and is worked on in his brain. It gets mixed and compared and organized. Then when he gets the cue, you get the feedback.

Once you've arrived at a way of playing a character, do you stick with that or do you keep changing it as you keep performing the role?

Once I've arrived at my performance, I pretty well hold to it. This play is a bit of an exception, mostly because of my relationship with Brian. But even in this play, what I think of as great swings, from night to night, are probably not even noticeable from the audience's point of view. Most other plays need a more rigid cleaving to them. Yet there, too, someone may read a line with a different inflection or emphasis and I find myself changing my reading because he's changed his. All of a sudden, the exchange lights up a line and I see it as I've never seen it in all the previous performances. Then later, I may decide, no, that's not it, I better watch it, keep it the way it was.

Is there some small point that you've been experimenting with in Da?

Well, there is something that I'm fiddling around with at the moment. When I receive that measly pension from the mistress after having been her gardener all my life, I'm sitting with my son and I say, proudly and sadly, "I planted them trees there, and I set up the tennis court." He tells me, "You've been diddled." And I say, not wanting to admit it, "What, diddled?" and then almost break into a tear, knowing he's right. But I've been wondering whether I'm taking that too far by almost breaking down; maybe I'm playing out the reaction that I want the audience to feel. If I play the emotion for them, you see, they don't have to feel it themselves. An actor should only suggest, suggest, suggest and let the audience do the feeling. Allow them to play out the emotions.

I remember when I was playing Kurt in *Watch on the Rhine*, I said goodbye to my children, and, my God, the tears just flowed. I could hardly control myself, hardly get through the performance. When I'd take my curtain call about five minutes later, I'd still be choked up. And everyone thought how wonderful it was that I could cry so facilely—but I really shouldn't have been crying at all. The audience should have been dissolved in tears instead. The very fact that people admired my ability to cry showed that I was not acting well: it reminded them that I *was* acting. Anything that draws attention to the fact that you're acting isn't acting.

You can drown your performance in a flood of technique?

Oh, I think so, yes. James Agate once said that when he looks at a watch, he does so to learn the time, not to admire the works, and I think that's a good thing for actors to keep in mind. These fancy actors who call attention to their technique are keeping the audience aware that they're actors. And yes, I'm afraid that I might be playing that moment in *Da* a little bit too strongly for the audience; they might not empathize or sympathize with me because I'm playing it so fully that they don't have to. I think I'll play it cold turkey, hold back the tear, at the matinee today. I'm glad you came; you helped make up my mind!

Do you find that the longer you play a certain role, the greater the temptation to make it fancy, to embroider on it?

Yes, that's what you have to guard against; in a long run, you feel you should be filling the role out, making the moment larger. And yet the whole trick of it is to hold onto yourself, to keep the reins on. Because you're so tired, the temptation is especially great on a Wednesday or Saturday night, after you've done a matinee; since acting is so physically demanding, you find yourself pushing to make the performance. It takes so much energy to act in the theatre—energy not only to fill up the house but to make people attracted to you, to command their attention.

Acting used to be much more dependent upon technique than it is today. This is the age of realism. In your forty-five years in the theatre, you must have seen many changes in acting styles taking place.

Oh yes, there have been great changes. I still find myself taking three-quarter turns to the audience. If I'm playing a scene with someone, we should, as in life, play the scene facing each other, but we always used to turn three-quarters toward the audience to get the voice out. The Lunts were the first actors to turn their backs on an audience and continue a scene. They were the first actors to clip cues and talk at the same time and tumble lines one over the other. So the techniques, you see, are changing all the time, just as they are in film.

When I think of the old actors I used to play with, I know that

I've changed a great deal. I worked with people who came up in the Delsarte method, with all those harmonic poises and poses—how wonderful those things were! They probably did not use them as flamboyantly as they had when they were younger, but they were still modifications of the thing. And it was just delicious to look at, to hear actors giving tones to their words, baying like hounds. I'm sure that when I first began I used to have a much more heroic style of acting; now it's settled down. But I think that I can probably lift myself back into those larger styles when I need to.

In the conventional modern theatre, of course, different plays call for different treatments. A farce needs big broad strokes, but when you're involved in a realistic play, your preparation is more internal. There are still some pretty flamboyant performances around, though; certainly Richard Burton uses his voice beautifully. That's another thing that's changed over the years. An actor used to try to paint his words—happy, sad, those were colors that could be added to a speech. But that isn't common anymore. Our whole society is kind of blanding out—bread isn't bread, ice cream isn't ice cream, and God knows, bologna isn't what it used to be. Hopefully, the theatre will be able to put that excitement back into life, and actors will show flashes of lightning occasionally.

Have you found that acting is easier for you now than it used to be?

No, I wouldn't say so, because I expect more of myself the older I get. When I was younger, I was more easily satisfied—just to learn the parts, to get through them. I had a photographic study, I could memorize everything I looked at—menus, signs, headlines. And I got in the habit of getting roles together so fast. I wouldn't know what the lines meant, but I would know that they were the second speech down on page eighteen. I had to break myself of that because I found I was learning chunks of material superficially.

And as the accepted performing styles have become more realistic, do you find that your approach to a role, your mode of preparation, is changing as well?

Yes, just the mechanics of acting used to concern me a lot more. I no longer read a part and think, what am I going to do with it, how am I going to enlarge on it, what do *I* want to do? Now, I take the material and try to see how best I can serve it. I look for what is there, and hope I can find it.

Would you say that you now work more from the inside of a character than from the outside? Is your preparation less dependent upon external elements, like costumes and walks?

Yes, generally. When I was a kid, I was big for cigars and moustaches and all that. Although surprisingly, a character still sometimes comes from the externals, and costumes can be terribly important. My wife and I were once doing a popular comedy called *Anniversary Waltz*; it was a very simple play and one that didn't present any great problems to me. I had just bought one of those Rex Harrison tweed hats, and, for some reason or another, I wore it on opening night. Suddenly, the whole part came together for me in an entirely new way. Taking it off and tossing it up and around, fiddling with the crease in it, turning up the brim and pulling it down—all those things filled in the part for me as it had never been before. It was later I heard that Olivier was once having trouble feeling comfortable with a role. He picked up an umbrella, walked on stage and, God, that was it! He could play with it, put it over his shoulder, swing it. . . . And now, when he finds that moment in a play when it all falls together, he says he has found his green umbrella.

I'm not as big on walks as I used to be, but I notice that I still use distinctive steps now and again. It's just that I no longer start out to do a particular walk; I let it develop of its own from the material. A lot of gestures and ways of speaking come naturally, too; they come by way of an internal identification with the character. When I say internal, of course, I'm talking about emotional identification and not cerebration. If I thought intellectually about my characters, I'd only get in over my head.

Maximilian Schell once summed it up by saying that getting a part together is like having two men inside you talking and questioning; when they finally agree, you're right.

In the years that you've been acting, you must have seen enormous changes in the audience, too. The emergence of film and television has no doubt affected viewing styles as much as acting styles.

Oh, audiences used to be much better educated in the conventions of the theatre than they are today. Audiences now are much too literal. They are not as willing to give themselves up to the make-believe of the theatre. When I first went into the business, as many people went to the theatre regularly as now go to the movies. That's why farce and melodrama were more popular back then: those forms depend upon the suspension of disbelief. You know, in order to give yourself up to an experience in the theatre, you have to be able to ease your better judgment. But reality has gotten so popular these days, and plays that depend on sheer theatrical convention have all but disappeared. It's a shame. Anyone interested in reality should go out on the street and take a look. We're in the dream business here!

Da has gotten so much critical acclaim and won so many awards. I was wondering if you can feel an appreciable difference in the audience. You're not trying to prove yourselves to them, but on the other hand, they come in expecting to be wowed out of their seats.

It's amazing how much an audience affects a play. They are fifty percent of the theatrical experience and so few people realize it. Yes, in a play like this, which has gotten such attention, the audience comes in with a preconceived idea of what the play is all about. If it has won all these prizes, then it must certainly be this kind of a play. And yet as an actor, I don't feel I can let them sit out there and determine what kind of a play they're going to see. I've got to stand up on stage and *show* them what kind of a play it is. That's another reason why it's very important that I don't overact that line I was mentioning before; I would be giving into the temptation to act according to the audience's expectations, rather than according to the demands of the play itself.

You were talking before about the kind of energy that is needed to act in the theatre. How do you manage to produce that night after night?

It used to be easier, and I'm not just talking about the effects of age. Years ago, you'd be in the theatre at 8:30 in the evening and at 2:30 in the afternoon on matinee days, and in between you'd just go home, eat, rest, sleep late. Now, my God, you're up at 7:00 in the morning to do the *Today* show, you've got commercials to do, interview appointments, soap operas. . . . By the time you get to the theatre at night, you've put in a full day's work, and summoning the energy that's required to give a performance is so much more difficult.

How do you do it? Do you have any kind of exercise routine or special diet?

That's what helps me. [He points to a giant jar of honey.] I may have the energy but I'll die a diabetic!

Beyond the pure stamina that's needed, you have to find a way to leave the day's events behind and enter into the make-believe world of the play. I'm not sure whether that control over your mental attitude is a matter of concentration or of relaxation.

It's a matter of giving yourself up, of letting go. When they call your half hour and you're dressed, you're ready, you're waiting to go on, you have to wean yourself away from the dressing room and all that's going on around you. You begin to accept the fact that you're going to walk out the door, go around the back, walk on stage when your cue comes, and in that time you'll have moved all the way from your life in New York to your character's life in Ireland. It's a long journey; I'm not sure myself how an actor does it.

Are there some small things you can do to bring on the mood of a play before you step out to perform?

Oh, I have certain affirmations that I have made all my life. Just sitting and being quiet and thinking about where I pick up the play can help. Some people do voice exercises; E.G. Marshall does yoga; I pray. Yeah, I do. I pray not only for help, but, as Teilhard de Chardin says, "Your life is prayer." You offer up works to God, and that's what I do.

How about at the end of the play? How do you come down after being so keyed up?

That's a great exhilaration. I remember when I was a young actor, oh God, I used to love to come off, especially in those farces where you've just been galloping. Even now, I come off soaking wet; my clothes are absolutely drenched. I don't sing anymore, but I used to when I was young—I just used to sing at the top of my voice. I still feel that elation, of course, and I come down naturally. The play itself is the release that you've been waiting for.

Do you find yourself becoming kinder and happier or more bitter and nasty depending on the role you're playing?

It's often struck me that way, yes. I really do think that you eventually become the person you play. With Reverend Anderson, who starts out as a dour minister and turns into a firebrand patriot, I lost thirteen pounds! It was not that demanding a part, but it made me think of myself as younger and I fitted myself into that image. When you're playing a part, you're giving up not only two-and-a-half hours for the performance, but also about an hour and a half to prepare, so that's four hours, half your day, and if you're playing an old bastard, it's bound to color you.

I wonder about the toll Da will take; I try *not* to let him affect me too personally. He's a gentle old gink but monumentally stupid. Well, not stupid so much as just not touched by the things that are important to him, and his interests are so narrow. I used to be very shy about playing up his attitudes toward Hitler and England—his expressions of sympathy for Hitler and antipathy for England. But when I thought about where he came from, it became a little more understandable. Indeed, the English Black and Tans did come into Ireland and commit absolutely dreadful acts. There were *pogroms*, just as in *Fiddler on the Roof*; the English would shoot and kill and destroy, and that's all Da knows about. So anybody who was going after the English certainly had a point in their favor as he would see it. It took me a while, though, to come to that understanding. I was so disturbed that he could think that way and I'd be too timid to hit his attitude as big as I should have. Yet if you're going to editorialize, you're not going to make your point in the theatre, so I just had to force myself.

What is it that attracts you to a role?

The first things, of course, are the character's responsibility to
the whole, how he serves the play and whether it's well written.
Those kind of things apply, however, to any part. What you really
want to play is the part that says something *you* want to say. You
don't always get that opportunity, though, nor should you expect
it. I suppose that great surgeons aren't always doing open-heart
surgery and actors aren't always privileged to play the really wonderful, totally motivated parts. Plums like *Da* don't come along
very often. So you've got to be prepared to do the ditch-digging
part of acting, and there's a lot of it. In a career that spans forty-
five years, you have to expect to shovel a bit. And I have.

*What proportion, would you say, in your forty-five years of act-
ing, were really challenging, satisfying roles?*

I find that I'm getting an opportunity now, in these later years,
after having been a character man all my life, to play the parts
that I've been fiddling around the edges of for a long time. When I
think of my role in *Da*, I think that I must be living at the right
time. This part came along when I was ready in life to play it.
And, of course, that's the trick: being ready to play it when you
get the opportunity. Lots and lots of wonderful actors never get
that opportunity for the right part to come along.

What made this **the** *right part?*

I knew it immediately when I read it. It's a beautifully written
play; it says something that I feel very close to—about roots,
everyone's roots—and it reaches people deeply because it deals
so directly with the human condition. It doesn't matter whether
you're Irish, though I happen to be—and so, of course, I have an
afffinity for the material—but it doesn't matter who you are. This
play is about the fact that we've all got roots, and those roots have
affected our past and will color our future and we can't ever in
God's name get away from them. No matter how we change ourselves, no matter how we rail and fight and scream against them,
they're there and can't be avoided. So, I was wise enough to know
that this whole play was gold; I knew immediately who the char-

acter of Da was, where he came from, where I came from, and I knew that I could play him. I got the opportunity and I'll always be grateful.

Are there some roles which you just won't do?

Well, I think of acting as a calling; it's a vocation which isn't given to everyone. I think that we should use our talents, if we have them, for good. So I'm very selective about what I do. Certainly I have to get out and hustle to make a living, and I've found myself doing roles that I was not delighted to be involved with. But I won't do shoddy stuff. I won't take advantage of frailty to get laughs, for example. I think that my work should be a reflection of who I am and what I am—and I won't sell that cheaply in the theatre or anywhere else. Being an actor, after all, is a wonderful, useful, contributing way to spend your life and I think myself very fortunate to have stumbled onto this trick.

Do you draw your interpretations of dramatic characters from real people you have known? Does Da, for instance, have bits and pieces of your own father in him?

Da has bits and pieces of many, many people. When I went to South Carolina last week to see my son's revue, we appeared together on a television program down there. My son was asked whether the part I play in *Da* was like the person I am in life, and he said, "That's not my father on stage, that's a totally different man, that's creation, something that came out of his head." My children have always called *me* "Da," but I'm not that character, nor is that character my pa at all. Maybe a reading here, a gesture there, has been culled from reality. There are bits of a lot of people in that performance, and most of them would be staggered to find out that I thought they resembled Da in any way.

The only part I ever based entirely on a real person was old Chris in *Anna Christie.* I based that on an old Dane I knew: I copied his accent, the way he walked and laughed, the way he lit his pipe. And yet when I told someone that, he thought I was a total raving idiot; he didn't see the man like that at all! And in fact, I suppose he wasn't really like that. I had presented my distillation, my impression of what he was like. I hadn't captured the total, real person.

Da is a play that seems to tap into the family feelings of everyone who sees it. I imagine for you actors it must have been almost a psychoanalytic experience to prepare.

Oh, it was. *Da* was put together entirely with memories. It was a kind of group therapy for the cast. I've never seen a rehearsal before where everybody felt so compelled to tell stories about their childhood, their mother and father. You'd start to talk about remembered incidents and then realize there wasn't much to tell, but you'd just ramble on anyway, letting it dribble out because it seemed important somehow just to say it. A lot of time was given up to that, especially in the early part of rehearsal before we were really moving the play. It was just a wonderful, wonderful way to ease yourself into the material, to give up the "now" of wherever you were and get into the "then" of the play. And finally, as the material itself became more and more involving, we all gave ourselves up to the play and left our own personal involvements behind. It's so important to be able to "give yourself up" in that way; it's something one should do in at least some way every day.

What is the relationship between actor and audience in the theatre? You mentioned earlier that you were "showing" them the play, but it sounds as if, in large measure, you're sharing it with them.

Yes, I've always felt that I went out there to love and be loved, not to fight them, not to beat them into subjection. A lot of actors go out there to tame an audience, yet I've never looked at it in that light. I've always felt that it is kind of a love feast. Of course, I can be as surly as the next guy if the audience turns on me and I miss a couple of laughs! But generally, my attitude is one of sharing, yes. Sounds kind of simple, doesn't it?

Sounds like you find a great deal of pleasure in what you do.

Well, my wife and children tell me I become very disagreeable during rehearsal periods, especially if I have a problem with the character. It's something I'm totally unaware of, but they all say it's true.

Being an actor who is married to an actress, do you talk shop at home all the time?

As a matter of fact, I never discuss my work at home. Years ago, when my wife and I were acting together, we talked about it constantly. We learned our lines together, we cued each other, we talked shop endlessly. And finally, one night we just decided, oh my God, if we're going to live together we can't go on spending twenty-four hours a day in the theatre. So we decided never to bring our work home. After that, I'd go to see my wife work in rehearsal just as I would any actress who had her own ideas and inspirations that I was seeing for the first time.

Do you find you get bored with a long-running play?

No, I can't say I ever do. Every performance is so totally different. The audience, as I've said, is such a big part of the proceedings and they're all new every night. So many things will change. The news will affect an audience; the weather certainly does— fallen barometers just dampen comedy. So, though you don't get bored in a long run, you do need your discipline. You have to keep the energies high, the interest up, and you can't just go out and perform automatically. You've got to remind yourself of your responsibilities before you get out there so you can hold onto the show.

Has it made much difference to you that people see you acting a character, and remember the character without necessarily remembering who played the character?

No, that hasn't bothered me at all. What was always more important to me was that people were reached somehow; that was enough. I've been getting more and more exposure all the time, though, so people are beginning not only to place my face but also to remember my name. And yeah, I like that, I enjoy being recognized and I like it when people come up and tell me my work has meant something.

You've done comedy and more serious drama. Which do you find more difficult?

I find comedy more difficult. You have to be so aware of all the things that are going on around you. Bill Bradley, the basketball player and politician, wrote in his book about having "a sense of where you are." Being out on the basketball court, he had to know what was happening in back of him, on the sides of him—and that's what it's like to do comedy. You have to be aware of everything. I try, for instance, to hold a certain line in the play that I know will get a laugh; I hold it and hold it and let the audience build its anticipation so then when I do drop it, it explodes. But last night, just before I popped the line, a man down front coughed very loudly—you could see that laugh splatter like a rotten egg all over the stage.

Do you get a great satisfaction out of doing comedy since it does require so sharpened a skill?

I do. I like the precision of it, the cleanness of it. It's monk-like. But I love to wallow in drama on occasion, too.

The communication between actor and audience is so direct in comedy.

Yes, it's right there and you're getting it right back. In drama, there aren't the same sign posts; the feedback isn't as immediate, it's more internal. If you're playing comedy and the lines are missing the audience, you know right away something's wrong. You can miss points in drama, they can go flying, but eventually the accumulation will tell you something.

After you play comedy a lot, you long to get out and be released from the responsibility of making every line all the time. And after you play drama for a while, you just can't wait to get back to the sharpness and discipline of comedy. So you're never happy. Oscar Wilde said smoking was the perfect vice, and acting is like smoking in that way—it never totally satisfies you.

*Getting a Tony for **Da** must have satisfied you enormously.*

Well, the Tony is the same way really. You think, ah, wouldn't it be wonderful to get that award? But then you realize that success is in the eyes of other people, it's not measured by you, and so you're always itching for more confirmation and always doubting whether you can keep up with their standards.

I have a few moments when I'm sitting in the Morris chair on stage and some of the other actors are playing out a scene a few feet away. Occasionally, my attention will wander off, but right after I was nominated, I'd find myself thinking, "Good gosh, don't just sit there. You were nominated for a Tony for this! Why don't you start juggling or something. . . ." But that's when I'd remember my character; I'd say: refrain, do without, do with less, drop it, stop it, behave yourself!

Do you read your own reviews? Do you ever learn from them?

I never read reviews. My wife reads them to me. No, really, I do read them and I agree with them always, even when they say bad things.

And it doesn't affect your performance? If they say something bad, it doesn't depress you?

No. Frankly, over the years they haven't said a lot of bad things. Criticism is necessary and not everything I've been in has been a pearl. I'm doing a play sometimes only because I'm a professional. And most critics don't want either to kill you or see to it that your children starve or that your furniture is put out on the street. I myself often fall into the trap of thinking that critics should serve the theatre, should be encouraging. And yet that isn't their function or their job, nor do they see it that way. They're there to review and it's your job as an actor to serve the theatre—it's *your* job to reach *them*.

You know, in talking to you now, I can't help but feel how much you love being an actor; it shines through in all that you say.

Sometimes, as I'm waiting for my cue to go on stage, I wonder, my God, how did I ever get here, how was I ever lucky enough to be an actor. What a strange thing it is to be, and how few of us are blessed with the opportunity. Just think, to be so happy and to make a living at it—all the things that people hope they'll be able to do in life—and to find that, yes, you've actually done it. How it happened is just as big a mystery to me today as it ever was. I suppose I never will know how or why I was one of the anointed ones, the chosen. I wonder, do many actors have that feeling?

Index